Cambridge Historical Series.

THE
FRENCH MONARCHY
(1483—1789)

CAMBRIDGE
UNIVERSITY PRESS
LONDON: Fetter Lane

NEW YORK
The Macmillan Co.
BOMBAY, CALCUTTA and
MADRAS
Macmillan and Co., Ltd.
TORONTO
The Macmillan Co. of
Canada, Ltd.
TOKYO
Maruzen-Kabushiki-Kaisha

All rights reserved

THE
FRENCH MONARCHY
(1483—1789)

BY

A. J. GRANT, M.A.

OF KING'S COLLEGE, CAMBRIDGE, PROFESSOR OF HISTORY IN THE
UNIVERSITY OF LEEDS.

VOLUME I.

CAMBRIDGE
AT THE UNIVERSITY PRESS
1925

GENERAL PREFACE.

The aim of this series is to sketch the history of Modern Europe, with that of its chief colonies and conquests, from about the end of the fifteenth century down to the present time. In one or two cases the story commences at an earlier date: in the case of the colonies it generally begins later. The histories of the different countries are described, as a rule, separately; for it is believed that, except in epochs like that of the French Revolution and Napoleon I, the connection of events will thus be better understood and the continuity of historical development more clearly displayed.

The series is intended for the use of all persons anxious to understand the nature of existing political conditions. "The roots of the present lie deep in the past"; and the real significance of contemporary events cannot be grasped unless the historical causes which have led to them are known. The plan adopted makes it possible to treat the history of the last four centuries in considerable detail, and to embody the most important results of modern research. It is hoped therefore that the series will be useful not only to beginners but to students who have already acquired some general knowledge of European History. For those who wish to carry their studies further, the bibliography appended to each volume will act as a guide to original sources of information and works more detailed and authoritative.

Considerable attention is paid to political geography, and each volume is furnished with such maps and plans as may be requisite for the illustration of the text.

G. W. PROTHERO.

PRINTED IN GREAT BRITAIN

TITLE IN BCL 2nd ED

PREFACE.

IT was my original intention to compress the history of France from 1483 to 1789 within the compass of one volume that should not exceed four hundred pages; but the part played by France during these centuries was so far-reaching and her internal development so full of important and interesting matter that I was glad to accept the suggestion of the Editor that I should allow the subject to fill two volumes of about the ordinary size of the series.

I have attempted to give a fair and impartial account of the chief events of French history, both domestic and foreign, during the period covered by these volumes. But I have always had before me a desire to represent in its proper light the growth and influence of the Monarchy and of the institutions developed by it. The French Revolution is often represented as being an attempt on the part of France to sever her connection with the past, and, in spirit and policy and ideas, a violent reaction against all that the Monarchy had done. I have tried to follow in the steps of de Tocqueville and others, and to show that the Revolution did not cause so complete a breach with the past as many of the actors in it imagined; and that the Absolute Monarchy, in spite of its dismal corruption under Louis XV and its catastrophe under Louis XVI, rendered nevertheless great services to France, anticipating in many points the beneficent work of the Revolution and in many others preparing the way for it. I have tried to show that the Monarchy was, at its best, the maintainer of order, the promoter of national unity and the protector of the commons against the nobles. But it is written also very plainly on the page of history that by the beginning of the eighteenth century it had outlived the circumstances which justified its power; and, having no longer useful functions to perform, it fell into hopeless corruption and disorder. The rise, the greatness and the decline of this great monarchy form an unsurpassed object-lesson in the laws that govern the life and health of institutions and societies; and one great advantage of the study of foreign history is that, while it enforces the solidarity of the civilised nations, it allows also the various political and social problems to be studied, without the distortions and exaggerations often produced by national egotism.

My debt in the following pages to the historians of France is great and constant, but the character of the series has not allowed me to load my pages with references to them or to other writers whose names and works are mentioned in the bibliographical Note at the end of the second volume. But I must here express my deep obligations to many who have assisted me during the course of my work; to Dr Prothero, the Editor of the series, for invaluable assistance in the general planning of the book, for many suggestions on points of detail, as well as for minute care in the tedious work of examining the proof-sheets; to Professor Tout of the Owens College, Manchester, who has read over nearly the whole of the proof-sheets and given many valuable suggestions and corrections; to Mr Oscar Browning, of King's College, Cambridge, who was kind enough to read chapters XIV and XV in manuscript; to Miss Thompson, of Scarborough, for much help given in the correction of proofs; lastly to my sister, to whom I am indebted for the Index.

A. J. GRANT.

September, 1900.

CONTENTS TO VOLUME I.

CHAPTER I.
PAGE
A SURVEY OF FRANCE AT THE END OF THE XVTH CENTURY.   1

CHAPTER II.
THE ITALIAN WARS 17

CHAPTER III.
THE RELIGIOUS SITUATION OF FRANCE AND THE REIGN OF
HENRY II 65

CHAPTER IV.
THE WARS OF RELIGION, PART I: TO THE DEATH OF
CHARLES IX 93

CHAPTER V.
THE RELIGIOUS WARS, PART II: THE REIGN OF HENRY III.   125

CHAPTER VI.
KING HENRY IV 152

CHAPTER VII.
FROM THE DEATH OF HENRY IV TO THE PEACE OF ALAIS .   189

CHAPTER VIII.

RICHELIEU SUPREME IN FRANCE 221

CHAPTER IX.

MAZARIN AND THE FRONDE 263

APPENDIX I. The French Kings of the House of Valois, from Charles V to the Extinction of the Line 306

APPENDIX II. The Bourbon Kings 307

APPENDIX III. The Family of the Guises, to illustrate the Wars of Religion 308

APPENDIX IV. The House of Condé, and its relation to the House of Bourbon, to illustrate the Wars of the Fronde . 309

APPENDIX V. The Peaces and Treaties of the Wars of Religion 310

MAPS.

France, 1483—1659 . . . . *at end of Vol. I.*
Northern Italy . . . . ,, ,,
Netherlands and Rhine Frontier, 1659—1789 . . *at end of Vol. II.*
France, 1659—1789 . . . . ,, ,,

First Edition 1900,
Reprinted 1905, 1914, 1925

THE FRENCH MONARCHY,

1483—1789.

CHAPTER I.

A SURVEY OF FRANCE AT THE END OF THE XVTH CENTURY.

FRANCE at the end of the fifteenth century had fully recovered from the effects of the English wars. The devastated fields were again cultivated: civilization had returned to the districts from which foreign invasion and civil war had banished it. Observers speak of the country as flourishing throughout its length and breadth: the population was increasing, and commerce showed an unprecedented volume and activity. The great towns, largely self-governed, were centres of industrial life: Rouen, Tours, Toulouse, Montpellier, Nîmes, Bordeaux, Bayonne, Marseilles, were the chief provincial capitals. Probably no country in Europe possessed such inherent power for resistance or attack. England had hardly yet recovered from the Wars of the Roses, and the Tudors did not feel themselves quite secure upon the throne: Italy was richer and more civilized, but so disunited as to be helpless: neither the Empire nor Spain possessed such a strong or popular Monarchy as France.

The European world generally was passing through a very critical stage in its perpetual transformation. Vast changes in the very constitution of European society had come in the last two centuries: the materials for further unsuspected revolutions in politics and religion were accumulated on every side. The mediæval conception of things was almost dead, and though the institutions that had been generated by that conception still presented an imposing appearance, they were seriously threatened—all the more seriously because they did not suspect the coming attack. The shock which the Church had received by the so-called Babylonian Captivity, the Great Schism, and the Great Councils of the fifteenth century, had shaken the very foundations of its power, both secular and spiritual, though the external traces of the blows had been very nearly smoothed away. The mind of Europe, no longer satisfied with the old ideas, finding what had once been a fortress against barbarism and anarchy now a prison-house, was feeling after new ideas and new guides and was developing new and unsuspected energies. Thus it had turned with eagerness to ancient Classical learning and seemed to find in the literature of Greece and Rome ideas more in harmony with its wants than in anything that the Mediæval Church had to offer: for good and for evil—and largely for both—the ideas of Paganism in art and in letters, in science, in philosophy and morals passed current in all the chief centres of civilization in Europe. Sometimes the Church adopted the new ideas, unsuspicious of their future effects: where it resisted them it was ineffective or despised. But the revival of the ancient literature was by no means the only great formative influence of the time. Printing had come on the heels of the New Learning. Columbus had found land beyond the Atlantic waters, and this and other geographical discoveries gave an incalculable impetus to men's thoughts and imaginations. Everywhere men were ready to push away from the old landmarks into unknown waters. Italy was the first country that was affected by these

Introduction.

new ideas. We shall see how they passed from Italy to France, how eagerly they were welcomed there, and how far-reaching were their effects. But in this preliminary chapter it is not the social and intellectual but mainly the political condition of France that we are to examine.

In France as in most other European countries the Monarchy and the Nobility were the two great antagonists whose combats and rivalries had filled the Middle Ages and given to French political life its most characteristic features. There had been since Charlemagne, perhaps since the Roman Empire, the tradition of a strong Monarchy in France, but during the ninth, tenth and eleventh centuries it had seemed to be overwhelmed by the centrifugal force of noble feudalism, which, at one time a principal support of order in a very dark age, had become in its turn the enemy of a higher order. Under Philip Augustus, Saint Louis, and Philip the Fair, the Monarchy had emerged into great dignity and power; but it seemed hopelessly ruined in the long agony of the Hundred Years' War. Every kind of force opposed to the Monarchy triumphed for a time. Many of the towns were almost independent: the nobles ruled their own territories almost without reference to the royal will. A new era had come with Louis XI. Romance has fixed his portrait in the popular imagination as the incarnation of cruelty, hypocrisy and superstition. But the verdict of history must be something very different. He curbed the power of the Nobility and sometimes broke it: in doing so he was neither scrupulous in his choice of means nor careful of the feelings of those whom he struck. But he gave to France the beginnings of the settled order that is the first condition of progress. A great historian has said of the royal authority in the days of Louis XI: "It towered over the great vassals, and even the provincial and popular elements, commanding peace, compelling obedience, concentrating in itself all the interests of the nation, terrible from the suddenness with which it punished, everywhere present, taking counsel from no one, firmly established in itself." When Louis's power passed in 1483 to his son Charles VIII, the Monarchy was one of the most powerful in Europe and incomparably the first political force in France. The period that we are to traverse in these volumes sees, with slight interruptions, a gradual increase in the power of the Monarchy until it culminates with Louis XIV about the year 1660: soon after this, it begins to decline.

The machinery of the royal government was very far from the full development that it received subsequently at the hands of Henry IV, Richelieu and Louis XIV: but already nearly all the future is to be found in germ. The Council of the King was the chief centre of power and from it are developed all the chief agencies of government. It was divided into three chief sections—(1) the *Council Proper* (the Small or Privy Council)—(2) the *Parlement* or supreme Judicial Court, whose attributes and functions we must examine more at length, and (3) the *Cour des Comptes*, the financial tribunal. All three are engaged not only in governing the country but also in sustaining and extending the royal prerogative against both Church and Nobility. We shall trace other divisions and developments during future reigns. Meanwhile it may be well to notice that the Council proper and the Parlement are far the most important. The chief royal officers were first and above all the *Chancellor*, the chief representative of the royal power and the head of the whole civil organization, the *Maître d'Hôtel*, at first the superintendent of the Royal Household, but later an important state functionary, the *Constable*, the head of the land forces, and lastly the *Admiral*, who was at first in command of the sea forces, but later merely a high military dignity. The Constitutional History of France shows how the royal administration encroaches upon all rival authorities whether of Church or State, until at last it rules in France without any effective limitation.

A French writer has noticed upon how widely different lines the French and the English nobility have developed. Both, in feudal times and in the times that follow after the decay of feudalism, possessed both political and pecuniary privileges. *The Nobility.* But while in England the nobles have in the course of centuries lost their financial privileges and maintain their special political powers, the opposite has been the case in France: there the Monarchy succeeded, as we shall see, in destroying their political power, and in practically excluding them from the government, but, until the Revolution swept away both Monarchy and Nobility, the nobles continued to possess most of their immunity from taxation.

That immunity had been natural and justifiable in the feudal period when their military service had formed the chief support of the State in war. But feudalism as a military system had virtually disappeared, and still the nobles retained, and for a long time were destined to retain, the powers and privileges that were only justified by that system. They paid none of the direct taxes of the State; they were free from both the property-tax that fell on the rest of the population (the *taille*) and from the salt monopoly or *gabelle*. And they had the right of exacting taxes or feudal dues of various kinds from the peasants who fell within their jurisdiction. Those who held their land on the tenure that was known as *censive* had heavy payments to make to their Seigneur quite apart from the taxes that were paid to the State. These varied in different districts and partly took the place of rent. Sometimes the peasant had to make to the Seigneur certain payments in kind, a certain proportion of his crops or of his sheep or poultry. All over France he was hard pressed by the cruel game-laws: great game destroyed his crops and he might use no violence in driving them out: his methods of culture were restricted lest certain manures or the reaping of the crops at a certain time should interfere with the breeding of partridges. The peasant too could be called away from his own work and forced for a certain number of days in the year to work gratuitously for his Seigneur. Dues and tolls were exacted on the roads or at the crossing of rivers, not by the State but by the nobles. In many districts he might not thresh his own corn where he could do it most cheaply, nor press his grapes in his own winepress. He must go to the wine-press or the threshing-floor of his feudal lord and there pay what dues were customary (*banalités*). Nearly three hundred years later the wife of a French peasant thus described her lot to an English traveller: "her husband had but a morsel of land, one cow and a poor little horse, yet they had a *franchar* (42 lbs.) of wheat and three chickens to pay as a quit rent to one Seigneur, and four *franchars* of oats, one chicken and one franc to pay to another, besides very heavy *tailles* and other taxes." It would be of course a very great mistake to transfer the feeling of the period of the Revolution about these matters to the end of the fifteenth century; but the position had not essentially changed during the interval.

Besides these rights and immunities the nobles also had considerable rights of administering justice, which varied according to the wealth, position, and birth of the noble. The chief clue to the domestic history of France during the first two of the three centuries that these volumes deal with is the constant encroachment of the Crown upon the prerogatives of the nobles. There is no need to paint the nobles in very dark colours. They were nearly always brave to recklessness and often generous and enlightened, but it is clear that France was wholly the gainer by the substitution of royal for noble justice, and would have been immensely the gainer if the royal taxes had extinguished the feudal.

The Clergy were the first of the three estates of the Realm—
The Church. Clergy, Nobility, Commons; but here for convenience they are treated after the nobility. The Church was very wealthy. Machiavelli says, "The Prelates

Introduction.

of France carry away two-fifths of the revenue of the kingdom," and he gives eighteen as the number of archbishoprics, and counts 146 bishoprics, and nearly 1000 abbacies. In France, as elsewhere in Europe, the question of the relation between the Government and this powerful and wealthy corporation was a very important one.

From 1438 until 1516 the relations of France and the Church were governed, except for a brief period during the reign of Louis XI, by the Pragmatic Sanction. That great State document had been adopted at a time when the great Councils were attacking and limiting the authority of the Papacy, and when the French Monarchy had not yet recovered from the crushing defeats that it had suffered in the Hundred Years' War. The character of the time is reflected in the Pragmatic Sanction: it was a rebellion of the great dignitaries of the Church against the authority of the Pope, and the King of France was too weak to turn it to his own advantage. Its chief provisions were the following: (1) the authority of Councils was declared to be superior to that of the Pope; (2) the elections to bishoprics and abbacies were placed in the hands of the chapters, which consisted of the cathedral officials and dignitaries; (3) all appeals to Rome in ecclesiastical cases were forbidden; and (4) nearly the whole of the payments hitherto made to the Papacy were cancelled: such as remained were to be regarded as free gifts.

The Pragmatic Sanction was popular with the bulk of the Church in France, and was eagerly welcomed by the legal corporation of the Parlement. But clearly it was not likely to please either Pope or King, and both were at the beginning of the sixteenth century far stronger than they had been in 1438. Accordingly upon the first opportunity a great change was made and, though to speak of this is to anticipate the progress of events by twenty years, it will be convenient to notice it here. In 1516 Francis I, flushed with his victory at Marignano in the previous year, met the Pope at Bologna and made a new agreement—the famous Concordat—which governed ecclesiastical appointments in France thenceforward down to the Revolution.

By the Concordat the right of self-government was taken away from the Church of France: in the new distribution the King got power and the Pope got wealth. The King of France procured the right of nominating to any vacancies in bishoprics or abbacies. The acceptance of the King's candidate lay, as a matter of form, with the Pope; as a matter of fact, the King's nomination was really final. To compensate this vast concession the Pope received the *annates*: that is the income of the first year after each new appointment. It seems that there is no stipulation as to *annates* in the text of the Concordat; but they were granted informally and the grant soon developed into a custom.

The Concordat was a fact of the utmost importance for the future of France. It was in harmony with the general tendency of the sixteenth century to subordinate the ecclesiastical to the temporal power. The Kings of Spain procured similar rights. The motives that actuated Francis I—the desire to efface the rival authority of the Church—were at the root of the more violent changes that were introduced by Henry VIII into England. After the Concordat there was little room for jealousy between the Kings of France and the officials of the Church: no more than between the Kings of England and the Church of England after the Reformation. It is the Concordat that gives to France her long list of ecclesiastical statesmen such as Cardinals Richelieu, Mazarin, Fleury, Dubois, Brienne. It was not so much that the Kings chose their ministers among bishops and cardinals as that they rewarded their ministers with ecclesiastical revenues and titles. The titles came to them, as it was said, from Rome by way of Paris. There was much natural opposition to the Concordat. Parliament for a long time refused to register it: the University protested against it; but in the end the royal authority overbore all resistance.

All the Clergy were privileged: they paid none of the ordinary direct taxes to the State. But their immunity was by no means complete. The King always looked to the Clergy to give him large contributions both for the ordinary and the special needs of the State. Their chief pecuniary privilege was indeed this: that what was exacted from others was granted by them, and they doubtless thus escaped from anything like the burden which their vast wealth would have justified.

Chief among all the agencies by which the royal power was advanced must be reckoned the Parlement of Paris. We have seen already how it formed at first part of the King's "Court," and, except in special circumstances and towards the end of the Monarchy, it remained faithful to its origin.

The Parlement of Paris.

It was the supreme judicial court of France, subdivided eventually into at least seven chambers, but at the time of which we are speaking into three, the *Grand' Chambre, the Chambre des Enquêtes,* and *the Chambre des Requêtes.* It is not necessary for our purpose to go into its methods of procedure: it is enough for the present to regard it as the supreme Court of Appeal for France, and in other cases besides those of appeal the most important tribunal.

The members of the Parlement held their office by right of purchase, and were not removable except for proved misconduct. The high prices that had to be paid for appointment raised the fees charged in its courts, and were said to lead to various kinds of corruption. The accidental political action of the Parlement has often overshadowed its normal judicial action: yet it is this that gave it its real importance. It had furthered the King's prerogative by finding expedients for withdrawing cases from the jurisdiction of the nobles on the ground that they were royal cases (*cas royaux*), and for interfering with the administration of the Church on the ground that its procedure was in conflict with the laws or violated the canons of the Church (*appels comme d'abus*). Pope Pius II had said "the Bishop of Rome, whose diocese is the world, has no more jurisdiction in France than what the Parlement is pleased to allow him." By the sixteenth century its supremacy in France was clearly recognised.

The political powers of the Parlement became during the period we are to deal with of great importance. All turned on one undoubted right that they possessed—the right of registering the King's edicts: until they were registered by the Parlement they were not binding. At first, it would seem, this registration had been a matter of convenience and a mere form. To the very end of the Monarchy there was always a dispute as to what it implied. Had the Parlement the right to discuss as well as to register? If it might discuss, might it protest? If the protest was not admitted, might it refuse registration? Sometimes Parlement advanced very high pretensions. Its members were, they said, the real though unelected representatives of the Nation—the States General in miniature. At other times they traced back their origin to the King's "Court," recalled its independent character in feudal times, and declared themselves equal in authority to the King. The view taken by the Kings themselves was of course something very different. They regarded the registration as a mere useful form. If the Parlement hesitated about registering, they first issued orders for immediate registration: if there was further resistance they went down themselves, held a session that was called a "bed of justice," from the throne on which the King sat, and enforced registration. In the King's presence registration was never refused, though often it was made with the appended note that it was only done "under constraint of force."

Besides the Parlement of Paris there were certain Provincial Parlements. At the beginning of the sixteenth century there were Parlements at Toulouse, Bordeaux, Grenoble, Dijon, Rouen, Aix and Rennes. Their functions were similar to those of the Paris Parlement, but their political importance was of course vastly less.

If the Parlement was during the greater part of its existence mainly the agent of the Monarchy, the States General were as a rule the defence and the stronghold of noble claims and privileges. They formed an assembly more or less representative of the people of France—as fairly representative probably as the contemporary Parliament of England. The three Estates of the Realm each had a separate representation: the delegates of the Clergy, Nobility and Commons were as a general rule, with a few exceptions, elected by their own order only. They failed, as is well known, to build up any representative or popular form of government in France, but it was not for want of trying. We find them at different times putting forward nearly all those claims which were enforced by the English Parliament, and which ended by annihilating the political power of the English Monarchy. Thus they claimed the right of voting taxes, of appointing ministers, of deciding questions of peace and war; and for a time their demands seemed likely to be granted. So late as the middle of the sixteenth century it appeared possible that the estates of France might gain their end and bring the Crown to submission: their position at that time was as promising as that of the English Parliament under the Tudor Monarchy.

The States General.

Certain points in their procedure may be noticed. Each representative brought from the district that had chosen him a statement of its grievances or aspirations. The first business of the Estates, and, in the opinion of the Kings, their only business, was to form from these separate statements a general one for presentation to the King. This task was performed separately by the three distinct orders, and their deliberations and voting were as a rule conducted separately.

The causes of the failure of the Estates have often been discussed and analysed. More than half a century before our period begins they had given away the most powerful weapon that the English Parliament possessed. In 1439, while the

Hundred Years' War was still proceeding and the hopes of France were rising, the Estates had authorised the King to maintain a standing army and to collect the property-tax called the *taille* to maintain that army. They did not imagine that they had thereby abandoned all control of taxation; but the *taille* was a somewhat vague and easily extensible tax, and we know from English History how powerful in such matters is the influence of precedent. If the English Kings had from the fifteenth century possessed the right of maintaining and paying an army, the seventeenth century would have had a very different character!

There are doubtless many other reasons discoverable for the failure of the Estates. Their triple organization was a source of weakness. By it the privileged classes were separated from the unprivileged in a fashion fortunately unknown to English History. By it a preponderance of two Houses to one was given to the privileged classes. Thus the States General became as a rule the mouthpiece of privilege rather than of the nation at large. Doubtless popular utterances are to be found in the history of their debates, but for the most part the occasional victories of the body tended indirectly to increase the power of the Nobility, with all its feudal leanings. It is this which makes historians acquiesce in its final failure.

We may trace the rivalry of the King and the Nobility not only in relation to the central government of France, but also in the provinces. The nobles retained political power and influence here after the Monarchy had established its superiority over the States General and had expelled the nobles from the highest offices in the State. All the Provinces of France had originally had Estates—representative Assemblies which, with a good deal of local variation, followed in general the pattern of the States General. But the Monarchy had not been more favourable to the local than to the national Assembly. A decided attack upon them had been made by Louis XI, and from that time onwards

Provincial Administration.

their power was gradually diminished. By the beginning of the sixteenth century we find that the provinces are divided into two groups, those wherein the old Estates were maintained (the *pays d'états*), and those wherein all self-government had ceased and public business was transacted by the officers of the Crown (the *pays d'election*—a title that has often proved misleading). Among the provinces that maintained longest something of their old liberties and privileges were Languedoc, Provence, Burgundy, Brittany, Dauphiné and Normandy : perhaps of all these Brittany and Languedoc were most tenacious of their rights. Their triple formation weakened them for reasons already examined in the case of the States General; and the triumph of the Monarchy in the central government gave it an overwhelming force in its struggle with the local liberties.

The title of the provincial officers in highest authority varied during the history of the Monarchy. At first they had been called *prevôts*, but from the reign of Philip Augustus onwards they had been called *baillis* or *sénéchaux*. Whatever their title, they represented the full authority of the Monarchy and had both military and judicial competence. All three titles that have been mentioned lasted down to the Revolution, but from the reign of Francis I were connected only with subordinate functions and districts of restricted area. The Parlement had eaten into their judicial functions; and it will be well here to glance forward and see how they were superseded in their general administrative powers. During the reign of Francis I after the early splendid promise of his reign had been wrecked by the battle of Pavia (1525) and his captivity at Madrid, it seemed necessary to take special measures for the defence of the frontiers. With this object Francis I created twelve lieutenants-general of noble birth for the frontier provinces. This was intended as a temporary measure, but it proved a permanent one and was extended to all provinces indiscriminately : during the troubles of the Wars of Religion the new officials gained further authority, and the lieutenancies were a much-prized possession of the great nobles. We shall see how the Monarchy pursued them and defeated them in this their last stronghold. The system of *intendants*, which dates from Richelieu, subordinated their authority to these low-born officers of the Crown. Like the *prevôts*, *baillis* and *sénéchaux*, the lieutenants-general last as long as the Monarchy lasts—a financial burden to the State with little real authority in the direction of the government.

To complete our survey of the institutions of France it is necessary to mention the towns; but our notice of them may be slight, for by the end of the fifteenth century the time of their political greatness was past. During the earlier centuries their powers had been very great and the Monarchy had usually supported their liberties and claims as tending to weaken the power of the Nobility. At the end of the fifteenth century the machinery of free municipal government was still there. There were still or there seemed to be free assemblies and a popular magistracy: the trades-guilds were still influential and wealthy. But really the towns were already far less self-dependent than they had been. The guilds were ceasing to represent the interests of the whole trade concerned: their management tended to fall into the hands of close circles of masters who were anxious to keep the workmen from rising to the position of masters and held the trade rigidly in the routine of past centuries. We shall see how, when the Revolution was approaching, the economists almost with one voice declared these guilds to be among the chief obstacles to the commercial progress of France. If we look to the form of the Municipal Government, we shall see there too signs of change and decay. The free assemblies were often free only in name. Where the election of the officers was genuine, the suffrage was very much restricted, and often it was not genuine at all. Royal officers found their way into the towns. It was not by any means always jealousy for municipal liberties that made the Monarchy interfere: it was often a genuine care for the welfare of the towns. The finances of the towns were in disorder and a royal officer was sent to superintend them. But whatever the motives, the royal interference which began to be evident in the days of Francis I developed by a series of ordinances until finally in Louis XIV's days the government of the towns was almost as much submitted to the royal will as that of the provinces.

We have already seen how unequal the pressure of taxation was, how the two most powerful and richest classes were exempt from the chief taxes. The chief tax was the *taille*—a tax levied in very arbitrary and irritating fashion on the land of the unprivileged class. On this class too rested the whole burden of other taxes that went to support the military service, the *crue* that paid the infantry, the *taillon* which supported the artillery. Next in importance to the *taille* and its developments came the *gabelle*, the most odious of all the taxes of the old Monarchy. Salt was a monopoly in the hands of the State, and every one in France not belonging to the privileged classes had to buy a certain quantity of salt at the arbitrary price fixed by the State. Nearly all the objections that can be urged against any tax could be urged against this; but it remained one of the most valuable resources of the Monarchy. Besides these there were a large number of indirect taxes in the nature of tolls on the rivers and roads (*péages*) and customs and excise (*aides*). It is almost impossible to reduce these to any system: they were of many different kinds and were not uniform throughout France. In addition to the taxes properly so called, the revenue derived from the royal domains defrayed a large part of the expenditure of the Crown.

The collection of the direct taxes was carried out by royal officers (*élus*) in those provinces that had no rights of self-government: but in the *pays d'états* it was largely left to the community itself to raise the sum that was demanded by the King. The indirect taxes were for the most part farmed out. The *fermiers* paid to the Government a sum down, and then made what profit they could from the collection of the taxes. The worst abuses were connected with this method, and we shall see all the financial reformers of France protest against it and try to alter it. The method was too convenient in case of financial emergency to be abandoned, and in spite of Sully and Colbert it lasted as long as the Monarchy. But in this and all other matters that have been mentioned in this chapter it is a mistake as dangerous as it is common to transfer to the early sixteenth century the feelings and protests of the latter part of the eighteenth. The system was traditional, and at the beginning of the sixteenth century no one thought of the possibility of altering it. We may add that in Europe generally the system of taxation was not more equitable.

In considering the general condition of France at the end of the fifteenth century it is well to look forward into the coming centuries which were to reveal its defects and its dangers. But they were not apparent to contemporary observers. France was then prosperous, united and hopeful. The burden of the taxes was not as yet seriously felt. The nobles gave little trouble to the King, and their courage, high spirits, and instinct for war were a valuable addition to the strength of the Crown. In whatever direction the energies of France were thrown they would produce a vast effect. We turn in the next chapter to a survey of the results they produced when she entered on the long struggle of the Italian Wars.

CHAPTER II.

THE ITALIAN WARS.

LOUIS XI was in every way the restorer of the power of France and of the French Monarchy, and yet at his death his work was popular with no one. Immediately on the accession of his son Charles VIII, the States General were summoned (Jan. 1484), and their debates show how every order—Clergy, Nobility, and Commons almost equally—desired the overthrow of the system that Louis XI had established. But their protests remained ineffectual, and France proceeded along the lines that Louis XI had marked out for it, under the careful management of Anne of Beaujeu, the sister of the King, who was as yet too young to reign. Shortly afterwards the Crown of France gained a very important addition to its territory. The Duchy of Brittany still retained its semi-independence, but a chance came of uniting it to the Crown. Francis II, the last Duke of Brittany, died in Sept. 1487, leaving only a daughter, Anne. The King of France at once claimed the control of the Duchy, and sent troops into it to secure it. So great an addition to the territory of the Crown of France, so very valuable because it excluded the entry of a foreign power, and especially the English, by that route, and gave to France excellent harbours and a vigorous seafaring population, was bound to be resisted, and was resisted, especially by England

and the Emperor. The struggle that ensued, whether of arms or diplomacy, does not fall within the scope of this book. Enough that a marriage treaty secured what arms had already gained. In 1491, under circumstances of some mystery, Charles VIII married Anne of Brittany, and the treaty of Plessis les Tours gave Brittany into the hands of the French King. Soon other treaties relieved him from all his other enemies. The treaty of Étaples (Nov. 1492) brought to an end the war with England. In Jan. 1493 the treaty of Barcelona ceded Roussillon and Cerdagne to the Crown of Aragon, and thus bought off hostility in that quarter. Lastly, in May 1493, by the treaty of Senlis, France gave up the claim to Burgundy, Artois, Charolais and Noyon in favour of the Emperor Maximilian.

But the acquisition of Brittany quite counterbalanced these concessions, which hardly diminished either the strength or the prestige of Charles VIII. No country in Europe was more powerful than France, none so ready for immediate action. The population had rapidly increased of late, and commerce had added to the wealth of the State. The art of war had nowhere made such great progress as in France. She possessed a well-trained and regularly-paid standing army, and her artillery especially was far better than any that could be found elsewhere in Europe. The young King, too, as he grew up, was eager to signalise his reign by some great enterprise. And in one direction a great adventure invited the adventurous. There was little inducement to attack England or any of the German states or Spain. But it was different with Italy; for Italy was rich and powerless. Her civilisation, on the intellectual and artistic side, was far in advance of anything else in Europe. Italy was for all countries beyond the Alps the fountain of the New Learning, the home of all the arts and graces of life. Her cities, especially the cities of the North, were rich with the results of the Mediterranean trade, which they almost monopolised. Contemporaries, especially those who lived through the troubled times that followed, were loud in their admiration of the fertility and luxury of the country. "It was cultivated," says Guicciardini, "through all its plains and to the very tops of the mountains, teeming with population, with riches, and an unlimited commerce; adorned by many munificent princes, by the splendour of many noble and beautiful cities, and by the majesty of religion." Yet Italy with her wealth, her grace, and her highly-developed intellect was also divided against herself, unwarlike and hopelessly corrupt. The Renaissance had not yet passed its most splendid moment in the arts of painting and sculpture, but the dark shadow that had always followed its course now lay blacker than ever across the land. Men had rejected the good with the evil in the mediæval scheme of morality and life. The passions and desires of the individual had been stimulated, and as a result the social feelings had declined in strength and warmth. Nowhere was there reverence or loyalty or mutual confidence between man and man or state and state. There was no vestige of political unity in the Peninsula. States great and small were huddled together from the North of Italy to the South. Dante's picture of Italy was as true as it had been two hundred years before. Not only were the city-states jealous rivals of each other, but inside each city, "within the same moat and the same walls," there were factions that hated one another more bitterly than the common enemy. Five states stood preeminent over the rest. Milan in the North commanded the central course of the Po. Her territory stretched, roughly speaking, to the Adda on the East and the Sesia on the West; the Alps on the North and the Apennines on the South. Next to the East stretched the territory of Venice, rich with the commerce of the Orient, enjoying a government of greater stability and excellence than any other state in Italy. Across the Apennines in the Tuscan plain lay Florence, the earliest home of the New Learning, and still at the very head of the movement. To the South and East of Tuscany, the Papal states stretched across from sea to sea, and from the mouths of the Po southward to beyond the Tiber; while all the southern part of the peninsula belonged reluctantly to the kingdom of Naples, now in the possession of the illegitimate branch of the House of Aragon. Sicily and Sardinia belonged without question to the legitimate branch, represented by Ferdinand the Catholic. The third great island of the Western Mediterranean, Corsica, long disputed between Genoa and Pisa, was now definitely held by the former. No principle of union could be found among these states. The possibility of a barbarian invasion was often talked about but not really foreseen or dreaded. Even when it came it failed to produce anything but the most temporary union. If voluntary union was impossible, so also it seemed was any forcible welding of the states together by the strongest of their number. They were too much on a level of equality for that. The Papacy had no desire for a union, for the Popes were usually chiefly bent on pursuing the material interests of their own families; and, if they had tried, the prestige of the Papacy in Italy was so sunk that their efforts would have been foredoomed to failure. As a matter of fact, no power worked so constantly against Italian union as the Papacy. The divisions of Italy made her helpless in face of a foreign invasion; but her methods of fighting were in themselves a danger. The Italian states fought constantly, but the character of the people was eminently unwarlike. The cities entrusted their defence as a rule to mercenary captains (*condottieri*), who, though higher pay could induce them to change sides, were often faithful to their employers. The native population grew meanwhile unused to arms.

Diplomacy was not likely to find any difficulty in discovering excuses for attacking a prey so rich and so defenceless. Both France and Spain had colourable reasons for interference in the affairs of Italy. The King of Naples belonged to the illegitimate branch of the house of Aragon, and the King of Spain, as representing the legitimate branch, could always put forward a claim to supplant him. The King of France, too, could urge that he represented the Angevin Kings who had once sat upon the Neapolitan throne, and could thus at any time claim the rights of his dynasty. The moment was favourable for interference. A revolt of the Neapolitan nobles had just been suppressed. The people were still discontented and restless, and an invitation to invade could easily be procured. France could furbish up, too, other claims upon Italy. The Orleans family had claims on Milan, where the sovereignty had been usurped by Francesco Sforza in 1450, and was now in the hands of Ludovico "the Moor." No conqueror, however unjust his cause, likes to appeal merely to force; and both these claims were used in turn to excuse French descents upon Italy.

Charles VIII attacked this fair prey out of motives of ambition, greed, and a desire for romantic adventure. The legendary history of Charlemagne and the real stories of Cæsar and Hannibal and Alexander were before his thoughts when he began his great march. He listened readily to a party of Neapolitan conspirators, and consented to claim those rights which came to him as the heir of the house of Anjou. He put his claims before the Parlement of Paris, and the Parlement obediently recognised their validity. In the North of Italy Milan beckoned him on. For there Ludovico Sforza, already regent of Milan, was anxious to seize the whole control of the State, the "tyranny," and drive out his young nephew Gian Galeazzo Sforza, in whose name he ruled. And as his nephew was in alliance with the Aragonese party at Naples, it was natural that Lodovico should look to France for help. The support of Milan opened Italy to the invader.

Charles VIII and his gallant and war-loving nobles entered with a light heart and without much thought of the distant future into this great adventure. But the campaign thus lightly begun marks a very important epoch in European history and especially in the history of France. The immense successes that France gained at first seemed to add so much to her power that a general European coalition was formed against her, and the theory of the European balance of power began to be developed. In the course of these wars France found in Spain her chief antagonist and for a time her conqueror, and so began that long struggle between these two nations which is the chief permanent political factor in European history down to the time when, by the treaty of the Pyrenees (1659), the struggle ends in the victory of France. The reaction, too, of Italy upon France, the influence of the art, the language, the thought, and the morals of Italy, is of the first importance, for the next century. Meanwhile, outside of the merely political world forces of the utmost importance had accumulated which largely influenced the course of the struggle. The increasing sense of nationality made men ready to shake off the connection with Rome, while the ideas of the Middle Ages, declining in power for more than two centuries, were now being replaced by others of a modern kind. Geographical discovery, soon to be followed by astronomical discovery, stimulated the imagination and opened a new avenue for trade; the increasing use of gunpowder and of printing played a very important part in the intellectual and military struggles of the time; the religious controversy, though no one suspected it, was rapidly reaching a revolutionary point. The mediæval passed by imperceptible stages into the modern world: *ab integro sæclorum nascitur ordo*.

No part of the long Italian wars of France is so interesting, none at least so full of romantic incident, as this campaign of Charles VIII: yet as belonging only to the prologue of this book it must be passed over in the most rapid fashion. It was known in Italy that the blow was coming, long before Charles VIII was ready to march. Representatives of the various Italian courts were busy in France gaining what information they could. Yet there was no real preparation to resist. The march on Italy began in September 1494. The Alps were crossed, in a march that the French compared to Hannibal's, though indeed little difficulty had been found. Turin gave Charles a hearty welcome. The Italians saw with astonishment his well-trained troops and, above all, his artillery, of a calibre so much greater than they were accustomed to, and yet moved about with so much ease. From Turin he advanced to Pavia, and there met Ludovico the Moor and the mother of Gian Galeazzo. The ducal crown of Milan was given to Ludovico and his rival was handed over to the French and died shortly afterwards. The belief in secret poisoning was so strong and so well justified in Italy at this time that it was generally believed that Gian Galeazzo had died no natural death. Ludovico, meanwhile, had thus attained the object for which he had called in the French, and having attained it, was perfectly ready to turn against them.

From Pavia the French army moved over the Apennines into Tuscany, choosing this route in order that they might secure the remainder of their artillery which had been transported from France by sea. As Charles VIII advanced, political revolutions occurred in the cities that lay upon his route: the situation was, in Italy, everywhere unstable and the presence of the French was enough to overthrow the tottering political systems of the cities. The chief of these revolutions was at Florence, where the population, already profoundly stirred by the teaching of Savonarola, was irritated against their "tyrant" Piero de' Medici. The King entered Florence and at first inclined to support the authority of Piero, but subsequently yielded to the popular demand, consented to see a republic established, accepted a subsidy and marched on to Rome.

Rome was entered on the last day of 1494. Alexander VI surrendered, and at once began plotting against the French, while he flattered them. But Charles, unsuspicious of the fierce animosities and the subtle intrigues that he was leaving behind him, marched carelessly forward to Naples. His knights and soldiers, French and Swiss, thoroughly contemptuous of the unwarlike Italians, rarely took the trouble to put on their armour. The march from Rome to Naples was accomplished in twenty-six days: and Naples was as little able or willing to resist as the other towns he had entered in his victorious march. Ferdinand, the King of Naples, fled at Charles's approach: on Feb. 22, 1495, he entered the city, and the object of his campaign seemed reached with astonishing ease.

But though it was easy to march through Italy, it was very hard to keep any firm hold on her astute and shifty statesmen. For the moment—though only for the moment—the common hatred of France thrust into the background many of the rivalries of cities and factions. Ludovico of Milan was as eager to get rid of the French as he had been ready to invite them. He busily negotiated a league for their expulsion. Not only the chief cities of Italy, Milan, Rome, and Venice, thus united against France; but also the Empire and Spain, alarmed at the rapidity and extent of the French conquests, joined the league: such leagues we shall see formed again and again for the same or similar objects. Charles VIII was warned by Comines of what was happening, and saw that it would be necessary to make his way home towards France. He left certain garrisons in Naples, and with the bulk of the army marched north: the stay in Naples had not improved the *morale* of his men.

The first serious difficulty that he met was at the passage of the Apennines. At one time it seemed as though the artillery would have to be left behind, so bad were the roads. But when the horses failed the Swiss soldiers harnessed themselves by hundreds to the guns and at last succeeded in bringing them down into the northern plain. But then in the valley of the Po, by the banks of its affluent the Taro, not far from Fornovo, the French found the army of the League waiting for them. In the battle which followed (July 6, 1495), the battle of Fornovo, the French and the Swiss showed all their accustomed military dash and skill; their King seemed to delight in exposing himself to the hottest of the fight, and some of the Italians were not anxious to bar his exit from Italy. The Italians were defeated, with a loss of 3000 men: while the French suffered but slightly. The troops, however, were weary of the campaign and decimated with illness. The victory of Fornovo gave them little else than a safe return into France.

Charles VIII was welcomed on his arrival as a conqueror, though he had lost a very large proportion of his troops and his retreat looked very like a flight. And soon it was clear that of all his victories nothing would remain to him. Immediately after his departure from Naples the garrisons that he left under the Count of Montpensier were attacked by a Spanish force. Gonzalvo of Cordova, a Spanish noble of the very highest type, commanded the Spanish troops. He had received his apprenticeship in arms in the difficult school of the Moorish wars, and now turned the tactics that he had learnt there against the French. At first he was driven back by the discipline and valour of the Swiss spearmen, but he was quick in learning from the enemy. The French troops could get no reinforcements, and failed before the numbers or the subtlety of their opponents. In October 1495, Ferdinand was again King of Naples. There were various French garrisons in different parts of the kingdom of Naples; but the last capitulated in July 1496, and nothing remained but the memory of daring and fruitless exploits.

Yet Charles had not by any means abandoned all hope of taking up again his Italian projects. Diplomacy was very busy, in the last months of his life, between France and the Italian states. The removal of the common enemy allowed all the old animosities to spring to life again. Florence especially feared the return of Piero de' Medici, and was anxious to see the French in Italy again. But nothing was settled when in April 1498 Charles died. The Italian campaign had been the chief interest of his reign, but at the very end of it he had shown some inclination to make improvements in the administration.

Charles VIII died without leaving male issue. The Queen became again the independent ruler of Brittany. The Crown passed to Louis of Orleans, who had been in opposition to Charles VIII. He was crowned as Louis XII.

The Reign of Louis XII down to the Treaty of Cambrai.

His reign has two faces widely different from one another. If we look at him in his relation to the domestic history of France we see him humane, merciful; a strong but not a despotic ruler, a friend of law and of constitutional procedure. The clergy were pleased with his cordial acceptance of the methods of election enjoined in the Pragmatic Sanction: Parlement was never stronger, purer or more influential; the taxes were low and the country prosperous. Louis showed more toleration for heresy than can be found elsewhere in his age, and allowed the players who were laying the foundation of the French drama to satirise himself so long as they left the Queen untouched. His care for his people and his good humour won for him the title of 'Pater Patriae' from the States General. "On no account," he said in his ordinance of 1513, "will we lay further burdens on our poor people, knowing the hardships of their life and the heavy burdens, whether in the shape of *tailles* or otherwise, which they have hitherto borne and still bear, to our great regret and grief." And such official utterances seem to reflect the King's real feeling. Yet we hardly recognise the same man in Louis XII's treatment of foreign affairs. Italy had as great a fascination for him as for Charles VIII, and in his dealings with Italy he shows a lack of high statesmanship and a carelessness for the best interests of France, as well as an entire absence of scruple. It is his Italian adventures which leave the most permanent mark on French history, and we must be careful to mark at least their chief crises and results. Yet before he turned to Italy he did, in however questionable a way, one good thing for France. The revived independence of Brittany threatened France in the most serious way: and if the widowed Queen married some foreign prince the threat would be still more dangerous. Louis XII was married to Jeanne, the daughter of Louis XI. The marriage had been forced on him by Louis XI, and had borne no fruit. The King determined to obtain a divorce and to marry Anne of Brittany. Alexander VI, the most infamous of the Popes, sat on the Papal throne, and was devoted to his son, Cæsar Borgia, the most infamous of all Italian princes. Cæsar was made Duke of Valentinois in Dauphiné, and at this price the divorce was procured and Brittany was reunited to the Crown of France, never again to be parted from it.

The King's designs on Italy were clear from the first. At his coronation he had been proclaimed King of the Two Sicilies and of Jerusalem, and Duke of Milan. The first title was simply the resumption of Charles VIII's claims: the shadowy Crown of Jerusalem was attached to that of Naples. Louis found in his own ancestry a plausible claim on the Duchy of Milan. It was against Milan that his attack was to be directed in the first instance, and diplomacy carefully prepared the way for it. He had little interference to fear from the outside. England was thoroughly pacific under Henry VII. The Empire was altogether incapable of rapid and effective action, for the liberties and privileges of the various princes and states of Germany allowed the Emperor little control of either money or troops. In Italy there was a great field for the action of diplomacy; for it seemed possible to make any combination of states for a moment and impossible to maintain any for long. The Papacy, as we have seen, had been won to the side of the King of France. Spain favoured his designs with a view to a subsequent attack on Naples, of which we shall see more shortly. The Italian states for the most part preserved neutrality. The friendship of Savoy opened the gate of Italy.

In 1499 the French army began its march under d'Aubigny, Trivulzio, and the Count of Ligny. Ludovico was unpopular in Milan, and found resistance impossible. His general, Galéas, deserted Alexandria, and Lodovico himself, despairing of success, fled from Milan and crossed the Valtelline passes into Tyrol, to beg succour of the Emperor Maximilian. The French army entered Milan in September, and was welcomed by a population which Ludovico had crushed with taxation. Genoa fell immediately afterwards into the hands of the French. But again the first conquest of Italian soil proved to be much less difficult than the maintenance of the conquest. Ludovico had been successful in collecting a force, mainly consisting of Swiss mercenaries. He advanced to the recovery of Milan in January 1500. The city rose in revolt to assist him, and Trivulzio, the French commander, had to flee from the city. Ludovico entered in triumph—a triumph more shortlived even than that of the French. In both armies Swiss mercenaries formed a large and important part. Their military value was as great as ever, but mercenary warfare had had its natural effect in weakening their loyalty to their commanders. The Swiss troops now refused to fight against one another. They demanded pay from Ludovico, and when he refused, negotiated with Louis XII. In the end Ludovico found himself without support: he tried to escape, but was captured, and ended his days in a French prison. His fate deserves little pity. He had been the first to call the foreigners into Italy, and he was among the first to feel the bitter consequences of that act of folly. Milan was again and more firmly in the hands of France. There was no power in the north of Italy that could rival hers. And now Louis XII advanced to the realisation of a greater ambition. He was master of Milan: he proceeded next to the conquest of Naples.

No remonstrance was to be anticipated from the Italian powers. The Papacy was allied to France, and the other states were either friendly or impotent. Maximilian, the Emperor, grumbled at the French occupation of Milan, a part of the Empire; but he was inactive, penniless, and not implacable. The most serious danger was to be anticipated from Spain. The house of Aragon had claims on the Two Sicilies which it conceived to be as strong as those of the house of Anjou, and we have already seen (p. 20) that it was in a position to dispute the validity of Frederick's title. The rival claims of France and Spain might seem likely to produce a collision between the two powers, and they did so eventually, when the question of the division of the spoil arose. For the present they agreed to cooperate in the attack. By the treaty of Granada (Nov. 1500) they agreed to partition the territories of the King of Naples. France was to take Naples, the Abruzzi and the Terra di Lavoro, with the title of King of Naples and Jerusalem. Spain was to take Apulia and Calabria, and the title of Duke. In the history of European diplomacy there is no more cruel or unrighteous compact, and few that have been more productive of fatal results to the contracting parties.

The approaches were prepared by the unscrupulous diplomacy that is characteristic of the age. The Pope ratified the terms of the treaty of Granada and excommunicated Frederick, the King of Naples. Frederick saw the storm approaching but could find no means of averting it. The Pope rejected his overtures; he tried in vain to conciliate the King of France by offering him tribute, fortresses and land; he turned at last to Bajazet, the Turkish Sultan, but equally without avail. The French army, strong in artillery and Swiss troops, left Milan in May 1501 under D'Aubigny and Cæsar Borgia, or the Duke of Valentinois, to give him his new title. The French navy was to cooperate under the Duke of Ravenstein. A Spanish armament was already in Sicily under Gonzalvo of Cordova, on the pretext of assisting Venice against the Turks. Frederick could make no opposition to such a mixture of force and treachery. Capua made some show of resistance; but it was speedily overcome and the inhabitants massacred, to the number of seven thousand. The Neapolitans quickly conceived feelings of fear and hatred for the French, which had an important influence on the subsequent history of the Italian campaign. On August 25 Frederick surrendered Naples into the hands of the representatives of Louis XII. He had stipulated for leave to retire to Ischia, but the stipulation was not kept. He was sent as a prisoner to France, where he died three years later. France and Spain could now divide the spoil. Maximilian grumbled disapproval, but all immediate danger from that quarter disappeared in 1501, when a treaty of marriage was made between Claude, daughter of Louis XII, and Prince Charles of Austria. Claude was to bring Brittany with her as her dowry, and the impolicy of such a division of the territories of the Crown was already apparent, though none could foresee the immense importance that would attach to Charles, who, now in his cradle, was destined to occupy the imperial throne as Charles V.

But soon the inevitable quarrel between the conquerors broke out. The treaty of partition had been indefinite—perhaps intentionally indefinite. Two central provinces, the Basilicate and the Capitanate, were claimed by both kingdoms. If these claims had been the real ground of the quarrel, diplomacy might have settled the matter, but they merely covered rival claims to the whole kingdom. Negotiations were conducted with little sincerity and no success, and soon the allies were definitely at war. The French were much better prepared for hostilities than the Spaniards, and at first the fighting went in their favour, but in Gonzalvo of Cordova the Spaniards had a general of unsurpassed courage and resources, while the French commander, the Duke of Nemours, owed his post to court favour and was deficient both in skill and energy. Already, in 1502, while elsewhere victory attended the French arms, Gonzalvo sustained a siege in Barletta, on the Adriatic coast, in which he was said to have shown every quality, moral and intellectual, that marks the great commander. In 1503 he showed equal talents in attack. Italy, which could only shake off one conqueror by supporting another, was turning against the French. Moreover, Louis XII believed that he had concluded arrangements with Spain through Philip, governor of the Netherlands and son-in-law of Ferdinand and Isabella. By a treaty signed at Lyons in April 1503 it was agreed that Charles, the infant son of Philip, the grandson of Ferdinand, and the future Emperor Charles V, was to be betrothed to Claude of France. The Neapolitan kingdom was to become theirs at once, but until the consummation of the marriage it was to be administered by representatives appointed by the kings of France and of Spain. Relying on this treaty, Louis XII sent no reinforcements to Italy; but its terms were at once repudiated by King Ferdinand, and Gonzalvo of Cordova refused to act upon it when it was communicated to him by the French. At the end of April 1503 he faced the French army at Cerignola. The French, under the Duke of Nemours, had not yet learnt the dangerous strength of their adversary. Though the sun was nearly setting when they came upon the Spaniards strongly posted near the historic field of Cannæ, they insisted on attacking at once and overcame the reluctance of the Duke of Nemours. The battle was over in the space of an hour. The advantage of position was with the Spaniards, and Gonzalvo used it to the best effect. The French attack was driven off; Nemours himself was slain; the retreat was turned into a panic rout, and the French fled as best they could, leaving three thousand men upon the field, most of their colours, and all their artillery. The waning prestige of the French sank completely after this defeat. They retained only a few places in the south of Italy, of which Gaeta was the most important, and those were menaced by the Spaniards. Gonzalvo entered Naples in the name of his master in May 1503.

The lost battle was followed at once by a diplomatic loss equally serious. The support of the Papacy was the keystone of French policy in Italy, and on the 18th August Alexander VI died. In vain French diplomacy tried to procure a successor who should be favourable to their ambitions. The aged Archbishop of Sienna held the Papal throne for a few weeks as Pius III, and then was succeeded by Julius II, "the belligerent pontiff who made his tiara a helmet and his crozier a sword," a declared enemy of Alexander and of the French. Cæsar Borgia was seized and sent to Spain. Henceforth France must count on the hostility of Central Italy. But Louis XII had not yet abandoned all hope of regaining Naples. Another army under La Trémoille was sent to reinforce the fragments of French garrisons that were still to be found in Neapolitan territory.

But ill fortune followed this army from the first. La Trémoille fell ill, and the command was left in the incompetent hands of the Duke of Mantua. Upon his approach Gonzalvo broke up from before Gaeta and fell back to the south of the Garigliano. On Nov. 6, 1503, a fierce but indecisive battle was fought near the bridge over the river which was in the hands of the French. Gonzalvo then retired a little from the river and strongly entrenched himself. The French, unable to drive him from his post, encamped on the north side of the river and watched him. The autumn rains were of unusual duration; the ground was naturally swampy and malarial. The sufferings on both sides were extreme, and the Spaniards were even more exposed than the French. But Gonzalvo kept his ascendancy over the minds of his soldiers in spite of all and carefully watched the enemy. At last, late in December, 1503, having secured some reinforcements, he made his way across the river and attacked the French. The attack was so sudden that the French retreated in panic to Gaeta, and the retreat was soon a rout. In their despondency the French even surrendered Gaeta to the Spaniards. The French occupation of Naples ended, leaving behind it the memories of an extraordinarily rapid initial success, of much military heroism and of complete failure at last. Of the conquests of Charles VIII and Louis XII, Milan alone remained. The victory of Spain had been due not only to the military genius of Gonzalvo but also to the great tact and humanity which he had shown in dealing with the Italians, who had been outraged by the contemptuous and cruel treatment of the French.

During the next four years European diplomacy was busy with schemes that had no definite principle or aim and that usually proved abortive; then the crowned heads of Europe coalesced again, and again for the old purpose, the plunder of an apparently helpless state. It will be enough to note the chief events that come between the defeat at Garigliano and the Treaty of Cambray. There are two main incidents in the history of France during these years—the Treaties of Blois, and the States General of Tours.

Louis XII had made a truce of three years with King Ferdinand, and thus abandoned, at least for the time, his claims upon Naples. But he still regarded Ferdinand as his enemy, and was soon busy negotiating against his interests. Both Philip and the Emperor Maximilian had their grievances against Ferdinand, despite their relationship to him. In Sept. 1504, three treaties were concluded at Blois. The first contained a first hint of the subsequent alliance of France and the Empire against Venice, which was declared to be the enemy of the Catholic Church, the Empire, and the King of France. By the second, the Emperor at last consented to give Louis XII formal investiture of the Duchy of Milan. In the third, Louis XII promised as a dowry to his daughter Claude—who was already betrothed to Charles of Austria—Milan, Brittany, Genoa, and Burgundy. All French historians have denounced this treaty, which dismembered France in the hope of obtaining a faster hold upon Milan. Naturally enough, the notion of Brittany passing to the heir of the Netherlands and of Spain roused the gravest anxiety. The King himself seems speedily to have repented of his decision. If he was to break his promise he determined to shelter himself behind the national will, and in 1506 he summoned the States General to Blois.

Louis XII was undoubtedly popular. The French nation,

strange as it may seem, had hardly been affected by the Italian wars, which were conducted by the monarch rather than by the State, and were largely self-supporting. Taxes were light, the country orderly, and agriculture flourishing. "Never for three hundred years," said a speaker, "has there been such prosperity in France as now." The King was greeted with genuine enthusiasm, and the title of "Pater Patriæ" was bestowed upon him. Then the deputies presented a request, of which no doubt the King had had full notice. He was implored not to give his only daughter to Charles of Austria, but to bestow her hand upon his nephew Francis, the heir to the throne, who was recommended as being thoroughly French. The King yielded to a pressure that he very probably prompted. His coronation oath, he remembered, forbade him to do anything which threatened "to diminish the realm." Philip was busy at that moment with complications in Spain and could not resent the affront. Next year he died, and soon the Venetian question monopolised the diplomatic energies of Europe.

From the League of Cambray to the Death of Louis XII.

Many states had grievances against Venice that with a little trouble could be amplified into causes for war; but the root of all these grievances was that she was strong and prosperous. Alone among the Italian states, her government was uniform, continuous, and successful. Her commercial establishments covered the East of the Mediterranean. In Italy she had encroached upon the territories of the Duchy of Milan (now held by France), of the Empire, and of the Papacy.

We have seen how, as far back as 1504, the Emperor had been thinking of an attack on Venice, in accord with the French King. But when in 1506 Maximilian attacked her it was alone, and though Louis XII had no love for the Republic, he felt himself bound by treaty obligations to oppose the passage of Imperial troops through Venetian territory. Maximilian had to accept a truce and retire. But France felt herself neglected and despised by the proud Republic, and soon the diplomacy of the time, so fertile in new combinations, was building up a league against her that has been called the conspiracy of kings.

Maximilian and Louis XII were the two chief conspirators, and France was easily induced to join by the haughtiness of the Republic and the hope of regaining the lost fragments of the Duchy of Milan. The treaty between the two leaders was signed in December, 1508, and other powers soon joined. Venice was so rich and so powerful, the jealousy of all powers concerned with Italy was so intense, that no power except England refused, and most were willing to take an active part. Ferdinand of Aragon joined, hoping for additions to his Neapolitan territory. Other reasons induced the Dukes of Ferrara, Mantua, and Savoy, and the Republic of Florence to come in. The list was completed by the Pope, Julius II, who had succeeded to the Papacy in 1503. He entertained the hope of driving all foreign powers from the peninsula, and had his doubts about the expediency of joining a league that would introduce so many foreign powers armed into Italy. But Venice would not yield on debated points, and the Pope signed along with the rest. He issued a bull against the Republic, declared the Venetians guilty of high treason against God, and called on all princes to attack them.

The Empire was as usual slow in getting its forces ready. The first campaign was over before they appeared. The Venetians knew the greatness of the danger, but thought it better to meet it with courage than to wait for the chances that delay might bring. They advanced boldly to the frontier of the Milanese, there to meet the French, who, they knew, would be first in the field. The two armies manœuvred for some time in the valley of the Adda. The Venetian force reflected the variegated character of the dominions of the Republic: Italians, Cretans, and Greeks, mercenary soldiers and peasants, jostled one another in the ranks. The force of

Louis XII was admirably equipped, and the infantry had been especially organised with great care on a new plan. On May 14, Louis XII caught the enemy's rear-guard at Agnadello. Alviano, who commanded this division of the Venetian army, though he was quite unsupported by the rest, offered a gallant and desperate resistance. The French, however, acting under the direction of their King, himself an eager combatant, at last carried all before them. Alviano was captured; the Venetians were defeated; and many thought that the partition of the territories of Venice might begin at once.

But the Venetians showed themselves both in courage and in astuteness worthy of their past. It was clear that some part of the Venetian domain must be abandoned: it was abandoned with an appearance of spontaneity that gained for Venice a reputation for generosity and humanity. The invaders could no longer count on the goodwill of the populations they subdued. Venice tried even to buy peace from the Emperor at the price of a tribute of 50,000 ducats: but Maximilian was not satisfied with the offer, and blundered on to his ruin. Padua had passed into the hands of the Emperor, but the peasants, when they felt the weight of imperial taxation, regretted the milder rule of the Republic. In July, 1509, they rebelled, and were assisted by the Venetians. Maximilian laid siege to Padua with the largest army that Italy had seen on its soil for many years. But the attack was directed without skill, and broke down before the stubbornness of the defence. The Imperial army was withdrawn, and the Venetians reoccupied other places in the neighbourhood. In the early spring of 1510 they made terms with the Pope. They yielded on most of the points that were matters of dispute between them, and surrendered some of their possessions in the Romagna. On these conditions the Pope abandoned the League of Cambray.

Next year the Italian states entered upon a quite new combination. Julius II saw his mistake in summoning France

and the Empire into Italy, or felt that the humiliation of
Venice had gone far enough. The only principle of Italian
diplomacy was to unite against the strongest state for the time
being, and Venice was that no longer. So Julius II, as the
representative of Italy, was now anxious to prevent the further
advance of the French and the Imperialists. He won over
Ferdinand of Aragon by giving him the investiture of Naples
and Sicily; he joined himself closely to the Venetians; and,
most important of all, he made terms with the Swiss. Switzerland was then the great hive of mercenaries for all Europe.
The mountaineers were really the best infantry in the world,
and they no doubt overrated their own importance. They had
just rejected the terms of Louis XII as insufficient, and readily
accepted the proposal of the Pope that they should enter into
his pay and serve him against the French and Imperialists.
Henry VIII, the newly-crowned King of England, also declared himself on the side of the Pope.

Louis XII entered with reluctance on the new phase of the
struggle. The name and authority of the Pope were not what
they had once been, but they still carried weight. Louis XII
called together an assembly of the clergy at Tours to consider
the propriety of the Pope's action in making war for an object
not purely religious. The assembly denounced the Pope and
supported the King. But the exigencies of the war soon
made more direct action against the Papal authority inevitable.
Louis XII summoned a council to Pisa to consider the condition of the Church and the reforms that were needed.
Julius II summoned an opposition council to St John Lateran
in Rome, and soon advanced to a bolder project. In October
1511 he made the Holy League with Ferdinand of Aragon
and the Republic of Venice for the defence of the interests
of the Church. The Pope appeared now definitely as the
champion of Italian independence against 'barbarian' interference. The situation grew rapidly more favourable to him.
Henry VIII joined the Holy League and threatened the

northern coasts of France. The Emperor himself showed himself willing to be reconciled to the Pope.

But though dangers were thus thickening round the French, they acted in Italy with surprising vigour. Their army was under the command of the nephew of the King—Gaston de Foix, Duke of Nemours. He was only twenty-four years of age, but already he displayed a military genius which promised to enrol him among the greatest commanders of European history. He could plan a campaign as well as direct a battle: he had the great man's power of infusing something of his own fiery will into the more sluggish minds of his subordinates. Italy was astonished at the rapidity of his marches and the energy with which he pressed on his sieges, and, though he made such demands from his soldiers, he had the art of winning their love as well as their obedience. He has been compared to the very greatest soldiers: had he lived he might at least have been for the sixteenth century what Condé was for the seventeenth. Early in 1512 he attacked and took Brescia, which had revolted from the French. Then, eager to bring on a decisive action, he marched on Ravenna with surprising rapidity. His first attack on Ravenna failed, and he immediately turned on the army of the Holy League, which had slowly come up to the relief of the place. This battle, if we judge by the numbers engaged on either side, the fury of the struggle, or the numbers of the slain, was the most important that had hitherto been fought in the Italian wars. Cardona, the commander for the Holy League, was so strongly posted that his slight deficiency of numbers seemed quite counterbalanced. But Gaston de Foix knew that delay would be favourable to his adversary and that he had no time to manœuvre. He ordered the attack to take place at once. The engagement opened with a long and ineffective cannonade, but when the troops came to blows the French carried all before them. The Spanish infantry fell back in good order after having fought with their usual stubborn valour. Gaston de Foix, at the head of a handful of men,

France during the Italian Wars.

charged them, but was beaten from his horse and killed. Ravenna fell into the hands of the French after the battle, but the French were more depressed by the loss of their leader than elated by the victory.

If Gaston de Foix had lived, men thought that he would have marched at once on Rome and secured the predominance of France in Italy by a *coup de main* against the Holy City. The Pope himself is said to have expected such an advance, and to have trembled for the consequences. But La Palice, who took the command of the French troops after Gaston's death, had no heart for such daring enterprise. He fell back on the Milanese, leaving only a garrison in Ravenna, which was promptly expelled by a rising of the people. Julius II, who, on receipt of the news of Ravenna, was preparing for a desperate resistance, found it possible at once to attack the French. A strong body of Swiss troops came to his assistance: the Emperor had made up his mind to join the League and allowed them to pass through Tyrol into Venetian territory. The prestige and popularity of the French had both disappeared with the death of Gaston de Foix. Everywhere the population rose against them. Soon the citadels of Milan, Cremona, and Brescia alone remained in their hands. Genoa revolted against them: Florence passed under the influence of the Papal party: and while Louis XII was thus suddenly awakened from his dream of Italian conquest the soil of France itself was attacked. A force of English and Spanish troops entered and occupied Navarre.

But Louis XII was not in the least prepared to abandon Italy. A French garrison still held out in the citadel of Milan. The Holy League, too, was no more stable than the League of Cambray. The Venetians were offended by the claims of both Emperor and Pope. There was no reason to despair of making some fresh combination that should favour the hopes of France. But an attempt to strengthen into reality the alliance with the Emperor, which still nominally subsisted, failed; nor had Louis XII better fortune with the Swiss: they believed themselves invincible, and regarded northern Italy as their own. He had better success with Venice, the state which he had once regarded as his bitterest enemy, and which had most cause to complain of him. For the immediate present was everything in the diplomacy of the time: men thought neither of past nor future. In March 1513 an alliance was made with Venice for the reconquest of the Milanese. Fortune favoured France too elsewhere: Julius II died in February of the same year: the greatest enemy of France and the most skilful statesman of Italy was thus removed. His successor Leo X was reckoned an enemy of France, but he had not the same strong political and military interests. Louis XII yielded on the religious questions that were in dispute between them, and Leo X showed an inclination to come to terms on other matters.

So, full of hope, he despatched La Trémoille with an army into Italy in April 1513. At first all went well: the French and Venetians carried all before them. The population seemed to recognise that the chances were with France, and showed an inclination to join them: Milan and Genoa declared for them again. But these appearances were illusory. An alliance against France had already been concluded between England, Spain, and the Emperor, and in Italy itself the Swiss troops had yet to be accounted for. These, eager to sustain their military reputation, although outnumbered by the enemy, attacked the French army at Novara before daybreak. The artillery tore their ranks, but could not force them to retreat. They captured the guns, turned them on the French, and then falling on the infantry gained a complete victory. La Trémoille with the fragments of his army thought himself fortunate to be able to repass the Alps.

Louis XII meanwhile had other enemies to face at home and other defeats to suffer. Hitherto the war had been fought beyond the bounds of France and had been almost self-supporting. But now the recently-formed triple alliance of

England, the Empire, and Spain, openly aimed at the dismemberment of France herself. The thing was perhaps no longer possible, for France was far more united than she had been in the days of Edward III and Henry V. But the allies began the campaign successfully. The English troops entered France by the always open door of Calais, and were joined by Maximilian and the Imperial troops. Together they laid siege to Térouanne, a much-prized French stronghold. It was necessary to relieve it, and yet both men and money were hard to find. At last a force was sent forward under La Palice and Bayard—the latter the flower of French chivalry and a skilful soldier. But while this army was cooperating in an attempt to introduce food into Térouanne, it was unexpectedly attacked and entirely defeated by a small English force, in what was subsequently known as the "Battle of the Spurs." La Palice and Bayard were taken prisoners. It was followed immediately by the surrender of Térouanne. Before the siege was finished a force of Swiss passed over the Saône and laid siege to Dijon. La Trémoille was in command of the place with a paltry force. When a breach had been opened he treated with the enemy and offered them, as a price for their withdrawal, a large sum of money and the abandonment of all the places still held by France in Italy—the citadels of Milan, Cremona, and Asti. The terms were not kept; perhaps there had never been any intention of keeping them; but this, the third serious defeat of the year, humiliated deeply the pride of the King and nation. The situation, however, though serious, was not desperate. It would be easy to fill up the gaps in the army, and diplomacy might make the coalition as short-lived as all its predecessors had been. Already the prospect of success had brought discord among the victors. Leo X was fully reconciled to France. The Emperor was the first to negotiate. Then in April, 1514, Ferdinand of Spain signed a truce for a year. The King of England, indignant at the treachery of his allies, stood out for a time. But he too came in at last, and the marriage of

Louis XII to the English King's sister Mary, was to be the symbol of the reconciliation.

The marriage took place on the 9th October. A round of *fêtes* and gaiety followed, which exhausted the already declining strength of the King. He died on 1st Jan. 1515. His Italian policy had been the chief object of his life, and it had resulted in entire failure, and was destined to lead his successor into failures still more disastrous. And yet his reign has always been considered a fortunate and a prosperous one. For, as we have seen, the disasters of the French arms did not touch France herself until the very last years of the reign. The country was prosperous, the population was increasing, the people were orderly, and the oppression of the nobles had ceased[1]. As men looked back to the reign of Louis XII across the grave disasters of his successors it seemed to them a sort of golden age.

II. The Italian wars of Francis I. and their consequences. The Accession of Francis I. and the Battle of Marignano.

French historians have usually shown a fondness for the memory of Francis I. His reign saw a remarkable development of art and literature in France, and his name shines with some of the glory that is always reflected upon a ruler by such a circumstance. His policy too was never commonplace or cautious: if it had its periods of tragic rout and failure, it had also much splendid ad-

[1] A contemporary (Claude Seyssel) thus describes the well-being of the country in this reign. "The revenue from benefices and from the property of the nobles has generally and largely increased. The sums paid for the gabelle, the tolls and legal dues, and all other sources of revenue have also risen vastly, in some places by two-thirds, in others by nine-tenths....For one rich and prosperous merchant that you could find in the days of Louis XI at Paris, Rouen, Lyons, or any other of the great cities of the realm you may find in this reign more than fifty....Merchants take a journey to Rome, Naples, or London more lightly now than formerly to Geneva or Lyons." This is not an isolated passage. The evidence as to the prosperity of France in this reign seems convergent and conclusive. It was to be shaken by the long struggle of Francis I with Spain, and finally overthrown by the "Wars of Religion."

venture and many striking successes. The King's personality too was at first attractive. He was handsome, and of engaging manners and witty conversation. As a soldier he was brave to recklessness, and naturally the idol of his war-loving nobility. He has also a claim to our liking in that he sympathised with the new movement in art and letters and thought that passed into France as a result of the Italian campaigns. He was the admiring friend and patron of Leonardo da Vinci, and was keenly interested in the new style both of writing and building which the revival of classical studies had introduced. We can understand why two women—his mother, Louise of Savoy, and his sister, Margaret of Valois—loved him always so tenderly and worked for him so devotedly. But history, which is concerned almost exclusively with the public acts of Kings and with their private characters only as they affect their public acts, cannot share the affection of his mother and sister. His gaiety and courage covered a thoroughly egotistic nature. He showed no skill either as general or statesman: above all he showed no power of following, even in disaster, the line of policy that he believed to be right. It would be difficult to point to any act of his reign which really conferred benefits on France. Yet, if he is far from a great King, his reign is a very important one. And its chief importance is this—a new and a strong motive enters into European politics. The hostility between France and the Spanish-Austrian House becomes a constant factor in the international relationships of Europe, and is destined to remain so for more than a century and a half.

His reign was a stirring one from the very first. He gave little attention to questions of domestic policy. Antoine Duprat, First President of the Parlement of Paris, was made Chancellor and exercised a dominant and sometimes an unfortunate influence on internal affairs. The Constable's sword was given to Charles Duke of Bourbon. Military projects against Italy engaged the King's attention from the very first. He possessed indeed no foot of soil in Italy, but he claimed both Milan and Naples as his predecessor had done, and was prepared to enforce his claim against both the Emperor and the King of Spain. He protected his own frontiers on the north and west by arrangements with Henry VIII of England and Charles of Austria; he had as yet no suspicions that the latter would turn out to be his lifelong and victorious rival. Assured then for the present of the neutrality of these two great powers he next looked for allies in Italy. Pope Leo X refused to countenance a new French invasion. Active assistance could only be expected from Venice.

By Midsummer 1515 he was ready for the invasion of Italy. He had only been on the throne six months, and was not yet 21 years old. But throughout his reign his action depended rather on hope and imagination than on experience and a well-considered policy. His wildest hopes were flattered by the events of the first year of his reign; but after that fortune had in store for him little but disillusionment. When he arrived at the foot of the Alps in August he heard that the chief passes were occupied by Swiss in imperial pay. To force them was out of the question. But guides suggested another pass to him, over the defiles of Guillestre and Argentière. It was a mountain path possible to pedestrians, but untraversed by horses, and apparently quite impossible for artillery. A Spanish engineer in the French service, Navarro, believed that it could be made practicable, and the King sanctioned the attempt. The road was found to be unusually free from snow, and in five days, after a very adventurous march, the French army came down into the Marquisate of Saluzzo. The astonishment produced by this exploit was so great that at first it seemed as if Francis I would conquer Milan without a battle. Maximilian Sforza began to negotiate. The Swiss troops, on whom alone he could rely, were mutinous through deferred pay, and seemed inclined to come to terms with the French King, who made them very liberal offers. But when affairs were at this point, a new force of 20,000 Swiss came down from the mountains under Matthew Schinner, the warlike cardinal of Sion, and were determined to force on a battle. Francis I, believing that his arrangements with the Swiss and the Duke of Milan would soon be completed, was moving leisurely from Pavia and Milan when near Marignano he was suddenly confronted by the new Swiss army, and had to prepare for battle (13th Sept.). The ground was marshy and did not allow the French generals —the Constable Bourbon, La Trémoille and Trivulzio—to draw up their troops to the best advantage. The Swiss attacked in three dense columns of about 10,000 men each, and though their ranks were torn by the French cannon they reached their enemies' lines, and at first seemed as though they would force their way through. The situation was saved by a charge of cavalry, headed by the King himself; but the battle raged till sunset—a fierce disorganised struggle, in which neither side could claim the advantage. After sunset the fight still continued by the light of the moon, and when at last darkness came the troops rested on the field of battle. The King himself slept on a gun-carriage at a few paces from the enemy. But during the night the French ranks were rearranged, and when the battle recommenced the Swiss suffered again very severely from the artillery, and were already giving way when "San Marco," the battle-cry of the Venetians, was heard, and it was known that Alviano was coming up to the help of the French. The Swiss broke and fled. The 'combat of giants,' as Trivulzio called it, had been a day of glory for France, to which her annals could hardly find a parallel. The Swiss infantry, that counted itself invincible, had been broken by a force that was thoroughly French and national. It was this which made the day seem so much more glorious than even the battle of Ravenna. Milan at once surrendered. The Pope made terms. The Emperor tried to recover his lost ground, but the only instrument that he possessed was the mercenary Swiss, and they refused to fight against the

French, whose ranks had been largely recruited from their compatriots. Francis signed the Peace of Viterbo with the Pope in October, 1515; preliminary terms were concluded with the Swiss in November. In August, 1516, the treaty of Noyon was signed with the Archduke Charles, who was now also King of Spain, and the Emperor gave his adhesion a few months later. In November, 1516, came the final Peace of Fribourg with the Swiss cantons.

There was much in these treaties that was quite transitory. The Empire was soon to fall into stronger hands and to continue the war against Francis, in spite of the treaty of Noyon; nor was all settled between France and Spain when Francis I gave up his claims to Naples. The really permanent parts of the treaties were the arrangements with the Swiss and with the Papacy. The Peace of Fribourg was called perpetual, and justified its name. It established friendly relations with the cantons, and they formed henceforth a constant recruiting ground for the French armies. More important still was the arrangement with the Papacy—the Concordat, which has already been examined in the introductory chapter. Henceforth the Church in France was as thoroughly subject to the Crown as it was in England after the changes of Henry VIII.

The negotiations of the year 1516 gave Europe peace for four years; but they were years full of preparation for war, and they saw the entry of a new champion into the European arena who disputed the first place with Francis I, and finally gained it for himself. A politic series of marriages and much good fortune concentrated in the hands of Charles of Austria the greatest extent of territory that had obeyed one ruler since the days of the Roman Empire; and if the extent of the territories in the new world claimed by Charles is taken into account even Rome had not ruled over so vast an empire. His father was the grandson of Charles the Bold, the great Burgundian duke, who had struggled on terms of equality

The Imperial Election; the rivalry between Francis I and Charles V; the Battle of Pavia.

with Louis XI. From him he inherited the Netherlands and
Franche Comté and indefinite claims on France besides. His
mother Joanna was the daughter of Ferdinand and Isabella,
and through her there came to him the Crown of united Spain
with its vigorous and warlike population, its fierce Catholic
enthusiasm, and its vast territories in the Americas that were
believed to contain inexhaustible mines of gold. Spain too
brought him the kingdom of Naples. He became King of
Spain in January 1516, and even then the prospect of another
throne awoke his ambition and the jealousy of rival powers.
He was the eldest male descendant of the Emperor Maximilian.
The Empire was not, indeed, hereditary, but for a long time past
the electors had not looked outside of the House of Hapsburg
for a candidate; and as the eldest representative of that House
Charles had more than a slight chance of the imperial Crown.
But if he gained it, if the real strength of the Archduchy of
Austria and the shadowy glory of the Empire were added to his
other dominions, the balance of power in Europe—a principle
which statesmen were just beginning to hold sacred—would
seem to be entirely upset.

The years 1517 and 1518 in France were quiet in comparison
with the previous years so full of stirring events. The chief
effort of Francis I was to induce the Parlement to accept the
Concordat which he had recently made with the Pope. It was
not until March, 1518, that Parlement registered the edict, and
then only by express command of the King; for the Parlement,
hitherto the chief engine of the royal power, resisted so great
an innovation as the Concordat implied. But these years were
full of intrigues with a view to the approaching vacancy in the
Empire. Margaret of Austria, in the Netherlands, and the
Emperor Maximilian, eagerly supported the cause of Charles.
Francis had only himself to rely on. The diplomatists on both
sides met in every electoral court in Germany, and no weapon
was so frequently employed, none was so effective, as direct and
shameless bribery. Maximilian died in Jan. 1719, and the

question was not yet settled. Both sides renewed their efforts; both sides had some chances in their favour. Germany, threatened by the Turks and torn by the Lutheran movement, wanted—so many held—a strong ruler, and the fame of Francis I was far greater than that of his younger opponent: the Pope, though with some hesitation, threw his influence on the same side. But the traditions of the Empire supported the House of Hapsburg: the official machinery was in the hands of the supporters of Charles. There was uncertainty up to the last moment, and the candidature of the English King created a momentary diversion. But on July 5, 1519, in the Diet at Frankfort, the electors pronounced in favour of Charles, who was henceforth known as the Emperor Charles V. So long as he lived, the Empire and the Netherlands, Spain and Naples, were bound together in a coalition against France which diplomacy could not hope to dissolve.

From the first, hostilities between the two great rivals were probable. England, under Henry VIII and Wolsey, had risen to a new importance in Europe and seemed likely to give victory to the cause that it supported. Both sides tried to gain England's support. But Francis I at the Field of the Cloth of Gold (June, 1520) displayed in vain the wealth of his country and his own grace and skill. The more private interviews that Charles V had with the English King at Canterbury and at Gravelines had a greater effect. Henry VIII did not yet commit himself; but Francis I was his most dangerous rival, and he leaned towards an alliance with the Emperor.

Troubles in Navarre were the excuse for the beginning of hostilities, which came in 1521. The long series of wars which followed have almost as much claim to the title, the "Two Hundred Years' War," as the struggle between England and France has to the title of the "Hundred Years' War": for the antagonism between France and the Austrian House counts as a central motive in European politics until the Treaty of Utrecht in 1713. Perhaps the best policy for Francis would have been to abandon Italy and to restrict his efforts to the defence of France: but the Italian war had become a point of honour with the French Kings, and Francis I followed it to an even greater disaster than had fallen upon Louis XII.

The French held their own on French soil in 1521; but in Italy things went against them from the first. The Italians could always be trusted to rise against the last conqueror. The Milanese rose against Lautrec, the French governor, who had not received from Francis I the supplies and money that had been promised him, and in consequence could only maintain the citadel against them. At the end of the year Leo X died, and the new Pope, Adrian VI, was a Hollander, formerly tutor to Charles V. It was probable that his influence would be thrown on the Austro-Spanish side. In 1522 the Italian campaign was wholly unfavourable to France. In April, Lautrec was defeated at Bicocca, chiefly through the insubordination of his Swiss troops. The waning prestige of France encouraged revolts everywhere. Genoa fell into the hands of the Emperor. Soon nothing in Italy was left to the French except the citadels of Milan, Novara, and Cremona. But the chief event of the year is not military but diplomatic. Henry VIII joined heartily with Charles V and projected a partition of France. Charles, according to this grandiose scheme, was to receive "the inheritance of the Duke of Burgundy," which would take him far towards the heart of France; Henry was to take Normandy and "all that had ever belonged to his ancestors." The projected invasion of France failed in 1522, but another plan was arranged for next year. The year 1523 saw, however, no military events of importance. The meditated attack on France failed rather ignominiously. In Italy Bonnivet prevented the scanty French possessions from further diminution. But diplomacy was busier than arms, and here Charles V gained successes of the utmost importance. In August the Spanish Pope, Adrian VI, made a league of

Italian powers against Francis, which all the important states joined with the exception of Savoy: even Venice, seeing the balance inclining strongly against France, threw in her lot with her enemies: worse still, secret enemies within the realm were cooperating with the open enemy outside. We come to the great treason of the Constable Bourbon.

No subject of the King had shared so much in the early glories of the reign as Charles of Bourbon. One of the King's first acts was to make him constable. His had been half the glory of Marignano. But he very soon had his grievances against the King. He had been recalled from Milan, and his expenses had not been paid him. No great command had been given to him. The Duke of Alençon had been preferred to him for military posts. But none of these things lay at the root of his treason. He was the last remnant of that 'Princely feudalism' against which Louis XI had to struggle, and he was bound to provoke the hostility of Francis, who praised Louis XI "for having freed the Kings of France from tutelage." He held his court at Moulins in almost royal state, collecting taxes and administering justice. He was too great for a subject of the new *régime* in France, and the King was glad when a pretext rose for diminishing his power. Certain of his dominions had belonged to his wife Susanna. As she had left no issue it was not certain whether they did or did not belong to her husband after her death. Francis, eager to divide Bourbon's possessions, put the law in motion, and doubtless pressed every advantage that the law gave him. In defence of his feudal claims the Constable turned, in the old feudal fashion, to the foreign enemy. At the beginning of August he signed a promise to help Charles V and Henry VIII in their plan for dismembering France. Charles promised to give him his sister in marriage, and of course to support him in his claims against Francis. The conspiracy was only to take effect when Francis I had led his army beyond the Alps into Italy. If it had been carried out according to the intention of the conspirators, France might have reeled under the blow, but Francis received information of the plans. He at first refused to believe in them, and only determined to arrest the traitor when it was too late. In Sept. 1523 the Constable Bourbon fled from France and joined himself to her enemies.

Despite this accumulation of dangers, the autumn of 1523 passed without disastrous results to France. Bonnivet held his own in the Milanese, and if his skill had equalled his courage he would have improved his position. The English armies penetrated into the neighbourhood of Paris, but were then driven off by La Trémoille with some disgrace. It was clearly no easy task, even for an European coalition, to partition France.

But the year 1524 had a worse fate in store for France and her King. In March Milan was entirely overrun by the Austro-Spanish army. Bonnivet was defeated, and the heroic Bayard, while trying to bring off the rear-guard, himself received a mortal wound. His death caused a great sensation. This "chevalier sans peur et sans reproche" shows us chivalry at its very best just as it is disappearing from the world. The story of his life and death became one of the most treasured memories of France. Elated with victory, Bourbon persuaded his allies to undertake the invasion of France. Like all exiles, he exaggerated the discontent of the country, believed that France was ready to revolt from its rulers out of sympathy with him, and would have liked the Spanish and Austrian army to press straight for his own territories on the Upper Loire. But Charles V insisted on the siege of Marseilles, desiring, as Henri Martin says, "to have a Calais of his own." The fortifications of the city were out of repair, and Bourbon prophesied an easy conquest; but the place was very stubbornly defended. Francis I marched to its relief and Bourbon had to fall back into Italy. But it was not enough for Francis I to repel invasion: he must answer blow with blow, and thought that the Spanish failure at Marseilles gave him assurance of success in Italy. In October, 1524, eager to repeat his success of Marignano, he passed the Alps with a force of about 40,000 men. Italy, as usual, was ready to reject an old conqueror for a new one, and was already alarmed by the victories of Charles V. Milan was occupied in October. The Marquis of Pescara evacuated the city, leaving, however, a Spanish garrison in its almost impregnable citadel. In December, Pope Clement VII, who had succeeded Adrian VI in 1523, made a treaty of neutrality with Francis, and Venice soon made similar terms. Pavia alone held out in the Milanese, and Francis eagerly undertook the siege. But its commander, Antonio da Leyva, showed military skill of a high order, and the siege was prolonged into the spring of 1525. Great efforts were made on the Imperialist side. The generals of Charles V worked for him with the utmost energy. Money was the Emperor's great want, for his German subjects would grant him none for an enterprise in which they were not interested. But Bourbon, Pescara, and Lannoy used every means, public and private, to collect money, and had a great measure of success. Bourbon had time to collect a force of Swiss and Germans and to march to the relief of Pavia. The King found himself caught between two fires, and yet he was so strongly posted in the park of Mirabello that there was no reason for despondency. For some time he stood on the defensive. Bourbon and the Spanish commander, Pescara, tried to bring on a battle by attempting to throw supplies into the besieged city. But as the enemy tried to pass the French position they were exposed to the fire of the artillery and retreated in disorder. The King, believing himself secure of victory, charged at the head of his cavalry, and silenced his own artillery by getting between the guns and the enemy. Da Leyva saw his opportunity and sallied out from the city to attack the French. After a very fierce struggle, the French infantry—mostly Swiss and German mercenaries—were defeated, the Swiss hardly showing their usual stubborn courage. Then Pescara, at the head of the Spanish horse, intermingled, after a novel fashion, with Swiss musketeers, fell fiercely on the French cavalry, who were commanded by Francis I in person.

The King did nothing to belie his reputation for courage. Most
of the leading officers of the French army were killed—La
Palice, Trémoille, Bonnivet, Lescare. The King, wounded in
two places, still fought on until his horse was killed and fell
upon him. He was made prisoner, but refused to give his
sword to Bourbon: Charles de Lannoy, the vice-king of Naples,
received it on his knees. The French power in Italy collapsed
at once. In fifteen days the only Frenchmen left in Italy were
prisoners. "Nothing is saved," said Francis in a letter to his
mother, "except life and honour[1]."

The news of the King's captivity was received with consternation in Paris. It recalled men's memories to the battle of Poictiers and the captivity of King John. It seemed as if Bourbon might play over again the part of the Duke of Burgundy, and all the disasters of the English wars be renewed. *From the Battle of Pavia to the Peace of Cambray.* A closer examination showed that the dangers were not so great as they appeared to be. Though France was hard pressed by taxation, and there was perhaps some sympathy with Bourbon, there was no sign of rebellion.

The apparent magnitude of Charles's victory told against
him. The Italians, true to their past, at once began to intrigue
against the ally whom they had helped to make so strong.
Henry VIII of England was uneasy at the immense acquisition of prestige that had come to Charles. He still made
warm profession of friendship; but really friendship had given
way to jealousy, and he drew near to France.

Further, it was soon seen that the Emperor was not in a
position to press his advantage. Germany was divided by the
Lutheran movement, harassed by the Peasants' War, and fearful
of an attack from the Turks. The exactions of the Imperial
armies in Italy provoked the bitterest resentment. The possession of the Milanese and of the person of the King of France

[1] Such seems to be the proper form of an often misquoted sentence (*de toutes choses ne m'est demeuré que l'honneur et la vie qui est sauve*).

were the only advantages which the battle of Pavia gave the Emperor; but they were very great. His great task for the next few months was to turn the captivity of Francis I to the best account. The King had at first been lodged at Pizzighettone, and treated with much respect and deference. But in June, 1525, he was taken to Spain. He welcomed the change, for he had a firm belief in his powers of charming and persuading, and hoped that in a personal interview with the Emperor he would be able to gain better terms than through representatives. The Emperor however, much to his chagrin, refused to see him, made his imprisonment much more severe than it had been in Italy, and moved him to Madrid, where escape was impossible.

Negotiations were carried on between the representatives of the two monarchs, but it seemed impossible to come to any conclusion. Charles at first demanded such concessions both to England and the Empire as would have amounted to the break-up of the French monarchy, and to the last he insisted on the abandonment of the Duchy of Burgundy and its dependencies, and of all claims to Italy. For some time Francis I stood out against these terms; he had rather remain in prison all his life, he said, than consent to the enslavement of France. In the autumn his sister, Marguerite of Valois, whose affection for Francis remained to the end romantic, passionate and almost beyond the love of a sister, was allowed to see him. Finding that Charles V would not give way, the King sent back by his sister, when she returned to France, letters patent directing that his son Francis should be crowned King: he himself seemed prepared to face a long imprisonment. But the confinement told heavily upon his spirits. Charles V yielded something of his former claims. Francis already comforted himself with the thought that whatever promises he made would be made under constraint, and would therefore not be binding upon him. In January, 1526, he signed the Treaty of Madrid. To gain his liberty he ceded Burgundy and all its dependencies to the Emperor; abandoned all his claims or rights in Flanders and Italy; promised to reinstate the Duke of Bourbon in his possessions, and to marry Eleanor, the sister of the Emperor. As a guarantee for the fulfilment of these terms he was to leave his two children as hostages, and he promised upon his honour and oath that if within a stipulated time he did not fulfil the terms of the treaty he would return to Spain and surrender himself again a prisoner to the Emperor. On the 13th of March all preliminaries were arranged: he crossed the frontier of the Bidassoa, and felt himself again a King. He had been a prisoner rather more than a year.

He had no intention of keeping the terms of the treaty. His contemporaries judged this breach of faith much more leniently than we are inclined to do. Charles V knew that a repudiation of the treaty was very probable. The King of England acquitted Francis of bad faith. Most important of all, Pope Clement VII, fearful of the Emperor's power in Italy, drew near to Francis, made alliance with him, and solemnly freed him from the obligation of his oath. Francis maintained that Burgundy could not be alienated without the consent of the people themselves; and the Estates of Burgundy at once declared that their Duchy was an inalienable part of the realm of France, and that Francis I was transcending even the powers of the monarchy in proposing to alienate it. Charles V had the French princes as hostages, but he could not think of putting pressure on such young children; and the only appeal left was to the sword.

The situation was not very favourable to Charles. Italy, as usual, turned against its master, and in May, 1526, an Italian alliance threatened the Spanish power both in Milan and Naples. In July the Italian states joined hands with France in the "Holy League" for the deliverance of Italy, and a month later the King of England joined. This amounted to a very considerable diplomatic success, but Francis was using his long-deferred liberty in the pursuit of pleasure, and showed little energy in his military enterprises. Consequently the war, so far as France was concerned, languished just when Europe expected to see it assume its vastest dimensions. Italy proved as fatal as ever to the French. It was upon the Papacy that the heaviest blow fell. Charles of Bourbon was in command in the north of Italy. He took and plundered the citadel of Milan in 1526. Then in 1527 he turned his eyes towards a greater prey. His army was insubordinate—his master rather than his servant. The pay of the soldiers was in arrears; a large proportion of them were Lutherans, and both religious hatred and avarice made Rome and the surrounding territories a tempting bait. An attack upon the Papal States, too, would not be altogether displeasing to Charles V. He had not forgotten Clement VII's union with France, while other events had occurred of late to increase his dislike for the political action of the Pope. The hungry army, therefore, turned aside from the territories of Venice and Florence, which had once been suggested for attack, and marched on Rome. Clement was entirely taken by surprise: he had recently dismissed a large part of his garrison. Bourbon's army appeared before Rome on May 5, 1527.

It does not fall within the scope of this book to describe in any detail the course of the siege which was the most renowned event of the first half of the century. There were no adequate preparations for resistance, but, as the Imperialists were almost unprovided with artillery and siege apparatus, the position was not quite hopeless. The first assaults were repulsed, and Bourbon, conspicuous by his dress and his courage, was killed. But his death infuriated rather than depressed his followers. The walls were carried with a rush. Clement, in helpless panic, threw himself into the Castle of St Angelo, and left his soldiers and the unarmed population of Rome to the unbridled fury of the invaders. Bourbon's army, consisting of Germans, Italians and Spaniards, hungry for money, food and slaughter, was soon master of the whole city.

These new barbarians had none of the reverence for the
Papacy that had restrained Alaric and Genseric; religion, so
far as it influenced them, incited them to pillage and slaughter.
Rome suffered more than she had suffered from any previous
conquest. Clement VII became a prisoner in the power of the
Emperor, and for ten months the ferocious conquerors pillaged
Rome at their leisure.

The catastrophe of Clement VII was a very heavy blow to
the policy of Francis, but he did not abandon all hope. In
August (1527) he renewed his compact with Henry VIII: the
two Kings declared themselves determined to liberate the Pope
and the French princes, who were hostages in Spain. In January,
1528, Charles V defied Francis I to mortal combat. The challenge was accepted and the preliminaries arranged; but the time
was passed when national quarrels could be settled by a duel,
and excuses were found on both sides for avoiding the combat.
The war therefore went on. In the autumn of 1527 another
French army, under Lautrec, had invaded Italy, and met with
those flattering successes that had so often duped the French.
Genoa and Pavia were taken. In December the Pope escaped
from his imprisonment. Encouraged by his successes Lautrec
determined to advance against Naples. The march recalled that
of Charles VIII in the absence of all resistance; it was fated
to recall it also in its disasters. The Spanish army withdrew
into Naples, and Lautrec blockaded it by land, while a French
and Genoese fleet, provided by the great Genoese admiral,
Andrew Doria, and commanded by his nephew, Philippino,
attacked it from the sea. The fall of the great city seemed
certain. But fortune and the blunders of the French policy came
to its relief. Andrew Doria was indignant with the French for
their arrogance towards himself and their unjust treatment of
Genoa, and, passing over to the side of the Emperor, sailed to
Naples and relieved the siege on the sea side. Plague broke
out in the French army, and Lautrec himself was carried off by
it. The Marquis of Saluzzo, into whose hands the command

came, was obliged to abandon the siege, and began his retreat northwards; but the Spanish troops followed and attacked his diminished and despondent army. He could make no resistance, and concluded a capitulation which allowed the French troops to withdraw unmolested beyond the Alps. Genoa immediately rose against them. Soon no French were left in arms in Italy. These events showed that Francis could make little impression on the Spanish position in Italy; nor, on the other hand, could Charles carry out his scheme for an invasion of France.

France was exhausted and weary of the war, and her King had lost something of his old romantic love of adventure. Charles had his own reasons for wanting peace. Germany seethed with commotions of various kinds: the social revolt of the Peasants and Anabaptists was added now to the Protestant revolution. Her eastern frontier too was in danger: for Solyman had overrun Hungary, and was now pressing upon Austria. The two great antagonists had lost nothing of their national and personal animosity; but a breathing space was necessary to both of them. To avoid the ceremonious delays of diplomacy negotiations were carried on by Francis I's mother, Louise of Savoy, and Margaret of Austria, governor of the Netherlands and aunt of Charles V, in a series of secret interviews at Cambray. The Emperor renounced his claim to the Duchy of Burgundy, and Francis abandoned all title to suzerainty over Flanders and Artois, and all his claims in Italy. The French princes were to be restored to their father on payment of two million crowns of gold, and Francis was now really to carry out his marriage with the Emperor's sister, Eleanor, which had been arranged at the Treaty of Madrid. The Treaty of Cambray proclaimed the superiority of Charles V, but could not end the rivalry of the two countries or give them a stable peace. It only marks another stage in the history of the long contest between France and the Habsburg power (Aug. 1529).

France during the Italian Wars. 59

More than six years passed before the rivalry of these two great powers again gave rise to war. What concerns the religious controversy in France must be left over for the next chapter. But during these years the prestige and power of Charles V seemed to rise, while that of Francis was stationary or declined. In February, 1530, Charles had received the imperial crown at Bologna with ceremonies of unsurpassed splendour. He had in Germany constant trouble with the Lutheran movement, which grew stronger year by year, and gave rise to political and social results of the greatest importance. But in spite of his German troubles Charles V had found it possible to accomplish one of the great purposes of his life. In 1535 he had struck a blow against the infidel. Tunis had long been a great stronghold and centre of pirates, and thousands of Christian captives were known to be rowing in the galleys of the Moslem or employed as slaves in the city. In June, 1535, Charles led an expedition against the place, took it, and set at liberty 20,000 Christian captives. The success of this crusade was received with enthusiasm by all civilised countries except France.

From the treaty of Cambray to the Peace of Nice.

Francis I meanwhile was forming new alliances and trying to strengthen his position. He made terms with Henry VIII of England, and yet at the same time joined hands with the Pope. The fateful marriage of his son, afterwards Henry II, with Catherine de Medicis, a relation of the Pope, was one result of this *rapprochement*. Francis entered also into close relations with the Protestants of Germany. But "the most Christian King" of France went even farther than an alliance with Protestant heretics. He needed a naval force before all things, if he was to cope successfully with Charles V: and he entered into relations with the Turk. Francis was neither infidel nor heretic at heart, but his master passion was a desire to humiliate Charles V, and he shrunk from no means that seemed likely to further his purpose. Europe was astonished to see France, once the foremost champion of the crusading movement, now in all but open alliance with Mahomedans. But he had no longer his old councillors to rely on. Louise of Savoy died in 1532. Duprat, his chancellor, and the great instrument, if not the real author, of his domestic policy, died in 1535. Francis's own health was showing signs of rapid decline: he would not be likely to repeat the daring adventures of his early years. New figures appear at court. Chief among them is Montmorency, soon to be made constable, an able soldier, devoted to Catholicism and anxious to establish good relations with Charles V. In the background the court was stirred, and public policy was sometimes influenced, by the jealousies of the Duchess of Étampes, the king's titular mistress, and Diana of Poictiers, whose influence was great over the future King of France.

In the year 1535 there was a sufficient pretext for war. Francis Sforza, Duke of Milan, died in October, 1535, and his territories were at once occupied by Charles V, while Francis claimed them for his second son. He claimed Piedmont also, as belonging to his mother, Louise of Savoy, and opened the campaign in the spring of 1536 with the invasion of Piedmont. The country was easily overrun. Turin and all the important towns threw open their gates to the invader.

Charles received at Rome the news of the invasion, and his feelings against his life-long rival found vent in a passionate outbreak before the Pope, the cardinals, and the ambassadors of Venice and France. He insisted on the justice of his cause; offered the Milanese to the King's third son, the Duke of Angoulême; and, if the King would not accept that offer, he proposed to meet him stripped to the shirt, in single combat with sword or dagger. But this challenge remained as fruitless as his earlier one. The Emperor therefore planned a double invasion of France, from the north and from the south-east. The blow was well planned, and the force at the Emperor's command very great, and yet failure met him at both points. In the north he laid siege to Péronne, and its early surrender was anticipated; but the place was splendidly defended by Fleuranges, and the invaders had to withdraw. In the southeast Francis held himself on the defensive. The country was ravaged by the French army as the Imperial troops approached; all but the strongest towns were abandoned. The sufferings of the inhabitants were extreme, but the object was gained. The invaders found no means of subsistence. Plague broke out in their ranks. Antonio da Leyva, the famous general, died. After having inflicted and suffered much, the Imperial army retired into Italy in September. So great was the prestige of Charles at the beginning of the campaign, that this repulse was reckoned to confer a glory on Francis second only to the battle of Marignano.

It seemed as if the struggle was only beginning, and yet the next year, 1537, saw the end. Francis, in spite of the Treaty of Cambray, declared himself sovereign over Flanders, and announced his intention of conquering it. But little had been done when unexpectedly peace was made. The new Pope, Paul III, was the chief agent in the matter. Charles was harassed by the Turks, and in France Montmorency threw all his influence on the side of peace. A truce was made for the Netherlands in July 1537, and for Piedmont in November. Negotiations for a real settlement took place at Nice in May 1538. The character of these negotiations was curious. The King and the Emperor would not see one another. Francis lodged in a village close to Nice; the Emperor remained in a vessel anchored off shore; all proposals passed through the Pope. It was agreed, as nothing more final could be arranged, to accept the *status quo* and agree to a truce for ten years. The chief results were that Charles kept Milan, and Francis Piedmont. Two months later the two rivals had a personal interview at Aigues Mortes. Francis behaved with that romantic gallantry that had gained for him so much admiration in the earlier years of his reign. He rowed up unexpectedly to Charles's vessel and entered it saying, "Here I am, once more your prisoner." He gave Charles a valuable diamond ring, and the most complete friendship seemed established.

In 1539 the new-made friendship seemed strengthened. Francis invited Charles to visit him in France, and as Charles had to go to the Netherlands to suppress a rising of the city of Ghent, he availed himself of the offer. Nothing could have been more hospitable than his treatment. He passed through France amidst continuous banquets and *fêtes*. He was detained by gaieties at Paris longer than he wished, but in February he appeared before Ghent and reduced the great city, his birth-place, to submission, taking away its charter of liberties and executing many of the opponents of his power. Had Francis taken the side of the insurgents he might have inflicted a very serious blow on the power of Charles. And yet these friendly relations were soon interrupted. Francis hoped, in return for his services to Charles, for some settlement of the Milanese question; but he hoped in vain. Charles had promised, with more or less of definiteness, that Milan should be bestowed upon one of Francis's younger sons. He would not fulfil his promise, and in October, 1540, gave it to his son Philip.

<small>From the Truce of Nice to the Death of Francis I.</small>

After that the renewal of the war was very probable. Francis sought for allies in England, in Germany, and again in Turkey. A most unexpected disaster to Charles encouraged Francis to attack him. His defeat of the Mahomedan pirates of Tunis was the purest glory of his reign. In the autumn of 1541 he attempted a similar feat by attacking the pirates of Algiers. The expedition was carefully planned, and richly furnished with ships and men: but it ended in utter failure. A storm destroyed the fleet before the provisions had been landed: the army suffered an entire defeat. The disaster was so great that it materially lowered Charles's prestige and crippled his resources for some time to come.

His extremity was Francis's opportunity. In July, 1542, he

France during the Italian Wars.

declared war, and arranged to attack the Imperial territories both in north and south, in Luxembourg and Roussillon. Luxembourg was captured, but the Duke of Alva, in a masterly campaign, forced the French to abandon Roussillon. In 1543 Charles was able to make an alliance with Henry VIII, whose policy it was to hold the balance even between the rivals. Yet the year passed without any military events of the first importance. The most important was the occupation of the Duchies of Juliers and Cleves by Charles, and the strangest the co-operation of a French and Turkish fleet in an attack on Nice, which was at first successful, though the town soon fell back into the hands of the Imperialists. But the next year, 1544, was destined to see greater events. The Emperor and the English King made preparations for a threefold attack on France from the north, the east, and the south-east. Their chances were made brighter by the disgust of the German Protestant powers with Francis for his cooperation with the Turks. France was really in serious danger, but she was saved by the want of a perfect understanding between the English King and the Emperor. For Henry VIII, instead of co-operating with Charles in an attack on Paris, turned aside to the siege of Boulogne, which he took in September. Charles, though he gained successes, could not push into the heart of France without the full support of Henry. He took St Dizier on the Marne and Château Thierri in August, and thought of marching on Paris; but he turned aside and captured Soissons instead, and then fell back upon the Netherlands. These were striking successes, but not enough to bring France to her knees. For earlier in the year (April) a last remarkable victory had been gained by the French on Italian soil. The young Count of Enghien was in command of the French army in Piedmont, and he had the orders of the King to stand on the defensive and not risk an engagement. Confident of the strength of the position, he sent one of his captains, Montluc, to gain from the King permission to fight. His vehemence gained the King to his side, and he hurried back to Piedmont, accompanied by many French nobles eager to take part in the coming battle. It took place on April 14, near Cérisolles. The battle bears some resemblance to Marignano, but this time the Swiss were on the French side. While Enghien and the cavalry on the left fought a desperate but losing battle, and the general was thinking of suicide to avoid the disgrace of capture, news was brought him that on the right the Swiss and French infantry had, after a fierce struggle with the German left, completely defeated them, and slain a large proportion of them. If the King had supported Enghien with troops and money the Milanese would have fallen into his hands. But Francis feared the fatal attractions of Italy and held him back.

Cérisolles, however, counterbalanced the loss of St Dizier, Soissons, and Boulogne. Neither Francis nor Charles threw into the war the eagerness that had once distinguished them. In October, 1544, the Peace of Crespy was signed, much to the astonishment of onlookers, who were expecting still greater military incidents. All conquests since the truce of Nice were to be given up. Beyond that, little more than the recognition of the *status quo* was accomplished. Savoy was to be evacuated by the French if Milan or the Netherlands came into the hands of the King's youngest son, as the dowry of a Spanish or Austrian wife. The real fate of both territories was left to the diplomacy and chance of the future. Henry VIII still continued the war; but Boulogne was blockaded and the Isle of Wight ravaged. In Jan. 1546 he signed a treaty at Ardres, and promised to surrender Boulogne at the end of eight years for 800,000 crowns of gold. Francis I therefore had more than a year of peace before his death in March 1546.

CHAPTER III.

THE RELIGIOUS SITUATION OF FRANCE AND THE REIGN OF HENRY II.

WE have seen how, during the reign of Francis I, France and Spain became the chief combatants in the arena of European war and diplomacy. But the same reign saw the appearance of two other combatants whose antagonism had an equal or greater influence on the future of Europe. The Reformation had come: Catholicism found itself confronted with an enemy ardent and confident of victory. We must see what shape the Protestant attack and the Catholic defence took during the epoch, and especially on the soil of France. Neither the Protestant movement nor the force that reorganised Catholicism had their birth on French soil, but there was no country in Europe where their conflict was more direct; for the central position of France, then as on many other occasions, made her the battle-ground of the various forces, both spiritual and temporal, that agitated Europe.

The Religious Situation in France.

The tendency towards some sort of reformation of the Church was common to all the countries of Europe. The Councils of Constance and Bâle had loudly proclaimed the need for it. More than one Pope had promised that an Ecumenical Council should be called together to consider the question of reform. The abuses of the monasteries, the avarice of the clergy, the very general violation of the vows of celibacy were complained of everywhere. In some respects France was particularly ready to receive and support some scheme of reformation. The Church of France, since the time of the Pragmatic Sanction, was peculiarly independent and quite ready to criticise the conduct of the Papacy, and its character had not had time to change since the Concordat. Francis I was devoted to the New Learning of the Renaissance—it was the most constant factor in his changeable nature—and the Reformation was at first closely allied to the Renaissance. His sister, Marguerite of Valois, whose devotion to him and influence over him we have already touched on, sympathised from the first with the New Learning, especially in its religious meanings. She strengthened her brother's tolerance for the opinions which subsequently were labelled Protestantism. On the other hand the Concordat, concluded by Francis after the battle of Marignano, had in the end an influence on the other side. Henry VIII in England broke the connection with Rome, in order that he might himself rule over the Church and add ecclesiastical power to temporal: but under the Concordat Francis already controlled the Church by the power which he possessed of appointing the Church dignitaries. The sense of nationality, therefore—one of the most powerful forces that made for the Reformation—had little influence in that direction in France.

The French historians are careful to show that several years before Luther's name was known in France opinions were being preached very closely akin to Lutheranism. Lefèvre d'Étaples, a Professor of Mathematics in the University of Paris and a profound student of the ancient languages, published, as early as 1508, works urging the study of the sacred Scriptures in the original. In 1512 he published his Commentaries on the Epistles of St Paul, urging the exclusive authority of the Scriptures, upholding justification by faith and not by works, and rejecting the mediatorial claims of the priesthood—expressing in fact those views that lie at

The Beginnings of Protestantism.

the very core of the Lutheran movement. The episcopal city of Meaux soon became the head-quarters of the new opinions. The bishop Briçonnet, a friend and *protégé* of Marguerite, the King's sister, accepted the new ideas with eagerness, but without any thought of schism. Lefèvre d'Étaples joined him, and at Meaux published a French translation of the New Testament. Farel, a name soon to be better known in Geneva, was for a time one of the group. They wrote and preached, not without occasional interference from the Sorbonne, but without serious danger. When, in 1524, the Sorbonne threatened proceedings against Lefèvre d'Étaples, the King interfered. Lefèvre, he said, was much honoured both in France and abroad: he ordered the proceedings to cease. There was no country where the outlook was more encouraging for those who loved the truth and hated fanaticism than France, when, in 1525, the defeat of Pavia altered the religious almost as profoundly as the military prospects of France.

The imprisonment of the King, after the battle of Pavia, brought power, as we have seen, into the hands of Louise of Savoy. It also made the mediation of the Pope a matter of the utmost importance to the imprisoned King. Moreover there had from the first been strong opposition to the Reforming tendency in quarters of great influence. The Sorbonne, the theological faculty of the University of Paris, was aggressively orthodox, and breathed out slaughter against all heretics. The Parlement of Paris was in close alliance with the Sorbonne. The King's toleration of heretics had been carried out in spite of protests from these two sources. We cannot wonder, therefore, when we find that the favour hitherto shown to the Reformers was at length withdrawn, and that a series of persecuting edicts were promulgated. Nevertheless it is clear that during the rest of his reign Francis I missed a great opportunity, one that we should have thought him peculiarly fitted to seize. War with the Spanish-Austrian power, whether conducted with arms or diplomacy, was in-

Francis I and the Reformers.

evitable, and the leader of that house had thrown in his lot with the cause of Catholic reaction. Francis I, by temperament and political interest, seemed called to lead the opposition in Europe, or at least to lend it valuable support. To do so he need not have called himself Lutheran nor have broken away from the Roman connection: it would only have been necessary to do what Henry IV, Richelieu, and Mazarin did afterwards— to put the interests of the State above those of the rival factions, to support the claims of the Protestants of Germany to independence, and to maintain the equilibrium of Europe. The Reformation struggle did not end until France adopted that policy; and for many reasons it seemed easier for Francis I to adopt it than for his successors. But he had no personal qualifications for the position of King of France at this hour of crisis; neither heart nor head was sound. He fluctuated for some time between contrary policies, but at last this "King of the Renaissance" declared himself definitely for religious persecution and the suppression of the New Learning.

There were times, indeed, when it seemed as if the influence of his sister would carry the day with him, and he would insist on toleration and some freedom of speech. In 1526, when Louis de Berquin, one of the leading Humanists of Europe, was arrested and in danger of his life, he was liberated by special order of the King. It seemed quite possible at one time that Francis would support the Protestant League of Schmalkalden, and the possibility awoke the keenest fears in Charles V and the Papacy. Even when that hope had passed, and heretics were being burnt by royal order, Francis still extended an invitation to the great German Reformer Melanchthon to come to Paris, promised him freedom from all molestation and expressed a hope that he might find some means of reconciling the opposing parties. Melanchthon never came to Paris; the persecutions continued; but as late as 1535 there issued a royal edict (the edict of Coucy) withdrawing the previous persecuting edicts and allowing all exiles to return to France.

But the swing of the pendulum was stronger in the opposite direction, and the influence of the King was thrown at last wholly on the side of repression and reaction. Persecution had begun immediately after the battle of Pavia. Briçonnet, Bishop of Meaux, recanted the opinions which had made him liable to an accusation of heresy. Lefèvre and the leading members of the 'reforming' group at Meaux fled to German soil. But though the leaders of the movement escaped the executioner, their followers were not so fortunate. In face of the decidedly aristocratic character that Protestantism subsequently assumed in France, it is well to note that it was not so at first. There were indeed gentlemen of good birth and scholars among the early victims (we may note especially Louis de Berquin, who, at first saved by the King, was in 1529 burnt by order of the Parlement of Paris with circumstances of special brutality); but the artisan class furnished at first the greater number of victims[1]. The most frivolous excuses were sufficient to send men to death. One victim was charged with having recommended a French translation of the Bible; another with having inserted sacred words in a drinking song. Heretics in France were not pursued with anything like the fierce fanaticism that the Government of Spain threw into the task; not perhaps with more rigour than fell in contemporary England upon the dissidents from the canon of orthodoxy adopted by Henry VIII; but the early hopes of the Protestants quite disappeared. Isolated acts of violence were followed up by still more infamous edicts. One, of 1535, declared death the penalty for all heretics (who are now called Lutherans); threatened all who concealed them with the same punishment; and bribed informers with a

The Repression of Protestantism.

---

[1] "We possess the official registers of the sentences passed by the Chambre Ardente of Henry II which generally give the profession of those convicted. They are chiefly drawn from the small tradesmen or artisan class, from domestic servants or petty officials." Armstrong's *Wars of Religion*, p. 3.

quarter of the property of the culprit. The same year saw an edict perhaps even more dangerous to the interests of the nation. The printing of any book of any sort within France was forbidden. It is difficult to estimate the strength of the new opinions in France; but they were propagated with extreme hardihood. Placards were affixed even on the doors of the King's room. The victims often showed a courage in facing their fate that proved at least the strength of their convictions.

The worst persecution was reserved for the last years of the King's reign. The downward plunge was taken in 1538, after his interviews with Charles V and the Pope, in Provence. The time of vagueness and indecision was passed, or quickly passing: on both sides opinion was growing definite. Calvin was already in Geneva: in two years the Society of Jesus would be founded. The line between the Protestants and the Catholic reaction was now plain. The intermediate party of the Humanists was clearly bereft of real power. The so-called King of the Renaissance threw himself heartily into the cause of the Catholic reaction.

In June, 1540, the Edict of Fontainebleau was issued, defining and extending the persecuting edicts; concealment of heretics was still counted as heresy; a quarter of the property of the condemned was still given to the informer. The Inquisition was established in France in all but name. Three terrible crimes spring from this final declaration of the King's policy. Worst of all was the extermination of the Vaudois Protestants in Provence. Unorthodox opinions had existed there ever since the time of the Albigensian crusade, but though the inhabitants were obnoxious to the orthodox they were otherwise harmless and useful citizens of France. For four years the King refused to give his sanction to the extirpation of these people. At last in January, 1545, the sign was given or forced from him in a moment of illness. The Baron of Oppède, first president of the Parlement of Aix, undertook the execution. The massacre that followed has its close parallel in other countries, and even in Protestant countries, but it has never been surpassed in cruelty or injustice. Three towns and twenty-two villages were destroyed; three thousand people were massacred; and after the massacre came a vast number of executions, without even the forms of justice. The other crimes of religious hate are insignificant beside these. But it is to be noted that fourteen of the reformers of Meaux were burnt in Paris on the same day (1546); and the same year saw the burning of Etienne Dolet, the great scholar and the friend of Rabelais. We may see of what manner of men France was thus robbing herself by the lines which Dolet wrote on the eve of his execution:

> "Si au besoin le monde m'abandonne,...
> Dois-je en mon cœur pour cela mener deuil?
> Non pour certain mais au ciel lever l'œil
>   Sans autre égard.
> Sus donc, esprit, laissez la chair à part...
> Si sur la chair les mondains ont pouvoir;
> Sur vous, esprit, rien ne peuvent avoir:
> L'œil, l'œil au ciel, faictes votre devoir!"

We have seen how the religious situation had changed in France during the reign of Francis I. At first men's notions of what the Reformation intended and implied were very vague. It was long before all hope of reconciling Lutheranism was entirely abandoned: it had not been entirely abandoned by the end of the reign of Francis I. But the first period of confused hostilities and vague hopes soon passed. The camps grew more distinct and began to know their leaders and the cause for which they are fighting. Luther's no longer was the only voice that was listened to by Protestants: Lutheranism itself ceased to be the most militant form of Protestantism. The German Reformer had been unequalled in the vigour of his attack; he had a power of winning sympathy which no other Reformer (except perhaps Zwingli) possessed. But when the time of mere negation and vague aspiration gave way to the

The new religious force in France. Calvinism and the Jesuits.

need of definite opinion and a constructive movement, the chief Protestant influence in Europe was no longer Luther but Calvin. He was a Frenchman by birth, but his career belongs not to French but European history. Still his influence on France was so great that it will be necessary to say something about his life and the general character of the movement that calls itself by his name.

He was born at Noyon, in Picardy, in 1509, and was thus only twelve years of age when Luther appeared before the Diet of Worms. He was at first intended for the Church and was himself an instance of those abuses which later on he attacked so violently. For at the age of twelve influence had procured him a canonry in the Cathedral of Noyon, and at eighteen he was nominally in charge of the parish of Marteville. He studied at Paris, but abandoned theology and embraced the study of law. He moved from Paris to Orleans and there became acquainted with the ideas of religious reform; for Orleans had for a long time been the favourite French University for German students. They were attracted by special privileges which were granted them there, and we are not surprised to find that Lutheran opinions had come with them. We know little or nothing of the circumstances in which Calvin adopted Protestant opinions; but we get occasional glimpses of him among the leading Reformers of France. When in 1534 Francis I was induced by certain Protestant placards that had been found even in his own chamber to order more rigorous persecution, Calvin retired before the storm. He went first to Italy, then to Bâle. At Bâle he wrote the first draft of his *Institutes of the Christian Religion* which, with its subsequent alterations, became the law for all Calvinist communities. It was prefaced by a dedicatory epistle to Francis I. Calvin, like the rest of the Protestants of France, still cherished illusions as to the toleration that the 'King of the Renaissance' might be willing to accord them. From Bâle he intended to go to Strassburg, intent on a life of study and teaching, but he made

Calvin.

a detour by Geneva, and there his destiny declared itself. Farel, one of the most ardent and militant of the French Protestants, was already there, anxious to find a will as strong as his own, and a keener brain to cooperate with him in his task. He persuaded Calvin to remain (1536), and henceforward his name is indissolubly connected with Geneva.

It is not necessary to follow his career in Geneva, or his struggle with his various opponents; but the characteristics of the man and his system are necessary for an understanding of French history. *Calvin in Geneva.*
It means much in French history that Protestantism came to France not in the loose form of Lutheranism, supported at first and subsequently enslaved by the secular powers; but in a form more definite, persistent, and independent. For in its creed Calvinism was more determinedly hostile to Roman Catholicism than any other form of Protestant belief. Calvin, indeed, never spoke of the Pope as Antichrist, but his followers soon did. And by virtue of its definiteness and comprehensiveness Calvinism excluded all possibility of conciliation with Catholicism as no other form of Protestant opinion did. For many years yet there was talk of a *via media* being found between Lutheranism and Catholicism: no *via media* was conceivable between Geneva and Rome: testimony to this is borne by the instructions to the Inquisition, in which Lutheranism is not mentioned, while the Calvinists are denounced by name. The religious struggle of the Reformation assumes its fiercest aspect when these two combatants are face to face. On the side of doctrine it is this definiteness and comprehensiveness of Calvinism that is most to be remarked. It is not necessary to do more than recall that Calvin's whole system is built upon his central dogma of predestination, enunciated by him without qualifying clauses; and that on the question of the Eucharist he rejected equally the Catholic doctrine of transubstantiation and the Lutheran of consubstantiation.

Calvin's doctrine with its logically complete formulæ was a

very important force in the European religious struggle: but Calvinism was much more than a doctrine. A great French Protestant (Guizot) has said that the three distinguishing features of Calvin's system are, (1) the independence of the Church of any temporal power, (2) the union of laymen and ministers in the government of the Church, (3) the enforcement of a moral discipline. All three points deserve a little further notice. Firstly, Calvin conceived of the government of the Church as emanating from the congregation itself, not, as in England or Germany, depending on the head of the State. This in itself goes far to account for the republican and democratic tendencies of Calvinism, wherever it is found. Calvin did indeed lay stress on the duty of obedience to the established authorities. "Private persons," he says definitely, "are not permitted to rise against tyrants"; and again, "I am not so savage or inhuman as to despise and seek to inspire contempt for princes and nobles, and that which belongs to the order and government of the world." But the spirit of his Church government was stronger than these isolated utterances. Everywhere, whether in England or Scotland, Holland or France, Calvinism fights for political liberty, or at least ranks with the forces that war against absolutism. The popularity of Calvinism among the French nobles is partly to be accounted for by this characteristic. They renewed under cover of religion that struggle against the monarchy in which they had been defeated when they fought on purely secular grounds. The second characteristic had for French history rather less importance. The Council in which the government of the Church and the enforcement of discipline was vested was called the Consistory. It was composed of laymen and ministers, and this arrangement was doubtless popular among a population weary of what was called the dominion of the priesthood, and constantly complaining of the way in which the Catholic Church subordinated the interests of the State to its own aims. The third point is the most important of all. Calvinism implied a severe moral discipline. Protestantism hitherto had not implied it. In Germany men complained that it seemed to be the unloosening of all morals, the consecration of mere individual impulse. The same complaints are loudly heard in England under Edward VI. But with Calvinism the Puritan element enters the Protestant movement. If we look at the details of the discipline enforced it seems to us harsh, inquisitorial, and often ludicrous. Dress and food are submitted to strict regulation; dancing is forbidden; foolish oaths are visited with heavy penalties. There was more in it, even, than unwise rigour and pedantic straining at trifles: it had its incidents of gross injustice and repulsive cruelty. The martyrdom of Servetus was accompanied by incidents as odious as those that are furnished by the records of the Inquisition; nor is the execution of Berthelier much better. But we blind ourselves to the real force of Calvinism if we fix our eyes on these incidents, which could not shock the 16th as they shock the 19th century. Without Calvin's discipline and all that flowed from it Protestantism would have been deprived of most of its energy in action and its moral earnestness: it would neither have won nor have deserved the success that it achieved.

While Protestantism was thus assuming a new and more militant form, Catholicism also was reorganising its force: the Counter-Reformation had begun. This was a movement more comprehensive in its scope, more far-reaching in its consequences even than Calvinism; one too on which it is much harder to pass anything like a certain judgment. The slightest survey must suffice.

The Counter-Reformation.

It was some time before the Papacy woke to an understanding of the danger of the Lutheran movement; it was at first too much occupied with its Italian interests to notice carefully what was happening beyond the Alps. But it was rudely awakened from its early security when Germany and England had passed from its allegiance; and when Protestant opinion was making rapid headway in every country north of the Alps, and was not unknown even in Italy, it was clearly time for the Roman pontiff to set his house in order. The Reformation era saw almost as great a change pass over the religious condition of those countries that remained in communion with Rome as in those that threw off its sway. The chief instruments wherewith the Catholic Church fought its enemies, and to a very large extent repulsed them, were the Jesuit order, the Council of Trent, and the Inquisition.

It was very natural that the Jesuit order should spring from Spanish soil. Spain, engaged in a long crusade against the Moors, had retained the religious enthusiasm which had sunk so low in most parts of Europe. If other countries were deserting the Virgin and the Saints, that seemed only one more reason to the ardent mind of Spain why she should remain firm in her allegiance. So naturally Ignatius Loyola, the founder of the Jesuit order, is a Spaniard. But it may be noted that France too played no small part in the foundation of the order. It was in Paris, in a church on Montmartre, that the oath was taken by Ignatius and his five confederates in 1534, which subsequently developed into the Jesuit rule. It was in Paris that Loyola chose the companions in whom he found such ardent cooperators in his work. The order did not, however, receive the Papal sanction until 1540—six years before the death of Francis I.

The Jesuit order.

The new order was unlike anything that the Church of Rome had known hitherto: it finds its closest analogy in the Dominicans. The Jesuits were no cloistered body intent on religious devotions that should save their own souls. Jesuitism, like Calvinism, was the product of an age of combat, and was specially constructed for the combat against Protestantism. "No storm," said Ignatius, "is so dangerous as a calm; no enemy is so dangerous as having none." The future of the order was to prove the truth of this saying; but during the stress of the Reformation struggle the Jesuit order fulfilled with wonderful success the task for which its founder designed it. Where the Jesuits resembled members of other religious orders, they carried their principles further than had hitherto been done. They were to be obedient up to—perhaps even beyond—the verge of sin. They were to be separated not only from the ties of family, but also from those of country. All this they had in common with the profession at least of other orders. What was special to the Jesuits was their rejection of any distinguishing dress, their busy occupation in the affairs of the world, and especially in education; in fact generally the definite practical objects at which they aimed. "Prudence of an exquisite quality, combined with average sanctity," wrote Ignatius, "is more valuable than eminent sanctity, and less of prudence." In the Jesuits the Papacy had an unequalled force ready to face all dangers, and trained with such skill that they were often able to surmount them. We shall see them often working with success in France, and we may often assume their action when we cannot see them.

The other elements in the reorganisation of the Papal forces may be passed with a brief mention. This is the period during which the Inquisition begins to show its most appalling activity. It is very questionable whether it was not a source of weakness rather than strength to the Papacy, as, while it cowed some districts, it generally produced an exasperation that often issued in rebellion. In its strict sense it was never introduced into France.

The Council of Trent.

The debates and decisions of the Council of Trent had a very direct bearing on France, though they belong rather to general European than to French history. The general result of the Council was to amend certain abuses in the Roman Church, to tighten the reins of discipline, and to remove all possibility of conciliation with Protestants of any kind: the Lutheran doctrine of "justification by faith" was denounced, the exclusive authority of the Scriptures was repudiated. There was much, too, in the decisions of the Council that conflicted nearly as much with the "Gallican" sentiment of the Church in France as it did with Protestant opinion: for the authority of the Pope was declared by this, the last of the great councils, to be superior to, and independent of, councils; and, further, the bishops were declared to hold their authority entirely from the Pope, who in consequence was intrusted with the reform of the various dioceses, to the neglect or even to the exclusion of the opinion of the bishop. This attack on the liberties of the Gallican Church was solemnly protested against by Henry II, and was never officially accepted in France. The first condition of success in spiritual as in temporal warfare is to have a clear plan of campaign and a recognised leader. After the Council of Trent the Roman Catholic Church had both.

Thus at the beginning of the new reign Catholicism and Protestantism faced one another in France with a definiteness that was likely to produce a more bitter struggle than anything France had known in the reign of Francis I. But it is well to remember that there was a considerable number of men in France (how large it is impossible to say) whose opinions were not in sympathy either with Calvinism or the Catholic Reaction. They were not numerous enough, their political action not important enough to warrant any examination of their opinions. They are perhaps best known through their great representative, Rabelais (1495–1553). Underlying all the riotous humour and coarseness of his works none can fail to detect a very great earnestness, and opinions that are in absolute conflict with received orthodoxy. He attacks under thinly-veiled satire the abuses of the Church of Rome— the monks with their idleness and vice, the Papal system, with its attendant injustices and cruelties—but he shows no leaning towards Calvinism. No writer of the time better deserves the high title of "Humanist" than he. It is on human, not on ecclesiastical objects that the gaze is fixed; it is to human virtues that he appeals. Justice, toleration, mercy, and freedom

The Humanists.

find in him a champion, though he cloaks his championship in an uncouth guise. It is clear that there were many in France who shared his views, but the times were too hard for them, their own views too vague, and perhaps their courage not high enough. France would have to wait for more than two hundred years before the ideas of Rabelais were supported by statesmen and translated into laws.

But though the spirit of Rabelais was not victorious in France it had adherents even during the worst period of the religious struggle. Before the civil wars began and during their first phase de l'Hôpital strove earnestly for the cause of toleration and humanity. And during the course of the religious wars themselves Rabelais' younger contemporary Montaigne (1533-1592) represents the same ideas, though with less enthusiasm and hope. For though Montaigne was less outspoken in his opposition to Catholic orthodoxy than Rabelais he stood really at nearly the same point of view, and preached consistently the foolishness of religious bigotry. He used the methods of philosophic scepticism to strike at the roots of religious persecution and urged the claims of humanity against the rival fanaticisms of both parties.

The new reign made no material change in the European situation and the policy of France. Henry II has none of the distinction of Francis I; none of the qualities which made him in spite of all his failures and crimes a popular King: but he continued the policy of his predecessor as it had manifested itself in the last years of his reign. He felt an implacable, jealous hatred of Charles V, and from the beginning everything pointed to the renewal of the war with Spain and Austria. From the first he persecuted Protestantism: not hesitatingly, as Francis I had done, but with a bigot's fury. Francis I's policy, then, was on the whole prolonged through the reign of his successor, but different instruments were used. Montmorency, who had been disgraced in the last years of Francis I, was recalled to

The Reign of Henry II.

court: there was no one in whom at first Henry II placed more reliance. But by his side there began to appear the great Guise family, which left so broad a mark on the history of France during the sixteenth century. This family sprang originally from Lorraine, but was now naturalised in France. They were related on the female side to the house of Anjou, and the relationship provided them with a pretext for their ambition: we shall see them, later, claiming the kingdom of Naples by this right. Already one member of the family, Mary of Lorraine, had married King James V of Scotland. Her daughter, Mary, Queen of Scots, as she is known to English readers, was shortly to become Queen of France. So highly connected and full of ability as well as ambition, it is hardly a matter of wonder that members of this family were found who even aspired to the French Crown. For the present the leading figures among the Guises were Duke Francis and Charles the Cardinal. From the beginning of Henry II's reign they acquired a great and increasing influence over the mind of the King. A third influence must be carefully noted. Queen Catherine de Médicis' time was not yet. She was neglected by her husband, and her word had no weight in state affairs: she was thrust aside to make room for the King's mistress, Diana of Poictiers. This remarkable woman, whose power over the King was due rather to intellectual than physical gifts, was some twenty years older than the King, but so long as she lived she retained her ascendancy over him. The religious and foreign policy of the reign bear the stamp of that ascendancy.

Europe was even fuller of the material of revolution than it had been in the days of Francis I. Protestantism was no longer a vague aspiration, but a definite and organised force, conscious of its own strength, which could no longer be despised or neglected. In England the death of Henry VIII had given the victory to the extreme Protestant party. In Germany Charles V tried in vain to find

The Reign of Henry II.

some *modus vivendi* that should allow him to rule on good terms with the German princes without forfeiting the name of Catholic; but the end of his reign saw the ruin of all his early hopes of establishing the Empire in Germany on a stronger basis. In France itself, as we have seen, Calvinism, aggressive and organised, had taken the place of the early vague Lutheranism. Nor was the religious movement an isolated one; it was closely allied in France, as elsewhere, with political and social questions. In 1548 a rebellion broke out in the great city of Bordeaux, which was nominally a protest against the salt-monopoly or gabelle, but covered a general rejection of royal authority. The King's agent Moneins was driven into the castle, but was forced to capitulate and was murdered. But the royal forces easily overcame the rebels. Order was restored and the city severely punished. A more serious danger was the alliance between the Protestant movement and the great noble families—an alliance the full meaning of which was not seen until the subsequent reigns.

The Austro-Spanish power in the person of Charles V was the great rival and enemy of France; but the first hostilities of the new reign were undertaken against England. *England and Mary Stuart.* The alliance between France and Scotland, which had existed since the reign of Edward I, entered now on a new phase. Mary of Lorraine, widow of James V and regent of Scotland, was supported by French arms. The future of Scotland seemed to turn on the disposal of the hand of the little Mary Stuart. The English Government tried to enforce her betrothal to the English King Edward VI that had already been arranged in the preceding reign. But the successful invasion of Scotland only increased the hostility of the people to England. Mary was shipped off to France and at once betrothed to the Dauphin. This implied war between England and France. The English Government, under the Duke of Somerset, was too much embarrassed with domestic troubles to conduct the war with vigour, and the recovery of Boulogne from England was the most important incident of the struggle. The King and Montmorency advanced against the place. The English fleet was beaten off and the fall of Boulogne was certain. Somerset negotiated and surrendered the town on promise of a payment of 400,000 gold crowns (March, 1550). The reign thus opened auspiciously: before it closed it was destined to see another far greater success at the expense of England.

The war with England was only an interlude in the great struggle with Charles V. Almost immediately after the surrender of Boulogne the preparations for the greater war began. It is usually classed as a phase and the last phase of the Italian wars; but really Italy, though the opportunity for renewing the war was found on Italian soil, plays an unimportant part in the struggle. France was awakening from her dream of aggrandisement in Italy. The past had shown how easy it was to conquer there and how impossible to hold what had been conquered. The true interest of France pointed rather to an extension of her frontier upon the north and north-east, and the chief interest of the war is for this reign to be found in that quarter.

The last phase of the Italian war.

Hostilities began without any declaration of war in 1551. French armies fought against Austro-Spanish armies on Italian soil, though Henry II and Charles V were not yet nominally at war. The course of French history would not be made clearer by any close examination of the causes that brought the French into Italy again. It is enough to say that the principalities of Parma and Piacenza had been granted by Pope Paul III to his son Pier Luigi Farnèse. But Farnèse was murdered and the principality claimed by the Emperor against the relatives of the deceased man (1547). In 1550 Paul III was succeeded by Julius III, who took the part of the Emperor. When therefore in May 1551 Henry II declared that he took Ottavio Farnèse under his protection, it meant war against both Emperor and Pope.

At first, as we have said, there was no open declaration of

The Reign of Henry II.

war between France and Spain, but that was certain to come, and Henry II proposed to isolate Charles by diplomacy before he attacked him in arms. Germany, full of religious and political animosities, offered an excellent field for diplomacy. The Protestants had been defeated at the battle of Mühlberg in 1547 and had been forced to accept the 'Interim'—the religious compromise by which Charles thought to pacify the religious disturbance of Germany until the Council of Trent had finished its sittings. But they accepted it only out of necessity: if zeal for the Protestant faith was weaker than it had been, hatred of Charles was quite as strong. Maurice of Saxony, whose support had won the battle of Mühlberg for Charles, was himself willing to play the traitor if treason would lead him to power. Henry II availed himself skilfully of the opportunity thus afforded, in a way that resembles the still more skilful use that Richelieu made a century later of similar German dissensions. Jean de Fresne, Bishop of Bayonne, was the French agent. In February 1551 a treaty was signed with Maurice of Saxony at Friedwald in Saxony, whereby Henry promised to provide a large sum of money towards the expense incurred by the Germans in their resistance to Charles V. The Germans on their side agreed that Henry II should take possession of Cambray, Toul, Metz, and Verdun. Charles V could hope for no help from England while Edward VI was on the throne, and even the Pope began to draw away from him and to show a disposition to join Henry. In February, 1552, before the Parlement of Paris, Henry announced that he was going to make war against the Emperor: he denounced the conditions of the Treaty of Crespy, and once more put forward the claims of France to Naples, Milan, and Flanders. Shortly afterwards Maurice of Saxony issued a manifesto against Charles V.

War began in April 1552. Henry II conducted the army in person, and marched no longer south-east to the fatal plains of Italy but north-east to a region where the French monarchy was destined to

War against Charles V: the Siege of Metz.

make constant acquisitions right down to the eve of the Revolution. He entered Lorraine and laid hands on the "Three Bishoprics" which had been claimed by him in the Treaty of Friedwald. He had little difficulty in achieving his purpose. The population spoke French and was favourable to France. Verdun and Toul received French garrisons readily; one was introduced into Metz partly by ruse and partly by force. But there the successes of France ended. It is true that Henry advanced as far as Weissenburg, and could boast that he had watered his horse in the Rhine; but he failed to gain over Strassburg. The thoroughly German population was hostile to him. He could hold nothing more than Metz, Toul, and Verdun, and it was clear that he would not retain these without effort. For in the autumn of 1552 Charles, having momentarily settled German affairs, marched into Lorraine with an army of 60,000 men, and undertook the siege of Metz. Things had gone hardly with him during this year—fortune, as he said, had turned from him to his younger rival. In Italy he had been defeated: in Germany Maurice of Saxony, after nearly seizing him at Innsbruck, had forced him to accept the humiliating Treaty of Passau. But the treaty freed him from German complications for the time; and he was resolved at all risks to regain Metz. Francis, who had become in 1550 Duke of Guise, was entrusted with the defence; he was joined by large numbers of volunteers and prepared for a stubborn resistance. The attack was opened on the 19th of October, though Charles was warned that the season was too late to make success possible. The natural defences of the place were very strong, for the Moselle and the Leille surrounded the place on three sides, and the fourth was very strongly fortified. The Imperial troops, encouraged by Charles's presence, fought well, but they failed to make any impression on Metz. When the frosts set in the mortality among the soldiers became very great. At last the Emperor had to recognise that he was engaged in a hopeless attempt. On

December 26 he abandoned the siege, and drew off, leaving his sick and wounded—a vast number—to the mercy of the French. The Duke of Guise ordered that they should be fed and carefully attended to—an instance of humanity that finds too few parallels in this cruel age.

The repulse of his army at Metz was a severe blow both to the prestige and the strength of Charles, but it was not in the least decisive of the war. The next three years on the contrary showed a considerable turn of fortune in favour of Charles. *The Abdication of Charles V.* On both sides there was great financial exhaustion which prevented them from any decisive action; but Charles V got decidedly the best of such military operations as there were. The northern frontier of France was crossed in the spring of 1553. Terouanne was taken in April, Hesdin in July. In 1554 there was a complete absence of serious military incidents. In August the French under Francis of Guise and Coligny met the Imperialists at Renty near St Omer. The French were victorious after some hard fighting and took seventeen ensigns, but there was no important result. The diplomacy of the year was more important than the fighting. Charles succeeded in negotiating a marriage between his son Philip and Mary of England. The marriage ensured the neutrality of England and held out hopes of her alliance. On the other hand the French position was strengthened in March 1555 by the accession of Cardinal Caraffa to the Papal throne under the name of Paul IV. He was very hostile to the Spaniards and their King, and consequently inclined to a French alliance.

But here the abdication of Charles V gave a new turn to the policy of Europe. This step, to which it is impossible to find a parallel in modern history, was due to many causes. Charles's health had completely broken down: he was chagrined by his failure to repress Protestantism in Germany and to crush the rival power of France: he wished perhaps to see his son Philip take his first steps in statecraft. The decision moreover was no sudden one. There was in him a vein of deep, almost morbid, religious sentiment. Long ago he had communicated to his wife his intention of spending the last years of his life in devotional exercises. He laid aside the burden of rule piecemeal—first the Kingdom of Naples, then his Imperial title, which passed to his brother Ferdinand, next in October 1555 his authority in the Netherlands, and last of all the Crown of Spain. Philip succeeded to all but Germany, Austria, and the Imperial title. Charles made his way back to Spain and went to the monastery of Yuste, near to which he lived until September, 1558, still in something like royal state, still watching the political affairs of Europe.

During the various stages of his abdication he had been trying to bring about at least a truce with France. The exhaustion of both countries made such a truce almost equally necessary to both. But the negotiations were not finished before his abdication was completed. At last in February the Truce of Vaucelles was signed: hostilities were to be suspended for five years. It was hoped by many that it would lead up to a permanent peace.

But the truce did not last a year; it did not last in reality more than three months. The Guises were the authors of this last act of the war, with its day of humiliation at St Quentin, which fell to their rival, and its day of glory at Calais, which came to themselves. They were eager for an opportunity that should allow them to assert their claim to the kingdom of Naples, and they supported the league of the King and Pope Paul IV. with this end in view. In November 1556 Francis of Guise was despatched into Italy with a well-equipped army. We need not follow him there. We need only note that he was repulsed from the very frontiers of the Neapolitan kingdom by the Duke of Alva, and quarrelled with his ally Pope Paul IV. Then there came the news of a great disaster which peremptorily recalled him to France.

Henry II and Philip II; the Battle of St Quentin and the recovery of Calais.

The Reign of Henry II.

In June 1557 the truce had been formally broken and war declared against the King of Spain. Philip, eager to signalise the first years of his reign by a victory, crossed the frontier with a considerable army and laid siege to St Quentin. The place was badly fortified and almost unprovisioned. Gaspard de Coligny threw himself into it to prolong the defence to its utmost possible limits. It was certain however that the place would fall if it were not relieved, and the Constable Montmorency tried to relieve it. The town was surrounded by marshy ground, and his efforts to force his way across this were repulsed. Then the Spanish army under the Duke of Savoy fell upon him, and, with the help of the Flemish nobleman Count Egmont, gained a complete victory. The French lost their flags, their artillery, and their provisions. Their leaders and entire divisions were taken prisoners, Montmorency among them (9 August, 1557). The French had suffered no such overwhelming defeat on their own soil since the battle of Agincourt.

Battle of St Quentin.

The road to Paris seemed open. Charles in his monastic retreat waited impatiently for the news that his son was before the walls. But as it turned out, the victory remained a singularly barren one, for Coligny, contrary to all expectation, prolonged the siege for eighteen days, and gave time for the French forces to gather for the defence of the capital. Philip, neither here nor on any other occasion during his reign, showed any power of rapid action: the Duke of Savoy advised him to march on Paris at once without waiting for the fall of St Quentin. Philip refused, and his refusal saved France from a very grave danger. The Spaniards took a few not very important fortresses in the north of France, and that was the sole result of the great victory.

Coligny, after the fall of St Quentin, went as a prisoner to Brussels, where he shortly afterwards embraced Calvinism. Francis of Guise was hurriedly recalled from Italy. His popularity was still very

The recovery of Calais.

great in spite of his failure in Italy. He now received the title of 'Lieutenant-General in Chief at home and abroad.' France expected from him something worthy of his reputation, and he was not slow to fulfil this expectation. Calais had always ever since its capture by Edward III been a threat to France; it was so more than ever now when England and Spain were joined in an offensive alliance. No project could be more popular, few could seem more difficult of execution, than the recapture of Calais; but it was to this that Guise addressed himself. The engineer Strozzi, who had assisted Guise in the defence of Metz, introduced himself under disguise into Calais. The fortifications were strong but the garrison small and the whole place neglected. Mary's Government was warned of the impending attack, but refused to believe it until it was too late to send effective aid. The outlying forts, Sainte-Agathe, Restaux, and Nieullay, fell quickly into Guise's power; and then, within ten days of the opening of the siege, the place was taken by storm. The jubilation was so great in Paris and in France generally that the disaster of St Quentin was almost forgotten. Guise became more than ever the popular hero: his popularity was an important force in France in the next reigns. He followed up his great success by the capture of Thionville, but in July the French army was severely beaten by the Spaniards in a battle near Gravelines.

The war had had its day of glory for France; but the tide of victory had been more constant on the side of Spain. France was exhausted and Henry II consented to treat. Negotiations began in October, 1558, and resulted in the very important treaty of Cateau Cambrésis in April, 1559. During the course of the negotiations Mary of England died and was succeeded by Elizabeth. Philip tried in vain to prolong the Anglo-Spanish alliance under the new reign, and even offered marriage to Elizabeth. She took her own course with the mixture of firmness and caution that was to characterise her throughout her reign.

The Treaty of Cateau Cambrésis.

Would France be able to hold Calais and the Three
Bishoprics, Metz, Toul, and Verdun? This was the most hotly
contested point in the negotiations, but in the end France
gained her point. Elizabeth, not yet firmly established on the
English throne, was anxious for peace. She yielded Calais to
the French under conditions that were adopted rather to save
her honour, than with any idea that they would be fulfilled.
France was to hold Calais for only eight years; she was then
to restore Calais to England or pay 100,000 crowns of gold.
With even less difficulty France procured the cession of the
Three Bishoprics. The treaty with Spain was a more complex
one. The conquests were surrendered on both sides, and
France definitely abandoned all claim to Milan and Naples.
On the side of Italy, France retained only Chieri, Pinerolo,
Chivasso, Villanova. These places were called the keys of
Italy, and by retaining them France showed that she had not
altogether abandoned the idea of expansion in that direction.
Lastly, to cement the treaty, and to ensure that for the future
hostility between France and Spain should be changed into
alliance, Margaret, the sister of the French King, was to marry
the Duke of Savoy, while Elizabeth, the eldest daughter of
the French royal family, was betrothed to Philip.

France, weary of war which had lasted with little inter-
mission for sixty-five years, welcomed the prospect of peace.
At the court the treaty was made the occasion for a round of
gaieties, banquets and tournaments. Henry II, who prided
himself on his skill in martial exercises, himself entered the lists
and was accidentally killed by a knight of Scotch extraction—
Montgomery (10 July, 1559).

The Italian wars were over. For more than half a century
the Kings of France had pursued an impossible ambition. We
have seen how profoundly the spirit of the French nation
had been modified during the same period. The next two
generations will mainly be occupied with the problem of the
new internal organisation of France, made necessary by the

Protestant Revolution, and the social and political aspirations that accompanied it.

The Protestants of France had suffered cruelly during the whole of the reign. Henry II had indeed been allied with the German Protestant princes, and even with the Turk, against Charles V and Philip II, but at home his policy was an unvarying one of cruelly repressive orthodoxy. There are none of the fluctuations that we have noted in the case of Francis I. Under Henry II, France, which had at first shown some sympathy with the new ideas and was before the end of the century to issue the first great edict of toleration, rivalled Spain in the cruelty and the folly of the measures that she took for the repression of heresy.

<small>Protestantism in France during the reign of Henry II.</small>

Henry II began by establishing in the Parlement of Paris a special chamber for dealing with questions of heresy (Oct. 1547). It soon received and deserved the popular title of the Burning Chamber (*Chambre Ardente*). Four years later the King issued an edict—the Edict of Châteaubriant—regulating the pursuit of heresy and increasing its vehemence. The edict included forty-six articles. All public careers were closed to Protestants: magistrates who showed too much leniency in dealing with Lutherans were themselves liable to prosecution: no petitions for mercy were to be allowed: all arguments on religious matters were forbidden: the reading of the Bible was forbidden: lastly, the reward for informers was raised from a quarter to a third of the goods of the condemned. But this was not yet enough. The Inquisition had not been introduced, and the Pope pressed for its introduction. Henry II might have been willing to yield, but the Parlement protested against the introduction of a foreign tribunal. The Inquisition proper was never introduced into France, but another and yet more stringent edict was issued—the Edict of Compiègne, 1557. This was directed against the lenity of the judges; it should be remembered to their honour. As they sometimes

The Reign of Henry II.

"through pity allowed the guilty to escape," it was declared that henceforth there should be only one penalty, and that penalty death. No modification of the penalty of whatever kind was to be allowed.

It is apparently impossible to estimate the number of victims that perished under these savage edicts, which far surpass in cruelty the religious legislation of Mary and Elizabeth of England. But the number was very considerable. During three years (1547—1550) the *Chambre Ardente* passed 430 sentences on heresy, of which 60 were capital. The stories of the deaths of the Protestant martyrs have been piously collected, and when all allowance is made for exaggeration and sympathetic colouring they allow us to see how real was the enthusiasm and devotion of these men, how grave a blow France was delivering against her own welfare in crushing their enthusiasm or driving it into rebellion.

The chief hope of the Protestants was to be found in the Parlement of Paris. Here, after the suppression of the first *Chambre Ardente*, jurisdiction in cases of heresy was disputed between two chambers— the *Chambre de la Tournelle* and the *Grand' Chambre*. Between them there was a wide difference of policy. The *Chambre de la Tournelle* did its utmost to avoid the capital condemnation of heretics. The *Grand' Chambre* was anxious to apply the edicts in all their severity. After many conflicts between the two it was decided that on Wednesday in each week the different chambers of the Parlement should meet together and give their decision in common (1559). The conjoint chamber, from the day of its meeting, took the title of *Mercuriale*. But the result did not in any way correspond to the wishes of the King: in the joint chamber the friends of toleration commanded a majority. The King, in order to enforce religious persecution, came down in person to the deliberations of the *Mercuriale*. One of the councillors, Anne du Bourg, seized the opportunity for making a strong

Protestantism and the Parlement of Paris.

appeal in favour of tolerance. "It is no small thing," he cried, "to condemn those who from the midst of the flames invoke the name of Jesus Christ." The King was moved to anger at his boldness, and ordered his guards to seize Anne du Bourg and to take him to the Bastille. A few months later he was burnt as a martyr for toleration rather than for Protestantism.

In spite of all this persecution—perhaps partly because of it—the Protestant movement grew and strengthened. In 1555 the first French Protestant Church was formed at Paris. In 1559 a Protestant synod was held in Paris. Representatives from 50 reformed Churches attended. The first Confession of Faith was drawn up. The Protestant Churches in France accepted the definite aggressive faith of Calvin and his system of Church government with all its republican tendencies. The Peace of Cateau Cambrésis was bound to usher in a period of religious wars.

CHAPTER IV.

THE WARS OF RELIGION, PART I: TO THE DEATH OF CHARLES IX.

THE treaty of Cateau Cambrésis terminates a long period of foreign war; and peace was, we have seen, the first requirement for the distracted state of France. But the peace was from the first precarious. A period of unrest and preparation ensued, and then the foreign war was followed by a long period of civil war, in every way more disastrous.

The situation in France on the accession of Francis II.

These religious wars form one of the darkest epochs in French history. They are paralleled only by the period of the Hundred Years' War. Henri Martin, recalling the terrible experiences of Creçy and Poictiers and Agincourt, and of the civil strife with which those wars were associated, says: "France has again to pass through the flames of Hell." But not only do these years form a very distressing period; they are also a very confused and difficult one, and it will be well therefore before we enter upon them to present, at the risk of repetition, the various great forces of the time and the leading personalities.

Foreign war did not add its complications to those of the civil war until nearly thirty years had passed, and yet France during this time was much influenced by the intrigues of her neighbours. It is well then to repeat that the treaty of Cateau Cambrésis had by no means ended the hostility of

France and Spain. Spain was pleased with anything that would weaken the strength of the French monarchy, and we cannot go through any year of this period of civil war without coming upon the intrigues or the influence of Spain. It is less important, but still important, to remember that Elizabeth was ruling in England,—that as her reign progressed she was more and more driven into a policy of hostility to Spain, and was drawn therefore into a co-operation with France that was practically effective even when it was not supported by treaties.

Little more need be said of the religious situation. Calvinism and Catholicism were definitely pitted against one another, each with a definite faith and scheme of life, each claiming not toleration but supremacy. But Calvinism in France soon enters on a new phase. Its early supporters for the most part opposed to the Government a passive resistance only, and were found chiefly among the poor, or at least in the ranks of the third estate. But from the end of the reign of Henry II onwards the Nobility of France gathered to the Protestant side in great numbers. It is difficult to be sure of the motives which impelled them to such a step. The names of Coligny and du Mornay will serve to remind us that there were many of the Nobility whose adherence was the result of conviction, and who are worthy both in character and ability to rank with the greatest Protestant leaders of the time. It is equally clear from the lives which many others lived that with them it was not so. Feudalism had been broken in France, but the aspirations of the nobles towards independence were not forgotten. The Protestant revolution in most countries strengthened the independence, the power, and the wealth of the nobles. It did so to some extent in England; it did so most notably in Germany and in Scotland. We cannot doubt that many of the nobles were influenced even more by the hope of seizing ecclesiastical property, and of securing immunity from the interference of the Crown, than by the logical power of the Institutes of the Christian religion, or by moral

The Wars of Religion, Part I.   95

indignation against the corrupt condition of the Church. The power too which the Guises had acquired at court worked in the same direction: many of the nobles would welcome any pretext for striking a blow against their excessive influence.

But though the striking political characteristic of French Protestantism is to be found in the adhesion of a large section, perhaps a majority, of the Nobility, it is not true that the movement, even in its later stages, was purely aristocratic. The armies that followed the Protestant leaders were at first themselves Protestant, and, numerous and often poor though the nobles of France were, they did not fill up the ranks. There were even cities—Rochelle is especially mentioned—where the Protestant zeal of the common people was keener and more tenacious than that of the upper classes.

The geographical distribution of French Protestantism is somewhat remarkable. It contradicts directly the theory which makes of the Reformation an affair of latitude and climate, and regards Protestantism as naturally limited to the northern and Teutonic peoples. For in France the main strength of Protestantism lay south of the Loire and west of the Rhone. There were also many Protestants in Normandy—a fact not without influence on the course of the war—and, despite the cruelties of persecution, a certain number in Dauphiné. But the valley of the Garonne and its affluents provided the larger number of the Protestants of France. Nor was this a passing accident. When the Edict of Nantes was revoked in 1685 the stronghold of Protestantism was still Gascony and Guienne.

Let us look at the leading figures in French history at this time. We need say little more of the Guises, for we have already noted their origin, their power, and their ambition. The reign of Francis II brought them into a dominant position. The King was young—he died at the age of 17: neither his character nor his age allowed him to rule. He was married to Mary of Scotland, a niece of the Duke of Guise. It was therefore natural that the reality of power should pass into the hands of the Guises. Francis the Duke —the Balafré, as he was called from a scar that dated from the siege of Boulogne—controlled all military matters: internal administration was in the hands of the Cardinal Charles of Lorraine. The Guises were the very foremost champions of the Roman Catholic cause in France: conviction no less than interest ranged them on that side.

The Queen-Mother's time had not come yet, for the Guises still kept her in the background: but it will be well to speak of her here. Catherine de Médicis is one of the few commonly known names of this period, and it is particularly necessary to guard against the traditional romantic colouring which has been spread over her career. Nothing can be further from the truth than the picture which is sometimes drawn of her as a Catholic fanatic tenaciously pursuing a scheme for crushing Protestantism through a long period of years: for in truth her life was little influenced by religion, and nothing is more striking than the rapidity with which she changed both her means and her ends. She was a characteristic Italian of the 16th century, quick-witted, fond of art, and to a certain extent of literature, clinging to the Papal system by tradition and interest rather than by conviction, not naturally cruel, but wholly egotistic, not recognising morality as binding on princes and statesmen, capable therefore, when circumstances and her own interest suggested it, of appalling crimes. She had been thrust aside in the reign of her husband by Diana of Poictiers; she was thrust aside in the reign of Francis II by Mary Stuart and the Guise family. Her opportunity came on the death of Francis II in December, 1560. She was not at all unwilling to intrigue with Protestantism; but when the time for intrigue and compromise was over it was inevitable that she should throw in her lot with the defenders of Catholicism.

At the head of French Protestantism regarded as a political movement stood two members of the princely house of Bourbon. The eldest, Antony, had married Jeanne d'Albret,

The Wars of Religion, Part I.

Queen of Navarre, a zealous Protestant. His little kingdom was partly occupied and always endangered by Philip of Spain, and fear for that country hampered all his actions; and even if he had been free from this preoccupation there is no reason to think that he could have played a great part in French history. He gives us the spectacle of a great ambition that shrinks from the use of the necessary means; of vacillation, and of consequent failure. His brother Condé was a more resolute character. He was, if not a great soldier, at least a daring and an enterprising one. So long as he lived he was the leader of the Protestant force. His private life was far from edifying, but this was overlooked in the need for having a Prince of the Blood Royal at the head of the movement.

Next in social importance to the Bourbon family, but far superior to them in character and ability, stood three brothers of the Châtillon family—the Cardinal, Gaspard de Coligny, and Dandelot. All had embraced Protestantism, and served it faithfully and without reserve. Coligny was the greatest of the three. We have seen him more than once already. His greatest feat of arms had been the defence of St Quentin against Philip, by which, though in the end defeated, he was held to have saved France from the very greatest danger. He held the title of Admiral, but the title was at this time in France a purely military one, and Coligny had never served at sea. Friends and enemies recognised in him a man incorruptible, incapable of meanness, a commander of considerable skill, merciful in victory, undaunted in defeat. He was dignified in his carriage, silent, and almost morose: yet able to inspire not only esteem but affection. Ranke calls him the greatest Protestant statesman of his age, and his name may without exaggeration be associated with William the Silent and with Cromwell. Yet he too bears the mark of his time. He knew of the proposal to assassinate Francis of Guise, and approved though he did not co-operate.

Besides the Calvinists and the Catholics we have seen that

there was a third party in France that stood apart from and above the religious fanaticism of the time. L'Hôpital, chancellor under Francis II, was the most prominent representative of this party. His policy was always consistent. He tried to procure toleration by subordinating the passions of the factions to the general interests of France. During his own lifetime he was unsuccessful: but when Henry of Navarre in a happy hour for France fought his way to the throne, he represented l'Hôpital's ideas far more truly than those of either Calvinists or Catholics.

The first act of the new reign was to dismiss the former servants of the Crown and to appoint new ones, subservient to the Guises. The nobles indignantly saw themselves thus deprived of all chances of power and amassing wealth. Immediately, too, the new Government showed clearly what its policy was to be in relation to religious dissent. Du Bourg, as we have seen, had been arrested for his championship, not of Protestantism but of toleration. It was hoped that the death of Henry II might save his life, but the Guises refused to show mercy. He was executed in December, 1559. The Guises would have liked to introduce the Inquisition into France in its Spanish form. France was saved from such a fate by l'Hôpital, who by the Edict of Romorantin, May, 1560, gave jurisdiction in religious matters to the bishops. The episcopal courts would doubtless be biassed against those who were accused of heresy; but it was something to have avoided the Inquisition, and l'Hôpital did his utmost to mitigate the execution of the Edict.

The Reign of Francis II.

The beginning of the year had been troubled with a conspiracy for the overthrow of the government of the Guises. In this—the so-called conspiracy of Amboise—aristocratic and religious discontent joined hands. There was widespread dissatisfaction with the rule of the Guises, both because of their policy and because they were "foreigners." The general scheme can be easily seen through all the very doubtful details. The person of the King was to be seized; the Guises were to be got rid of; the chief power in the State was to be given to the house of Bourbon. An attempt was made to secure Calvin's approval for the plan, but in vain: he saw the danger to his system which would come of countenancing rebellions; but the movement went on in spite of him. The chief agent was Godefroi du Barri, Sieur de la Renaudie, who gave himself out as lieutenant for a 'mute captain,' who doubtless was Condé. The secret was well kept for some time. It was agreed that a petition should be presented to the King at Blois; that under cover of this petition a band of armed Protestants should force themselves into the Castle and seize the King and the Guises. But a rumour of the plot was carried to the Guises. The King was removed to the strong castle of Amboise. Still the conspirators did not lose all hope: they gathered round Amboise to be ready for any opportunity. The plot, however, was more fully revealed to Guise, and he took prompt measures to disconcert it. The bands of the conspirators were hunted out and dispersed. La Renaudie himself perished in a chance scuffle.

The whole affair eventually increased the influence of the Guises. The Duke Francis was made Lieutenant-General of the kingdom with unlimited powers, and he punished those of the conspirators upon whom he could lay hands. Their lives were doubtless both legally and justly forfeit; but the character and method of the punishments showed the hero of Metz and Calais in his most cruel and vindictive mood. The leaders of the movement were not touched. Coligny and his brother had probably not been implicated. Condé almost certainly had been; but nothing could be proved. He was allowed to clear himself by a solemn declaration in presence of the King. The Duke of Guise himself pretended to be satisfied.

The conspiracy was crushed, but the opposition to the Guises still continued. It was rumoured that the house of Bourbon was still plotting. The King of Navarre was known to be in communication with Queen Elizabeth. The cry for reform was loud, and a convocation of the States General was demanded. The Government thought it well to yield, and summoned the States General for the 10th December, 1560. But Guise meanwhile was aiming at the destruction of the King of Navarre and his brother Condé, whose schemes did no doubt constitute a serious menace to the Crown. The two brothers were summoned to Orléans for the States General, but the implacable hostility of the Guises was notorious and they hesitated to come: it was only when strong assurances were given them that there was no danger that they consented to enter Orléans. Condé was almost immediately seized, and the King of Navarre was put under close supervision. Condé was tried for conspiracy, not by the chamber of peers, but by a specially appointed commission, and under such circumstances the verdict was assured. It was given at the end of November, and Condé was condemned to death. The execution was fixed for Dec. 10, the day of the opening of the States General, which it was doubtless intended to overawe by such a display of the royal power. But on Dec. 5, 1560, Francis II died. All Catherine's children had feeble health, and Francis was perhaps the weakest of all: he was carried off by an abscess in the ear. His short reign had so identified him with religious persecution that there was a great sense of relief in Protestant countries: Knox tells of his delight when the news came that the King of France was dead "of a rotten ear...that deaf ear that never could hear the truth of God."

Francis II was succeeded by his brother Charles IX, who was only ten years of age. Mary Stuart, the widow of the late King, went back to Scotland to the stormy and tragic destiny that awaited her there. The Guises thus lost their control of the State. Catherine de Médicis at last grasped the power that she had longed for, and for more than ten years she remained the most important influence in France. Her

Catherine de Médicis & l'Hôpital. The approach of the Civil War.

one great aim was to remain in power. With this object she coquetted with the Protestant party and toleration; with this object she kept her son back from education and such knowledge as would allow him to rule; with this object she assisted in carrying out the Massacre of St Bartholomew. But she was never in favour of violent means if gentler could prevail. As a woman she knew that her influence would be most likely to prevail in time of peace. She tried therefore to balance faction against faction and party against party, and from purely egotistic motives supported l'Hôpital in his efforts to find some basis for religious toleration. If we look at her aims, and not her methods or her success, she deserves much credit. Henri Martin has said of her, "Her egotism often made her swerve from her aim; but her aim should not be misunderstood. She tried to beat down the nobles; she struggled against foreign influences; she was anxious for the unity and independence of France." Her rule was spoiled not only by that absence of morality which had wrecked so many Italian States; but further by a lack of persistence, of courage, and of force[1]. The period of the Reformation was one in which the first virtue of a Government was power to govern. A cruel despotism would probably have caused less misery in the end than the weakness of the French Government from 1560 to 1589.

Catherine's efforts then were doomed to failure, but the years 1561 and 1562 saw a very noble attempt on the part of l'Hôpital

[1] Here are two contemporary opinions about her (both taken directly from Mr Armstrong's *French Wars of Religion*, p. 85). Henry IV said, "What could a poor woman have done, with her husband dead and five small children upon her hands, and two families who were scheming to seize the throne, our own and the Guises...I am astonished that she did not do even worse." A Venetian observer wrote of her, "There is no prince who would not have lost his head amid these troubles, much more a foreigner without trusty friends, constitutionally timid, never hearing the truth. Nevertheless all the respect that is still given to the Monarchy is due to her."

to avoid the civil-religious wars, which he in common with most clear-sighted statesmen saw to be impending. The States General were opened at Orléans in December 1560 in spite of the King's death. L'Hôpital opened them with a fine appeal for tolerance. "Let us," he said, "attack heresy with the arms of charity, prayer, persuasion, and the words of God that apply to such a contest. Kindness will do more than severity. Let us drop these wicked names—Lutherans, Huguenots, Papists,—names of parties, factions, and seditions. Let us content ourselves with the title of Christians." In the debates that followed, the representatives of the nobles and the third estate asked for religious toleration, and attacked the wealth and the power of the Church. It was agreed, when the financial situation came up for discussion, that a smaller body of representatives should be selected to discuss this and other matters. Accordingly, in August 1561, 26 representatives of the Nobility and the third estate met at Pontoise, while the representatives of the Clergy were at Poissy. The demands made and the reforms suggested were of the most far-reaching kind. Three, perhaps, deserve special note as showing the trend of opinion at this time, before war had come to enflame fanaticism on every side. There came from the lay members a very general demand for regular meetings of the States General, for religious toleration, and for the confiscation of the property of the Church in order to pay the debts of the State. It is probable, however, that the elections had been to a certain extent controlled by the Chancellor: these demands represent his opinions rather than those of France. It is worth noting also that among demands which seem a premonition of the Revolution there were others, in which the reactionary claims of the nobles made themselves heard. They demand, for instance, the reestablishment of the old jurisdiction of the Nobility which the growth of the monarchy had nearly killed, to the great benefit of France; they reaffirm their exclusive right to hunting; they claim further distinctions between themselves and the Commons. The whole course of the debates in the Estates shows an extraordinary fermentation of opinion, and brings to light ideas which if realised would have produced a new France, or at least given an entirely new direction to her development.

The Guises meanwhile were excluded from office. Condé was declared innocent. The King of Navarre was made Lieutenant-General of the kingdom. L'Hôpital continued to strive for religious toleration. In February 1562 he suspended all trials of religious offences on the ground that nothing should be done until the Council of Trent had finished its sittings. Then while the clergy were sitting as part of the States General at Poissy he brought about a colloquy between representatives of the opposing faiths. Neither he nor the Queen Regent understood—just as Elizabeth of England did not understand—how impassable was the gulf between them, how impossible it was to find any *via media*. Beza came as the representative of the Calvinists; Lainez, the general of the Jesuit order, was present; the Cardinal of Lorraine was the chief speaker on the Catholic side. Two points are notable in this colloquy—first the fierce invective of Beza against the Catholic doctrine of the Mass, secondly the distinction drawn by the Catholic speakers between Lutherans and Calvinists. The hostility between the two leading Protestant bodies was becoming acute in Germany, and the Catholic leaders hoped to play upon this hostility and cut off the Huguenots from the sympathy and assistance of Germany. L'Hôpital refused to be discouraged by the result of the colloquy. He called an Assembly composed of members of all the Parlements, and issued another Edict in January 1562 (usually known as the Edict of January), whereby Huguenots were authorized to hold religious services outside the towns.

But in vain l'Hôpital struggled for peace and religious equilibrium. France was being carried resistlessly and with increasing velocity towards war. The favour shown by the court no doubt caused an increase in the ranks of

Protestants. The number of Protestant congregations was estimated, though doubtless with exaggeration, at 2300. Calvin in a letter says that he is deluged with applications for ministers for France. "We are asked for preachers on all sides: inquirers for them besiege my door, and contend for them with pious emulation." The Catholics saw with anger and alarm this result of a limited toleration.

On the Catholic side Guise was of course the most prominent. During 1561 he drew to his side Montmorency the Constable and the Marshal St André. Influences of various kinds were brought to bear on the weak will of Antony of Navarre. During the year he came over to the side of the Catholics, much to the indignation of Jeanne d'Albret, his wife. The Government was not strong enough to enforce its edicts or to maintain the religious peace. Long before the leaders on either side had drawn their swords there was civil war in many districts. The Protestants erected 'temples,' sometimes seized Catholic churches, broke images, stained-glass windows, and carved work. The Catholic population saw with fierce indignation this attack on a faith that they loved. There were riots and counter-riots on every hand. Paris and Toulouse were distinguished for the zeal with which they struck down the Protestants. In such circumstances it would have required a very strong hand to maintain the peace. A Henry VIII or an Elizabeth, a Henry of Navarre or a Richelieu might have succeeded. It was far beyond the power of Catherine de Médicis. An incident not perhaps worse than many others of the time produced a collision between the two parties. On the 1st of March, 1562, the Duke of Guise was coming to Paris from the German frontier, and passed through a small place called Vassy. It was Sunday, and a Huguenot service was in progress in a neighbouring barn. The accounts of what followed are obscured by partisanship. But a fight took place between Guise's soldiers and the Huguenots. Guise himself was struck on the cheek by a stone: his soldiers killed

The Wars of Religion, Part I.

some 60 and wounded about 200. He entered Paris immediately afterwards. With the Parisians he had always been popular, and the incident at Vassy increased his popularity: no king could have had a more triumphal reception. With the nation in such a temper war was bound to come.

It is very difficult to get any clear idea of the struggle that follows. There is no great leader until quite the end of the war, and no definite plan followed on either side. Although the country was deeply stirred by religious passions, it is curious to notice how small the armies are, and how largely they are composed of foreign mercenaries. Both sides hire foreign troops without any reference to the religion of their auxiliaries. German, Spanish, English, Swiss, Italian, Albanian troops are all at one time or another engaged in the war. Infantry counts for very little: the battles are chiefly engagements between cavalry, and are rarely decisive of the fortunes of the campaign. On more than one occasion, when the fortunes of the Huguenots seemed at their lowest ebb, a change in the policy of the Queen Regent, difficult to explain and dependent probably on quite small causes, gave them better terms than they could have hoped for after victory. The real importance of the war is not to be found in its battle-fields or its campaigns: the chief loss of life even is hardly to be sought there. The darkest side of the war is to be found in the permanent condition of civil strife which was established in every town and district in France. The Protestants were not blameless. Where they were in the majority they misused their powers by plundering churches, breaking up monasteries, and often killing their religious opponents. But naturally the worst excesses were committed by the Catholics, who possessed a great majority in the country and thus had little fear of retaliation. The use of force in religious controversies had been definitely approved of by their leaders. They were roused to fury by the insults offered to their faith and the revolution that was threatened

The War to the Peace of St Germains.

in every department of their social life. It is impossible to give any statistical account of the loss of life and the industrial ruin caused by these tumults, but any detailed history of France shows them occurring on all sides. They were worst perhaps in Toulouse and Paris, but no part of France was free from them. When the wars were over it was found that certain districts had fallen out of cultivation during their course. Everywhere the course of civilisation had been retarded. Nevertheless, during these thirty years and more of confusion and war life still went on. The fields in most districts were still tilled; commerce still flowed, though with a weakened current. Doubtless the evils of the time were far more felt in some districts than others, but even in the most disturbed districts there were some fortunate enough to see the storm pass without sustaining personal damage. Montaigne (born 1533—died 1592) was one of the most fortunate of these, and his picture of his own life forms so agreeable a contrast to the scenes of anarchy and violence which were general during his lifetime that it may be well to quote his words. They are from his Essay "That our desires are encreased by difficultie." "Among other meanes ease and facility doth haply cover and fence my house from the violence of civill wars. I have abated and weakened the souldier's designe by taking hazard and all means of military glory from their exploit, which is wont to serve them for a title and stead them for an excuse. I yield them the conquest of my house dastardly and treacherously. It is never shut to any that knocketh. It hath no other guardian or provision but a porter, as an ancient custom and used ceremony, who serveth not so much to defend my gate as to offer it more decently and courteously to all comers." He goes on to speak of the universal distrust. "Your own servant may be of that faction you stand in fear of. And where religion serveth for a pretence, even alliances and consanguinities become mistrustful. Common rents cannot entertaine our private garrisons. We have not wherewith to entertain them without our apparent ruin, or more incommodiously and also injuriously without the destruction of the common people.... That so many strongly guarded houses have been lost, whereas mine continueth still, makes me suspect they were overthrowne only because they were so diligently guarded[1]."

Catherine de Médicis had tried in vain to maintain peace, and in the hope of doing so she had seemed to lean towards l'Hôpital and the Protestants; but, with the actual outbreak of hostilities it was inevitable that she should move over to the side of the Catholics, even though that side were led by the Duke of Guise, her rival for power. With much misgiving she joined herself to Guise, Montmorency, St André, and the King of Navarre. War was not long in coming. Condé gathered forces and money from the reformed Churches, and then conjointly with Coligny and Dandelot he entered into a sort of bond of association for the defence of Calvinism. But the Protestant leaders refused to regard themselves as rebels. They pretended that the King and his mother were captives, and declared themselves leagued for "the honour of God, the liberty of the King and his brother and of his mother the Queen, and for the maintenance of the Edicts." Everywhere there was a struggle to determine which party should have the mastery in the various cities and districts. The chief towns that were held for the Protestant cause were Rouen, Bourges, Orléans, Lyons, Montauban, Béziers, Montpellier, Nîmes. But though the Protestants held power in these and many other cities it did not by any means always follow that the inhabitants were with them. Often they held merely the citadel, and by means of its guns kept in check a resistance that was ready to break out at any time. In many places there was fierce fighting before the partisanship of the town was decided. In Toulouse 3000 Huguenots, who had surrendered upon the offer of terms, were massacred in cold blood.

[1] Book II. Ch. XV. Florio's translation, slightly altered.

There could be no question that the military strength of the Catholics was superior to that of their opponents. The Government had greater financial credit than the rebels, and could procure stronger mercenary reinforcements from beyond the Rhine. The King of Navarre now led the Catholic army, and advanced against Rouen in September. If it was to be saved the Protestants must have help. They looked naturally to England as the nearest and strongest Protestant country, and on the 10th of September they made terms with Queen Elizabeth. She was to receive Havre from the Protestants, and promised Condé in exchange three thousand men and a hundred and forty thousand crowns of gold. The help was very acceptable; yet this alliance with the traditional enemy of France perhaps injured the Protestant cause more than it helped it. But the Catholics as well as the Protestants looked for foreign assistance, and procured from Philip II of Spain 6000 veteran troops. The English help did not come in time to save Rouen, which capitulated on October 26. During the course of the siege the King of Navarre was wounded, and shortly afterwards died of his wounds. Guise was now leader of the Catholics without a rival, and in November 1562 arrived before Orléans with a strong following of German auxiliaries. Orléans, Lyons, and Montpellier were now the most important towns that remained in the hands of the Protestants. The course of the war had been a great disappointment to them: they had anticipated rapid victory, though on very insufficient grounds. Despite their enthusiasm and their undoubted courage, the general result of the unnumbered struggles that had taken place throughout France was decidedly in favour of their enemy. Province after province had been lost: it was chiefly in the south and in Normandy that they still had a strong foothold.

Condé, always energetic and daring, hoped to restore the fortunes of the Protestants by some bold stroke. Leaving the Catholic army unmolested at Orléans he marched on to Paris.

There was astonishment and even alarm at his approach, but no panic. He turned westward to join hands with the English forces in Normandy. The Catholic army threw itself across his course at Dreux and forced on an engagement (Nov. 1562). Guise, Montmorency, and St André were all with the Catholic army. The battle opened with a heavy cavalry charge, in which the Protestants were at first victorious; but they encountered a very vigorous resistance from the Swiss mercenaries, and then, when the battle hung in the balance, the Protestant foot was broken by the attack of the Catholic reserve under Guise. A curious feature of the battle was that Montmorency, the Catholic general, was taken prisoner in the first charge of the Huguenots, and at the end of the battle Condé had to surrender to the Catholics. St André was left dead on the field. In February 1563 Guise, who had just been named by Catherine Lieutenant-General of the kingdom, renewed the siege of Orléans. The place was hard pressed, and its capitulation seemed certain, but on February 18 Guise was assassinated by Poltrot de Méré. So fierce had the passions grown on both sides that the assassin was saluted by the Huguenots as a hero, and even Coligny spoke of the deed as "the greatest good that could have happened to the kingdom and the Church of God." The example found many imitators before the religious wars were over. Guise before his death with unexpected magnanimity urged his attendants to spare the assassin.

The assassination of Guise saved Orléans. Guise had been the great supporter of the war. In spite of him Catherine de Médicis had been negotiating with the Protestant leaders almost continuously: his death removed an obstacle to her schemes. She now with the help of l'Hôpital negotiated peace with the Huguenots. This peace—the Peace of Amboise (March 1563)—allowed Calvinist services in one town in each *bailliage*, and in certain other places under strict conditions. In Paris such services were strictly forbidden. The Huguenots on their side were to surrender all towns that they held and all prisoners.

They remained excluded from all offices. Few thought that this arrangement could be more than a truce, for on both sides it was equally disliked; but France had suffered so cruelly from the civil tumults that accompanied the war that even a breathing space was welcome to the Government. But the terms of the peace were never properly kept. The Government was too weak to enforce them in face of the violence of the passions that had caused the war, and were in turn stimulated by it.

This peace lasted without open rupture from May 1563 to September 1567. During these years no event of great importance occurs on French soil; the unceasing rivalry of the factions cannot be described without going into excessive detail. But before the end of the so-called period of peace the situation had considerably changed. The first result of the peace was to turn the arms of combined France against the English who were occupying Havre. There was a widespread fear lest Havre should prove another Calais in the hands of England. Elizabeth supported her garrison there almost as weakly as Mary had supported hers at Calais. Condé joined himself to the attacking force, which in July became master of the city. The incident had a lasting influence on Elizabeth's policy. She did not again for many years support the Huguenots except indirectly; and as events forced her into more decided opposition to Spain, she came to look upon the friendship of the French Government in all its variations as her strongest support.

Important as the recapture of Havre was, events beyond the French frontier exercised an even greater influence on the course of French affairs. In 1563 the Council of Trent at last finished its sessions. We have already seen how great its importance was in defining the position of the Roman Catholic Church and strengthening it for aggression. The conclusion of the Council made it somewhat more difficult to preserve the peace in France. L'Hôpital had always appealed to mutual toleration 'until the Council had finished its work.' Now that its work was finished and that work contained no hint of compromise or reconciliation, a powerful argument in favour of a truce was gone. In the Netherlands meanwhile the country was in dangerous ferment. The pressure of the Spanish Government and the work of the Inquisition had driven the country up to and beyond the frontier of rebellion. The Huguenots of France were elated by the example of their co-religionists: Catherine was alarmed by the spectacle of the dangerous union of political and religious discontent. Henceforth for many years French history and the history of the Netherlands were in very close connection. Nor were events in Scotland without their influence. Mary Stuart was finding her Scottish crown difficult to wear. A very close parallel might be drawn between the Reformation movements in Scotland and in France. Both were Calvinist, both were led on by the aristocracy: in both countries the Protestant leaders were anxious to limit the powers of the Crown. Condé, Coligny, and their associates watched, and sometimes imitated, the measures of Murray and Morton and Maitland of Lethington.

Catherine was anxious to maintain the peace, and it was due to her that it was maintained so long. In the year 1564 she took Charles IX, whose nominal majority at the age of fourteen had been declared in the previous year, on a progress through the provinces. The young King was not devoid of gifts capable of attracting the public favour. He was passionately fond of hunting and all physical exercises, and it seemed quite possible that when manhood really came he would be able to reign. For the present, power rested completely in his mother's hands. As the royal party approached the Spanish frontier Catherine was anxious for an interview with Philip of Spain, her son-in-law, in the hope of putting the relations between the two countries on a friendly footing—for Philip had frequently complained of the toleration which the French Government had shown for the Huguenots. Philip himself refused to meet Catherine, but he sent his wife as a mark of courtesy and his chief minister and soldier Alva to negotiate. The conference took place at Bayonne (June 1565). The meeting was at the time regarded by the Protestants as being of ill omen. Later, it assumed a still more sinister meaning: it was at this conference, so it was maintained, that the Massacre of St Bartholomew was arranged, and from this hour onwards Catherine had always that terrible crime in view. But though this belief was itself important diplomatic documents prove that it has little if any basis. Religious matters were discussed: Alva urged the Queen to greater energy in repressing heresy and perhaps suggested the destruction of its leaders: his own master was preparing just such a blow in the Netherlands. But no one now holds the view that the Massacre of St Bartholomew or any massacre was arranged at the interview. Catherine still pursued her policy of balance and pacification. In January 1566 an assembly of Notables was held at Moulins, and Catherine did her utmost to conciliate the great rivals of the hour. The Assembly of Moulins was not devoted only to religious questions. It is an important landmark in the judicial history of France, and it may be well to note that it formally recognized the Parlement's right of registering the royal Edicts. There was a formal reconciliation between the Guise family (the young Duke Henry had now taken the place of his murdered father) and Coligny and his brother. At the same time the Edict of Amboise was reaffirmed.

It was not Catherine's fault that war broke out again. It must be remembered that peace had never really existed in many of the country districts. Above all the minds of men were not at peace. The Huguenot preachers and writers breathed fire and slaughter against their enemies, and sometimes declared that it was permissible to slay Kings or Queens "who opposed the Gospel." Alva had been despatched by Philip to the Netherlands to cut with his sword a knot that ought not to have been beyond the powers of conciliation to untie. He

The Wars of Religion, Part I.

had set up the famous 'Blood Council' and had begun to establish a reign of terror. France was affected by all this. The reports of collisions between the two parties, of 'temples' and churches plundered, of assassinations and reprisals became more frequent. In many districts Catholic associations were formed which contributed to the growth of the Holy League that later on gained so great a notoriety in France. The Calvinist leaders protested: Catherine gave gracious answers to their protests, but nothing was done. In the autumn of 1567 the situation was more alarming for the Calvinists than ever. A considerable army, consisting largely of hired Swiss troops, had been raised—nominally, and perhaps really, to watch the march of Alva along the frontiers of France towards the Netherlands. But when Alva had reached his destination, and no Spanish attack on France could any longer be suspected, the French army was still kept on foot. The Protestant leaders suspected a design against themselves. From the Netherlands came news that Alva had seized the leaders of the opposition, and had determined on their death. Condé, Coligny, Dandelot, and other leaders of the Protestants held a meeting and decided to anticipate the blow which they believed to be impending. The King and Queen were to be seized at Meaux, and a policy more favourable to the Huguenots was to be forced upon them. But the Queen received information of the project, summoned the Swiss to her help, and fled to Paris: soon afterwards war began again (Sept. 1567).

The Huguenots were, as usual, numerically and financially weaker than their opponents, but they were strong in cavalry, and Condé was ready for a daring move. For the second time he decided to make a dash on Paris in the hope of frightening the court into concessions. But the Catholic army accepted battle at St Denis to the north of Paris, if a cavalry engagement that lasted barely an hour can be called a battle. It was indecisive in results, but the Protestant attack was beaten off. The Constable Montmorency was wounded in the battle and died soon after. Catherine did not appoint any successor, but gave the title of Lieutenant-general and command of the royal troops to her favourite son Henry of Anjou, who was sixteen years of age. And here unexpectedly the war ended, or rather there came one of those cessations of official hostilities of which there are so many in this war. Condé had been reinforced by German auxiliaries under John Casimir, son of the Elector Palatine. Catherine was always in favour of peace if she could find an excuse for it. The Peace of Longjumeau was signed in March 1568 and renewed the terms of the Treaty of Amboise.

The Peace of Longjumeau gave France six months of disturbed rest, and then war began again. It is hardly worth our while to examine how a peace broke down which had never existed except in name. Alva's executions in the Netherlands again had an important influence, and the rigorous and relentless policy of Pope Pius V, who succeeded to the pontificate in 1566, also made the Protestants despair of any real conciliation. He was the great Pope of the Catholic reaction, sincere to fanaticism, unsparing of himself and unwilling to spare any heretic: before he died the Church saw the tide flowing strongly in her favour even in countries like Poland and Germany where all seemed lost. Condé and Coligny believed that their liberty and life were threatened, and retired to La Rochelle, which now began to be the headquarters of the Huguenots. As they became conscious of their military inferiority they saw the value of a stronghold which should always give the great Protestant sea powers, England and Holland, access to them. Jeanne d'Albret, the widowed Queen of Navarre and mother of the prince Henry who was soon to champion the Huguenot cause, joined Condé with a considerable force. On the other side fierce counsels were gaining the ascendancy over the milder wisdom of l'Hôpital. The great Chancellor was dismissed from office because he was not willing to persecute. His place was taken by pliant instruments of the Catholic reaction.

The Wars of Religion, Part I.

Henry Duke of Anjou again commanded the royal forces, assisted by Tavannes and Biron. In order to cut off Rochelle from German and other reinforcements which were about to arrive he occupied the bridges over the Charente, and thus in March 1569 brought on the battle of Jarnac. Condé attacked with his usual vigour; but his troops were undisciplined and inferior in number. He was defeated and forced to surrender his sword: he had already surrendered it when he was shot by an officer of the Duke of Anjou. His death was an important event. Coligny drew off the troops in fair order but he could not quite take Condé's place, for he was not a prince of the blood royal, and was not as acceptable to the Nobility as Condé had been. The young Prince Henry of Navarre, though only 15 years of age, thus became an important person. The defeat at Jarnac does not seem to have weakened the fighting strength of the Huguenots very much. Coligny received assistance from Germany, and was the stronger power south of the Loire. Soon he was able to lay siege to Poictiers, but the siege proved unsuccessful and he had to withdraw. He hoped to join Montgomery in the south, but on his way he was attacked by the Duke of Anjou near Moncontour (3 October, 1569). Both sides largely consisted of foreign mercenaries, and the army of Coligny was in great disorder, the nobles demanding instant battle, the mercenaries clamouring for pay. The battle was the severest that had been fought during the war. The Huguenots were decisively beaten with very great loss. Coligny could rally after the battle not more than half of his troops: but with his usual firmness and resourcefulness he succeeded in saving the cause to which he had given his heart. At first indeed all seemed lost: the Catholic leaders believed that the final victory had been won. But there was bitter jealousy between the King and his more successful brother; the royal army failed to press its advantages; Coligny had regathered his forces; and so it came about that the Huguenots after two defeats, one a very decisive one, obtained the best terms that they had received since the beginning of the war. Coligny's recovery of strength alarmed the court: the country was in a deplorable condition: Catherine de Médicis as usual found her influence waning during a war. In August 1570 the Peace of St Germain was signed in spite of the protests of the Pope and Philip II. It was a very important document, and contained the germ that was afterwards expanded into the Edict of Nantes. The chief terms were, (1) free exercise of religious worship for the Huguenots in two cities in each province and in all places where it was already established: (2) all careers to be thrown open to them equally with the Catholics: (3) as security for the maintenance of the Edict they were to be allowed to garrison four towns, La Rochelle, Montauban, Cognac, and la Charité. Had the terms of the Peace been kept, the Huguenots could not reasonably have asked for anything more. The Pope called it "the most deadly blow that the faith had received since the beginning of the religious troubles."

The controversies as to fact and motive that beset the Reformation, like all other periods of violent revolution, are nowhere keener than for the period that now follows—for the events, that is to say, which lead up to the St Bartholomew Massacre and for the Massacre itself. The student of history must be content to leave much in doubt, but the general situation and the causes that led to the Massacre are beyond controversy. Questions of national and even of European policy are mixed up with questions of personal jealousy and ambition. Catherine de Médicis, her relation to her children, and her passion for power continue to form the very centre of this French drama.

The Massacre of St Bartholomew's Day.

Charles IX was 21 years old in 1570. He began to resent the insignificant rôle to which his mother's ambition had condemned him. He determined not only to reign but to rule, and he embarked on a fresh line of policy to which at first his mother offered no opposition. He saw, as all men saw, how much France had been weakened by these unceasing religious wars while Spain was advancing in apparent power. The rising of the Netherlands was crushed, to all appearance. In 1571 all Christendom rang with the fame of the great naval victory that the Spaniards had won over the Turks at Lepanto. The Italian wars had left in the minds of Frenchmen a strong feeling of jealousy and hostility to Spain. It was natural then that the policy should suggest itself of bringing these civil struggles to an end, and of attacking Spain with the united forces of France. Spain's troubles in the Netherlands supplied the necessary opportunity. Union in a war against the national enemy would be, it was suggested, the best means of making men forget their religious differences.

This was the policy that Charles IX favoured: it was on the lines of Catherine de Médicis' policy. The times were favourable and the men were ready to hand. The Guises were too devoted to the Catholic reaction and to Spain to support the scheme: the King therefore turned to Coligny. The Protestant leader came to the court at Blois in September, 1571, and from then to his death was the King's chief adviser. The new policy pleased him at every point; it would be, he maintained, the best thing conceivable both for France and the Protestant cause. There was no secret about the proposed change of front. Spain saw it with alarm and protested in vain. The way was to be prepared by marriages of great diplomatic importance. In 1570 the King married Elizabeth, daughter of the Emperor Maximilian II, who lived on good terms with his Protestant subjects. The year 1571 was full of negotiations for a marriage between Elizabeth, Queen of England, and Henry of Anjou, in spite of the wide disparity of age, and for an offensive and defensive alliance between the two countries: it was the fault of England, not of France, that the marriage was not carried out, that a defensive alliance only was made. A third and equally important marriage was actually arranged between Henry of Navarre, the rising leader of the Protestants, and Marguerite of Valois, the King's sister. The favour shown to the Protestant cause in this marriage was all the more striking because Marguerite of Valois herself disliked the match and was known to desire a union with Henry of Guise, the hero of the Catholic cause. Other and smaller incidents showed the same current of policy. Coligny was constantly with the King. An attack made upon the Protestants of Rouen by the Catholics of that city was severely punished. So convinced was Coligny of the sincerity of the new policy that he handed over the cautionary towns to the King before the appointed time. There was a general expectation that a large French army would enter the Netherlands to support the malcontents there.

It is impossible to regard all this as a trap dexterously baited. The Catholics and the Catholic leaders were furious, and the Pope protested both in public and private against the new policy. Foreign ambassadors reported the seriousness of the situation to their Governments. It is evident from the negotiations with England that the proposed marriage and union with England failed only because Elizabeth refused to cooperate.

The King then was willing to change his policy entirely; but it was far from being so with the country at large. The Guises did not conceal their hostility to the new move. The Catholic associations fomented the hostility to the Huguenots. Nowhere was the Catholic feeling more aggressive than in Paris, where public opinion was outraged by the insolent and defiant bearing of the Protestant nobles who had come up to court with Coligny. Coligny himself gave offence by his haughty manners and his assumption of power: he did not conceal his hostility for Henry of Anjou and Catherine. And yet up to a certain point the new policy was persisted in, in defiance of public opinion. The English marriage had fallen through, as we have seen, but the project of marriage between Henry

The Wars of Religion, Part I.

of Navarre and Margaret of Valois was carried out, and that too before the full Papal dispensation had arrived. The Queen of Navarre died suddenly in Paris in June, 1572, but even that did not much postpone the marriage. It took place on August 18. Huguenots crowded into Paris to be present at an event which seemed to insure them toleration and a share in the future of France. Paris was full of rumours of plots, but nothing occurred to interrupt the marriage. Abroad, too, everything was favourable to the avowed design of Charles IX. Elizabeth consented to an alliance, though not to the close alliance which had at one time been hoped. The revolt of the Netherlands against Spain had entered on a new and more dangerous phase. On the 1st of April, 1572, Brille and Flushing had been seized by the 'water beggars,' as the Dutch patriots were called who had been driven from Holland by the tyranny of Alva. In May, before the Spaniards had stamped out that rising, which proved indeed in the end unquenchable, the flames had broken out in the South. Mons and Valenciennes fell into the hands of Louis of Nassau, who had the assistance of French troops under La Noue. It seemed as though epoch-making events must follow—events that would herald in a better time for Europe.

Why did not these events come about? It is impossible to see clearly all the springs of what followed, but some may be pointed out. The enterprise against Spain turned out not to be so easy as some had represented: Genlis, who had been sent without open support but with secret instructions from the French Crown to the relief of Mons, which was being besieged by Alva, was overwhelmed and taken prisoner. But probably the cause is to be found in Catherine de Médicis' character. Power, if we understand her character aright, was her one passion, and it seemed as though power had passed to Coligny. Already he seemed to have complete ascendancy over the mind of the King: the outbreak of the war would see him in greater authority than ever. Catherine, moreover, timid by nature and disliking decisive measures, found that the war policy had great dangers. Elizabeth's attitude in the matter was doubtful. From Italy she was strongly advised not to commit France to war against Spain. She drew nearer to those who had the same animosities as herself. Both Guise and the Duke of Anjou hated Coligny, and they became now the confidential advisers of the Queen Mother. To a Florentine brought up in the school of Machiavelli the situation suggested one remedy. Coligny must be removed. An assassin was hired; the preparations were made. Coligny was shot at on August 22 as he was entering his lodging; he was wounded in both arms but neither fatally nor dangerously. The Queen Mother, whose policy never looked far ahead, had probably not realised the results of this act. The excitement on both sides was intense. Charles IX, accompanied by his mother, visited Coligny and expressed his anger and sympathy. The Huguenots demanded a strict enquiry. Clearly Catherine de Médicis and her confederates had got no good from this attempted assassination: the situation became, on the contrary, much worse. Panic-stricken at the thought of this crime being brought home to them, they decided to commit another and a far greater. They had failed to kill the leader of the Huguenots; they must now kill them all. It was possible if only the King's consent could be obtained. Every means was used: his own life, he was told, was threatened. At last his will was overborne. "If you must kill them," he said, "kill them all that no one may be left alive to reproach me." (23 Aug. 1572.)

The preparations were hurriedly made, and the signal was given shortly after midnight. Guise himself superintended the murder of Coligny, who was stabbed in his bed and then thrown into the courtyard that Guise might identify him. It was only necessary for it to be known that official sanction had been given to the killing of the Huguenots and that the royal troops were engaged, to induce the Parisian populace to join eagerly in the slaughter. "Comrades," Guise cried after the murder of Coligny, "continue your work, the King orders it." A score of Protestant noblemen of the highest birth were killed, and along with them Ramus, the great jurist, and Goujon, the sculptor. The slaughter continued for three days and extended from Paris to the provinces. It is impossible to reckon up with certainty the number of victims, but a very moderate estimate puts the deaths at 2000 in Paris, and 8000 in the provinces.

The official explanations of the Massacre varied widely as different influences were brought to bear upon the King. At first it was put down to a feud between the houses of Châtillon and Guise that had broken out in spite of the Government, and the King declared that in spite of what had happened the Edict of St Germains still subsisted. But the Guises refused to bear the responsibility that was thus unjustly thrust upon them. The King therefore was persuaded (26 August) to write to the Governors of the provinces, declaring that the massacre was due to the Admiral's "tyranny," which had at last grown insupportable, "and therefore I allowed justice to have its course, irregular, indeed, and different in its methods from what I could have wished, but inevitable considering the character of the person against whom it was aimed." On the 28th of August he went to the Parlement and declared that the Massacre had been carried out by his orders as the only means of crushing "a conspiracy for the extermination of the royal family." But this view of the case was not uniformly persisted in. While Rome and Spain resounded with praises of the deed, Charles found need to apologise for it to the Court of England and threw the responsibility for it on the ungovernable fury of the people. Nowhere were the effects of the Massacre worse than in the Netherlands. The hopes of the insurgents there were at once dashed to the ground. William the Silent had to face a long struggle against desperate odds. But eventually the force of circumstances brought French policy back into the former paths, and before long the

Protestant Netherlands were again looking to France for assistance.

The Massacre spread wide and struck deep, but, though the Huguenot party was terribly weakened, it was not exterminated nor completely overawed. The loss to the Huguenots indeed was irremediable. The death of Coligny was in itself worse than the loss of a great battle, for no one was found to take his place who had at all the same moral ascendancy, stoutness of heart or military and diplomatic skill. The blow, too, had fallen with especial violence on the smaller nobles, who had formed the most valuable part of the fighting force of the Huguenots. Henceforth the Huguenots could rarely bring an army into the field without Catholic cooperation; and we shall see that an increasing number of the Catholics were willing for political reasons to cooperate with the Huguenots. Henry of Navarre and the younger Condé had abjured the Protestant faith and gone to mass in order to save their lives, and this example was followed by a nameless crowd. But the towns of the west and south-west declared for resistance, and Rochelle was once again its centre. The Huguenots now adopted a far more definite organisation than anything they had previously possessed. None could now desire to keep terms with the Government; and few of the Huguenots could hesitate to set up an opposition Government. Their forces were to form a sort of federal republic. Each Protestant town was to have its Mayor and two councils: they in their turn were to elect a general chief and council. This republican organisation gave them strength for the time; but, in the future, embittered against them the monarchy of France. We shall see that Richelieu remembered it when he delivered against them his final blow.

The Fourth religious war and the death of Charles IX.

We might have expected that with the memories of the 24th of August in the minds of both parties the war would have been a long and stubborn one; and so it probably

The Wars of Religion, Part I.

would have been if its control had been left to the passions of the parties. But the Massacre had been to the Queen Regent merely an episode, not the end of one long political scheme nor the beginning of another. She had planned the assassination of Coligny partly in order to escape from a foreign war: she did not desire to substitute a civil war. So after the royal armies had besieged Rochelle in vain for five months (Feb. to July, 1573) the troops were withdrawn and terms were offered and accepted. The Huguenots were not to be persecuted; there was to be a very limited permission to hold Calvinist services; Montauban, Rochelle and Nîmes were to be held by the Huguenots as security for the performance of the treaty. It was a strangely colourless sequel to the St Bartholomew Massacre.

Catherine had other reasons for wanting peace, besides weariness of the war. Her favourite son, Henry of Anjou—the victor of Jarnac and Moncontour, after herself the chief author of the St Bartholomew Massacre—was elected in May 1573 to the throne of Poland, and, strange to say, was escorted to the throne by a body of German Calvinists. After he was gone, victory might easily strengthen some rival against the Queen-Mother. The Catholics, too, gave her nearly as much trouble as the Huguenots. Joyfully as the Massacre had been welcomed by some, there were more whom it offended bitterly. The Government was harassed by rumours of plots, no longer from the Huguenot side, but from the malcontent Catholic nobles. The party afterwards known as the 'Politiques,' began to form itself—a party which, in the interest of the tranquillity of the State, was willing to accord toleration to a religion that it disliked. Charles IX meanwhile was slowly dying. Romance has probably added picturesque incidents to his last days. But it is clear that the memory of August 24 lay heavy upon his conscience. He is sometimes spoken of as the author of the Massacre: he was more really one of its victims. His hopes were Coligny's hopes. When he saw power torn from his weak hands and France thrust back again into the dismal round of civil war and national weakness he sank into a morose and despondent apathy from which nothing could rouse him. He died on May 30, 1574. Because of his aspirations during 1571 and the early months of 1572 he is the one of Catherine de Médicis' children for whom it is easiest to feel something like respect.

CHAPTER V.

THE RELIGIOUS WARS, PART II.   THE REIGN OF HENRY III.

WHEN Charles IX died his brother Henry of Anjou was King of Poland. But his short residence in Poland had served to disgust him with the country and the country with him. The Poles had expected to find the hero of Jarnac and Moncontour a vigorous and ambitious soldier; they found instead an effeminate and luxurious prince. The King disliked the people, whose language and ideas he could not understand, and amidst the rough manners of Poland longed to return to all the civilised pleasures of Paris. When the news of his brother's death reached him his mind was soon made up. It was doubtful whether the Poles would grant him leave to go to Paris to claim his French crown, for the country was at this moment threatened with a Turkish invasion; he went therefore without asking leave. It is characteristic of him that he could throw no persistent energy into his quest of the French crown. He went through Austria and Italy. The pleasures of the Italian cities detained him some time.

The Religious wars to the treaty of Fleix.

The miserable future that was in store for France during the next few years, depended to a considerable extent on the character of the King or on his want of character. Of all the children of Catherine de Médicis he is the worst. The military energy that he had once seemed to show had completely evaporated. His life was divided henceforth between two chief interests—religion, or rather religious observances, and the pleasures of a luxurious and debauched court. His religion was of the most external, irrational and superstitious kind, but it was often sincerely held. He was seen walking in religious processions, and he allowed the lash to be laid upon his own shoulders in public until even strong Catholic opinion revolted against his hysteria and lack of all kingly dignity. His religious observances and beliefs had no effect on his conduct, and did not make him live more soberly or rule more wisely. He surrounded himself with favourites such as Joyeuse and Epernon, who had complete dominion over his mind, and for whom he squandered almost incredible sums, while the public service was nearly bankrupt, and the people were plunged deep in misery. His court was a scene of disorder and debauchery. Duels were of constant occurrence, and were often fatal. The memoirs of the time give an impression of licence which it is hard to parallel. Henri Martin has drawn at length a comparison between Henry III's court and the most corrupt courts of the Roman Empire. The only suggestion that can be urged in extenuation is that there was a strong vein of insanity in the King. Sully says in his Memoirs, "I shall never forget the extravagant and fantastic dress and attitude in which I found him in his Cabinet; he had a sword at his side, a Spanish hood hung down upon his shoulders, a little cap, such as collegians wear, was upon his head, and a basket in which were two or three little dogs hung to a riband about his neck. He stood in so fixed a posture that in speaking to me he neither moved his head, hands, nor feet."

There were new elements arising in France with which statesmen would have to reckon seriously. The Huguenots were not increasing in strength. This was due partly, but only partly, to the cruel persecutions that had been used against them. France had decided against the ideas of Calvin. At first the novelty had attracted many; but now, beyond those who had already thrown in their lot with the Huguenots, there were few who did not prefer the colour and grace and poetry of Catholicism to the austerity and coldness of Calvinism. Nor on the whole were the intellect and heart of France inclined to accept the doctrines of Calvin in preference to the Catholic theology and the worship of the Virgin and the Saints. But if Calvinism made few fresh converts or none, the middle party was rapidly strengthening. These men, who soon came to be known as the Politicians (Politiques), were Catholics, who were shocked by the cruelties of which the St Bartholomew Massacre was the culminating point, and impressed by the terrible evil that the civil wars were inflicting upon France: they were anxious therefore to find some compromise that should really allay religious passions and give France repose. Elements of a more questionable kind were also to be found in the party. Some joined it from motives of disappointment or jealousy or ambition. The Montmorency family was for the present the chief representative of this party; for l'Hôpital, who would naturally have directed its action, had died shortly after the Bartholomew Massacre. Damville, the second brother of the house of Montmorency, was governor of Languedoc, and he acted there quite independently of the central government. He allowed the Huguenots a large freedom of worship, openly declared that both religions must be accepted in France, and consequently spared Languedoc much of the misery that the rest of France was suffering[1]. Let us add that the zealous Catholics too were growing more zealous than ever. Despairing of the action of the monarchy, they formed a new organisation

---

[1] I owe to Mr Armstrong's *French Wars of Religion* a striking definition of this party given by the Catholic Tavannes. "They were," he says, "those who preferred the repose of the kingdom or their own homes to the salvation of their souls; who would rather that the kingdom remained at peace without God than at war for Him."

of their own—the League. We shall see to what lengths they were willing to go and what allies they sought.

War had broken out again before the death of the last King, and, though little fighting had taken place, the intrigues and preparations that were the inevitable preliminary of war had been busily carried on. Henry III had at once therefore to make a decision as to his religious policy. He seemed at first inclined to accept a policy of toleration, and on his road from Italy he had an interview with Damville. But after he had met his mother his weak will easily succumbed to hers, and his declaration that France could have only one religion was the signal for the outbreak of more serious fighting. It will be well to follow rapidly the course of the next three of these wars before examining the rise of the Holy League. These three wars are even more tedious than those which had gone before. There was lack of funds on both sides, lack of men on the side of the Huguenots, and on the side of the Crown lack of energy. At first, too, the Huguenots were without leaders. We have seen what a clean sweep had been made of them in 1572. Henry of Navarre was a prisoner at Court; the younger Condé had fled abroad; none of the nobles had the ascendancy over their party that had been possessed by Coligny. Their leader came from an unexpected source. The King's brother, the Duke of Alençon, was in no way superior to the other children of Catherine de Médicis: his future history was to exhibit him possessed of the same weakness, the same tendency to cruelty and treachery. For the present he was almost an unknown quantity, but he was furiously jealous of his brother. In September, 1575, he escaped from the Court and put himself at the head of the Huguenots, who welcomed him on account of his birth. By themselves the Huguenots could now have done very little, but many of the Politiques joined themselves to them. The war, if war it can be called, lasted only for a few months more, and shows us nothing of even second-rate military interest. Money came to the

The Wars of Religion, Part II.

Huguenots from England, and with money they could procure German assistance. In October, Montmorency-Thoré, the lieutenant of Condé, was defeated by Guise. But German troops were ready to enter France, and actually did so before the end of the year, under Condé and the Elector Palatine. They passed through Burgundy, crossed the Loire, and joined the troops of the Duke of Alençon at Moulins, pillaging the country remorselessly as they passed. Catholic France cried out for more energetic action; but energy could never come from Henry III. Catherine de Médicis too was now anxious for peace. Guise's victory had alarmed her: if Guise gained victories while her son was inactive, she saw how dangerous Guise would become as a popular champion. In May, 1576, therefore, terms were arranged through the Duke of Alençon (whose court title was "Monsieur"). This so-called "Peace of Monsieur" was of the usual kind. Its terms will be found given in tabular form elsewhere[1]. It lasted so short a time that they do not deserve close examination here. The point of chief interest is that a convocation of the States General was promised.

The war, we have seen, had been most ineffectual, and yet some very important incidents were connected with it. During its course, in February, 1576, Henry of Navarre, with a small band of followers, escaped from Court. He had lived there of course as a Catholic, and was not easily distinguishable from the other licentious and duelling nobles. But he was not at ease there, and soon after joining the Huguenots he again conformed to their religion. He was not immediately accepted as their leader. Condé was the greater favourite with the zealous ministers; but the great charm of Navarre's frank and daring character, his warm humanity and his considerable military talents, soon forced him up into the position of leader for both the Huguenots and the Politiques. His wife joined him. They held their court at Nérac—a court little different from the court at Paris, says Margaret of Valois, except that many of the

[1] See Appendix.

courtiers were Huguenots. It is to be noted too that this Peace of Monsieur gave a great impulse to the organization of the League. The King was believed to have abstained from crushing the Huguenots. France, as we have seen, was for the most part enthusiastically Catholic; so the League was formed in order to force the King to do what of his own accord he would not do.

The States General met at Blois. All the 312 deputies were Catholics. The meeting was in most respects abortive, for the reforms which it projected were never carried out. But it is very important as showing what the trend of Catholic opinion in France was. The States desired to extirpate heresy and to limit the powers of the Crown. The first object had been aimed at from the beginning, but the second had only recently been adopted. The parts of Protestants and Catholics had been, during the course of these religious struggles, inverted. It was the Protestants who at first had wanted to drag France back towards feudalism, but at the end of the struggle they appear as champions of the rights of the Crown. The Estates of Blois made demands which, if granted, would have superseded the Monarchy: they demanded that all Acts passed by all the three orders should be binding, even without the royal sanction, and that the majority of the King's Council should consist of commissioners nominated by the Estates. It was impossible for Henry III to accept such proposals. He thought to conciliate public opinion by accepting the League. He signed it himself, he induced his brother to do so, and declared himself its chief. At the same time he revoked the edicts that had accompanied the Peace of Monsieur, and thus a condition of war was at once created. But Henry III found that all his protestations were in vain. Catholic France did not trust either him or his mother. The deputies welcomed the withdrawal of the Edicts of Toleration, but they refused to trust the King with money. The debates on this subject were long and bitter and full of suspicion. The Estates refused, to the end, to make grants at all sufficient for a war of extermination against the Huguenots.

The Wars of Religion, Part II.

Hostilities, therefore, which had begun, were quickly dropped, and again there is no military event of much importance to chronicle. The great concessions that had been made to Alençon (who had now become Duke of Anjou) by the Peace of Monsieur had induced him to abandon the Huguenots. He was now made Lieutenant-general of the royal armies, and in April 1577 he captured the Huguenot stronghold of La Charité —a place very valuable to the Huguenots, because it assured to them a passage over the Loire for their German auxiliaries. But negotiations accompanied the fighting, and they resulted in the Peace of Bergerac, September, 1577. This was one of the most important of the religious peaces—next to the Edict of St Germain the most important—and it procured for France a troubled calm for seven years, interrupted only by a short splash of war in 1580. There was to be freedom of conscience for the Huguenots, and the Calvinist service was to be allowed in one place in each *sénéchaussée*, and in such places as it was carried on in at the time of the conclusion of the peace. There were to be mixed chambers—consisting, that is, partly of Huguenots and partly of Catholics—in the four Parlements of the South. Nine places were to be garrisoned exclusively by Huguenot troops, in the pay of the King. All offices in the State were thrown at least nominally open to the Huguenots.

Such were the terms of the most durable religious peace that France attained before the Edict of Nantes. It was interrupted, as we have said, in 1580 by a slight outbreak of war. Henry of Navarre held his Court at Nérac. "Nothing was seen there," says Sully, who frequented it, "but balls, festivals and polite entertainments." The name that French historians give to the events of 1580—la Guerre des Amoureux—indicates the trivial character of its causes: it is in no way properly one of the wars of religion. Henry of Navarre had many grievances against the French King: among others the whole of his wife's dowry had never been handed over to him. He determined to seize Cahors, which formed part of the dowry.

Cahors is extremely strongly situated, defended by its rocky approaches, and the river Lot which runs round three sides of it. But Henry of Navarre attacked it, and, after some desperate fighting, in which he was the most daring combatant in his army, succeeded in mastering it. The place was not in itself very important, but it was the King of Navarre's first feat of arms. From this time forward the stories of his courage and his humanity did much to conciliate public opinion to him. The war was ended by the Peace of Fleix, in November, 1580. The terms of the Peace of Bergerac were renewed.

There is nothing mysterious about the origin or general character of the League, though some details of its organization are obscure. It was, to begin with, an almost spontaneous effort of Catholic zeal to resist the advance of Protestantism. Then there gathered to it many whose hostility to the Government was political rather than religious; and thus it became an instrument for those who yearned after the feudal independence possessed by the Nobility in earlier centuries. Lastly, Philip of Spain, finding the Government of France thwarting his policy at several very important points, himself supported and stimulated the League, and used it as an instrument to weaken the power of the French Monarchy: he even, at one time, hoped himself to mount through its agency to the throne of France.

The origin and development of the League.

Catholic organization had begun very early in the course of the civil wars. It was an almost inevitable thing when the action of the central Government was so weak, and the Huguenots had already set the example of a well-organized religious union acting independently of the Crown. We hear of something like a Catholic League on a very small scale at Angers in 1563, at Dijon in 1567, at Bourges in 1568. But it was through the Peace of Monsieur, in 1576, that the first great impulse was given towards the League. The Catholics believed that the King had not thrown much zeal into the war against the Protestants. They determined to defend themselves and perhaps also to force his hand. At the same time the aristocratic aspirations which had at first attached themselves to Protestantism began to feel that they might find support as easily in a Catholic organization. In 1576, when d'Humières, Governor of Péronne, formed a league in Picardy to resist the claims of Condé to that province, he declared that its purpose was not only to re-establish the law of God and to defend the King, but also "to restore to the provinces of the realm, the rights, pre-eminence, franchises and liberties as they had existed in the time of King Clovis." No effort was needed to spread the League: it corresponded to the feelings and needs of the time, and soon covered France with a huge federal network. All members promised obedience to their chief. This chief was not mentioned by name, but all knew that he was Henry of Guise, the brilliant son of the Duke Francis, who had been assassinated before Orléans. He was handsome, liberal with money, of charming manners and address. A scar received in battle had won for him the title of "le balafré," which his father had also borne. The records of the time are full of the personal fascination that he exercised. "Whoever looked on him," it was said later, "became a member of the League." His uncle, the cardinal, had died in 1574, and after that event Henry was the most prominent member of the great house of Guise. His vast ambition was ready to seize any opportunity, and from an early date, certainly as early as 1576, he cast sidelong glances at the crown. He could trace his descent to Charlemagne, and the industry of his supporters undertook to prove that he had a right to the French throne, either because of the doubtful orthodoxy of the reigning line or through some actual flaw in its genealogy.

The League was also joined by many malcontent Catholics who could not bring themselves to enter into union with the King of Navarre; and the circumstances of the time made many men malcontent. The King, nerveless and unsuccessful, hedged himself round with a rigid etiquette that excluded his great Nobility from any intimacy, while he lived in a round of degrading pleasures with favourites of lower birth. Making all deductions for the exaggeration due to the party rancour of the time, the ferocity, folly and vice of Henry III's court seem barely credible. His favourites—men of little merit or ability—gained ready access to the King and exercised over him a boundless influence. It was not only that he poured the revenue of the State into their hands; the great posts of the State were also given to them. Thus after d'Arques had been made the Duke of Joyeuse he received the government of Normandy. Nogaret was made Duke of Épernon and Governor of Metz, Boulogne, Calais and Provence. In many instances nobles of high standing, even the Guises themselves, were forced to yield up their posts that they might be transferred to the King's favourites. Meanwhile the nobles themselves, where they had power, exercised it almost independently. The great towns managed their affairs on a democratic basis without reference to the central Government. The unity of France seemed in process of dissolution.

It was not until after 1584 that the League was closely associated with Spain, but, from the first, Philip's attention was called to the possibilities of such an association. He had causes of bitter complaint against the action of the French Government. The revolt of the Netherlands was still proceeding, engulfing the armies and the navies and the treasure of Spain. All along Spain had feared French interference there. We have seen how French help was actually given to the insurgents in 1572 and how much more was expected when the great blow of the St Bartholomew Massacre was struck. For a time the danger of French interference had disappeared; but it was soon revived. It was beginning to be plain that the insurgents must find foreign help, and as Elizabeth of England refused the offers and appeals that were made to

The Wars of Religion, Part II.

her, they turned to France. The Duke of Alençon, who had now become Duke of Anjou, embraced the opportunity. As early as 1578 he had been accepted as "Defender of the Liberty of the Netherlands against the tyranny of the Spaniards." But his brother did not support him, and he retired. He renewed his attempt in 1581 and seized Cambrai, without the direct help, but certainly with the connivance of Henry III. He entered then upon a wider intrigue. He hoped to procure the assistance of England; to win even the hand of England's Queen, and so to expel the Spaniards and make himself supreme master of the Netherlands. His failure belongs rather to English or Dutch history than to French. Elizabeth seemed to regard his suit favourably, but waited to see what measure of success attended him in the Netherlands. The taint of treachery was in the blood of all Catherine's children. The Duke of Anjou was not satisfied with the position of honour that the States gave him. He aspired to an absolute rule, and in January 1583 attempted to seize Antwerp. He was beaten off by the enraged inhabitants, and soon retired into France, where he died in June 1584.

But the failure of Anjou did not remove the danger. The States petitioned Henry III for help, and he did not give them by any means a decided refusal. There were troubles ahead unless Philip could find means to prevent them. But it was not only in the Netherlands that France was thwarting Philip. In 1580 he had made himself master of Portugal. No European state had put out a hand to save Portugal from attack; but through the influence of Catherine de Médicis the French Government tried to recover Portugal from Philip. A fleet, under Strozzi, was sent out to occupy the Azores. In July 1582 it was defeated and Strozzi was slain. We cannot wonder that, with France thus meeting Philip at every turn, he was ready to stir up a resistance to the Crown of France at home, which should prevent her from undertaking any scheme of foreign conquest. The League was the instrument that he naturally chose for such a policy.

The League, it is said, had made no progress since the Peace of Bergerac, but the death of the Duke of Anjou in 1584 roused it to new and far greater activity and importance. Henry III had married Louise de Vaudremont in 1575, but no children had been born of the marriage and none were likely to be. The Duke of Anjou had died childless. Who then was the next heir to the throne? If the custom and law of France, as it had been known in the past, were alone considered, there was no difficulty in answering the question. Henry of Bourbon, King of Navarre, was next heir to the throne. The difficulty arose chiefly because he was a heretic: but he was also a foreigner as King of Navarre, and so distant from the direct line of succession that there was room for doubt as to the validity of his claim. Would Catholic France accept a Protestant King? Ought she to do so? If Henry of Navarre mounted the French throne would he not bring about a schism like that of Henry VIII of England? The question was an anxious one too for Philip. If a divided France under the weak rule of Henry III gave him such serious trouble, what would happen if France were united under Henry of Navarre, whose energy and military ability were undoubted, and who had, as King of Navarre, a standing quarrel with Philip for having occupied some part of his territories?

The death of the Duke of Anjou at once stirred the League to new life and prompted important changes. Down to 1584, the League had been mainly aristocratic in its aim and composition. But now a side movement organized in Paris gave it an entirely new character. Paris was, beyond comparison, the most important city in France; for political purposes perhaps more important than all the rest of France. It had all along been strongly Catholic. When the Huguenots were allowed to worship elsewhere, the permission had never been

The civil-religious wars renewed.

The Wars of Religion, Part II.

extended to Paris. The inhabitants readily and, to a certain extent, spontaneously took their part in the St Bartholomew massacre. A branch of the League was now established there (1584). The founder was a lawyer, Hotman; and the League soon connected itself with the various guilds and trading companies. It at first numbered among its supporters many estimable men drawn from the ranks of the upper *bourgeoisie* and the legal classes: it was only later that it developed a revolutionary and anarchical character. But another and a greater change came about the same time. Not only Paris but also Spain joined the League. Philip had all along regarded it with favour; he now gave it his direct support.

Though Henry of Guise held no official position, it was known that he exercised a limitless influence over Catholic France. King Philip through his delegates Tassis and Mareo held long interviews with Henry of Guise and his uncle Mayenne at the castle of Joinville. The Guises had their doubts about the righteousness of what they were doing; but their doubts were dispelled by a guarded message from the Pope. They made terms with Philip at the castle of Joinville in January 1585. By this treaty, which was of course secret, the contracting parties promised (i) to extirpate heresy from France; (ii) to exclude from the throne of France heretics and the supporters of heretics; (iii) Cardinal Bourbon, the uncle of Henry of Navarre, was declared to be the next heir to the throne—a resolution adopted merely to gain time, for the cardinal was an ecclesiastic, childless and old, and his nomination postponed for the time the difficult question of deciding the rival claims of the several claimants to the throne; (iv) Philip on his side promised to give a large annual subsidy to the League. On March 31 the Manifesto of the League was published. Cardinal Bourbon's claims were again declared valid, and the exclusive supremacy of the Catholic Church was to be upheld; but further support was promised to the liberties of the nobles, to Parlement and all local authorities; the States

General were to be held every three years, and the taxes to be diminished.

The situation in France had become a very strange one. The Monarchy counted for very little. There were two other governments in France, each for the moment more important than the King's. In the South-West, Henry of Navarre directed the independent organization of the Huguenots and Politiques. In the North and in Paris the League had taken up a distinctly independent and really hostile attitude. Henry III must join himself to one of them, or he would soon have hardly the semblance of a crown. To which party should he join himself? Navarre made overtures to him, and upheld in theory the authority of the Crown. Queen Elizabeth urged him in the same direction. She offered him her support if he would fight against the League. But Henry III was, as we have seen, a sincere and even a fanatical Catholic. The power of the League, especially in Paris, alarmed him. In spite of all his jealousy of the Guises, he drew near to their organization, and at the beginning of July, 1585, signed the Treaty of Nemours. Henry III accepted absolutely all that the League had done; he approved of their rising, and took their troops into his pay. He apologised for the Edicts of Toleration that he had previously issued, and withdrew them. He threatened all heretics in the most explicit terms: "We have commanded and command that all who adhere to the new religion shall forsake the same, and within six months make confession of the Catholic, Apostolic and Roman religion; or, if they refuse to do so, that they depart from our kingdom and the lands within our allegiance." The King forced the Parlement of Paris to register the edict. At the beginning of September it was followed up by a bull of excommunication from Pope Sixtus V against Henry of Navarre. He was thereby declared to be for ever excluded from the throne of France. Even if he were to return to Catholicism, the Pope maintained, that would not give him the right to reign.

The Wars of Religion, Part II. 139

The Treaty of Nemours and the withdrawal of the Edicts of Toleration established at once a condition of civil war.

The news of this alliance between Henry III and the League came as a great shock to the King of Navarre. "Terror of the evils which he saw coming upon his party was so great," he said, "that one half of his moustache turned white." But he addressed himself to the contest with his accustomed buoyancy and energy.

The War of the Three Henries, down to the Day of Barricades.

The war that followed, known from its three chief combatants (Henry III, Henry of Navarre, and Henry of Guise) as "the war of the three Henries," is a very strange one. The King is allied to one party, but he feels that party even more his enemy than the other. He is overshadowed by both his rivals, and finally the family trait comes to light again, and he tries to do by treachery and assassination what he had not been able to do by arms.

We have already noticed the part played in the League by the city of Paris. Paris had all along been zealously Catholic. By the year 1585, political and religious feelings, both of extreme violence, joined to produce a condition of things very threatening to the Monarchy. All through this period of French history, the parallels with the French Revolution are very close and striking. The St Bartholomew Massacre has its parallel in the September massacres; the League is not unlike the Jacobin Society; the condition of Paris in 1586 and 1587 reminds us of Paris in 1791 and 1792. The leaders of Parisian opinion were chiefly priests who used their pulpits as platforms for the dissemination of the most violent opinions on religion and politics. The most prominent of these priests were Jean Prevost and Jean Boucher; other leaders were Mathieu de Launay, a doctor in theology, and Hotman de la Rocheblond. At the beginning of the civil wars the eloquence of the Calvinist ministers had been, in the opinion of all, far higher than that of the Catholic priests: their preaching was an important factor in the situation. But all that was changed now. The Jesuits had given new energy to the Pulpit, and no Calvinist could now rival the popularity of the Catholic preachers of Paris. Henry III had been more devoted to Paris than any of his predecessors. He had lived constantly at the Louvre; he had built largely, and he felt the conduct of the city in turning against him to be an act of ingratitude. A new and more democratic constitution was adopted, certainly without the King's approval, first secretly and then openly. The city was divided into five military districts, each with its colonel and captains. The supreme direction of affairs was vested in the "Council of the Sixteen," often called merely "The Sixteen." This was not a committee of sixteen persons: it took its title from the sixteen districts of Paris. It was largely swayed by clerical influence.

Navarre's chief hope for the war that now opened, after his own skill and the valour of his well-tried and devoted followers, was in foreign assistance. He determined to avoid pitched battles, to confine his attention to parrying the blows aimed at him, and to keep as far as possible behind the walls of cities. He got money and diplomatic support from England: as the crisis of the struggle between England and Spain approached, Elizabeth drew nearer to the party which in France was fighting against Spain. From Germany Navarre obtained, as he had often obtained before, large supplies of troops who would be very useful, provided they could be paid. It is more remarkable that he was successful in recruiting in the Evangelical Swiss Cantons. Since the time of Francis I they had remained faithful to their alliance with the French monarchy; but now their religious sympathies carried the day, and they seem to have imagined that they could supply troops to the King of Navarre, to fight against the League, without breaking their alliance with Henry III.

The year 1586 saw no military events of much importance, though there was a good deal of obscure fighting in the South and South-west of France. On the whole it went in favour of the Catholics. Condé was defeated near Angers: Épernon drove the Protestants out of Provence. In July, Henry III, feeling very uneasy in his relations to the League, and finding it impossible to obtain money, opened through his mother negotiations with Navarre, but they proved fruitless, and served only to raise further suspicions against him in Catholic minds. The year 1587 brought the struggle to a crisis. The German and Swiss troops entered French territory in January. It was necessary to devise some plan to meet them. The great thing was to prevent a junction between them and Henry of Navarre. So while the Duke of Joyeuse was despatched into the South to hold Navarre in check, Henry of Guise marched against the Germans and Swiss, who advanced under Fabian, Burgrave of Dohna. Joyeuse was eager to bring on a battle. He was considerably superior in numbers, especially in cavalry, the all-important arm, and his only fear was lest Navarre should escape him. The troops met in the plain of Coutras, at the confluence of the Isle and Dronne, affluents of the Dordogne. The battle is like one of Cromwell's battles. The gay dresses of the royal army contrasted strangely with the worn and stained clothes of their opponents, whom they nearly doubled in number. The Huguenots sang a psalm before the engagement. Henry called upon his followers to imitate the example he would set them of courage and enterprise. The Catholics gained at the outset a slight advantage on their left, but the real struggle was fought out on the other side of the field, and there the cavalry of Henry of Navarre resisted the attack of their opponents, and, then attacking in their turn, broke up their line in entire confusion. Joyeuse himself was killed as he was surrendering his sword: the whole Catholic army was broken up. It was the first victory that the Huguenots had won since the beginning of the war, and their exultation was naturally very great. But, for whatever reason, the victory was not followed up: the blame has been variously apportioned between Henry and his troops.

The death of Joyeuse was welcomed in France, for no one was more unpopular. But it only brought into clearer relief the dependence of Henry III upon his favourites. Much that had belonged to Joyeuse was now transferred to the Duke of Épernon. He held offices without number, and, besides being Duke and Peer of France, he controlled the governments of six provinces. He really held the power which was supposed to rest with the King.

Henry of Guise had meanwhile gained a success of a different but equally important kind against his German and Swiss enemies. The invading army consisted of 12,000 Germans, 20,000 Swiss, and 4000 French troops. If Henry of Navarre, after Coutras, could have joined hands with this great force he would have been master at any rate of the South of France. But as we have seen he did not follow up his victory. There was great confusion in this army of mercenaries. The discipline was slack; the numbers were not so great as had been promised; there was no definite plan of action. It was determined at last to cross the Loire at La Charité, and thus join hands with Henry of Navarre. But La Charité was guarded and the passage could not be forced. The army made its way down the Loire to the Beauce district, harassed all the time by the Duke of Guise. They had made their way as far as Auneau, near Chartres, when they were attacked at dawn by the Duke of Guise. They were driven out of the place with very considerable loss, and what little confidence they had in themselves vanished (24 Nov. 1587). Then Henry III negotiated with the Swiss, showed them that as a matter of fact it was himself that they were fighting against, and succeeded in inducing them to retire. He treated too with the Germans. They asked to be allowed to withdraw and promised never to serve against the French King again. On these terms they were allowed to withdraw, but Guise refused to recognise the compact made with the King, attacked them as they were retiring and slew a great number. The invasion, from which so much had been expected, ended therefore in a rather shameful rout.

There was a sense of relief but no exultation in the ranks of the League. They accused the King of having saved the enemy when Guise, if left to himself, would have crushed them. These negotiations of the King with the Swiss and Germans were regarded as high treason against the League. When therefore, in December 1587, Henry III made a triumphal entry into Paris he was very coldly received. "The King," men said, "had slain his thousands, but Guise his ten thousands."

But what a stormy and dangerous Paris it was into which Henry III had come, and how scanty were his own forces for resisting it! The government of 'the Sixteen' had grown stronger, its fury and passion had risen to boiling point. The hatred of Henry III himself, and the desire to pass over the legitimate claims of Henry of Navarre were now supported by political theories. The *rôles* of the Protestants and Catholics had been inverted during the course of the war. The Huguenots had at first been the liberals and federalists: but now they championed the claims of legitimacy in the person of Henry of Navarre: the League on the other hand—so ready are men to suit their theories to their actual aims—was now supporting political views of the most revolutionary kind. Ultramontane Catholicism joined hands with democracy: such views had found expression in the later sessions of the Council of Trent. The fundamental law of France, it was maintained, was that the King must be a Catholic and orthodox. Again, the elastic theory of "the Social Contract" was invoked. Monarchy rested on an implied contract between the King on the one hand and God and the People on the other. If he broke his agreement with either, the People were absolved from obedience and might depose their King, or even put him to death. Thus not only do the events of this period find a parallel in those of the French Revolution: there is a close resemblance also between their theories. Revolution was in the air, and those wild suspicions which in time of revolution take possession of men's minds were harboured everywhere. The King, it was said, had saved the Germans and Swiss; the King was meditating a massacre of Catholics; no charge was too absurd to be believed if it was brought against Henry III. The Duchess of Montpensier, the sister of Henry of Guise, exercised a great influence with the multitude, and her brother had become the idol, the passion of the Paris people. We have seen how well qualified he was by nature to play a popular *rôle*. He had every gift and grace that a popular leader requires and he had real talent besides.

Events had occurred which increased the long-standing jealousy between Guise and the King. The death of Joyeuse had left the government of Normandy vacant, and the death of Condé had similarly affected the government of Picardy. The Guises claimed both, the first for Henry the Duke of Guise, the second for Aumâle. But the King had given Normandy to his favourite Épernon, and Picardy to the Duke of Nevers. It was natural enough that he should distrust the Guise party; for he suspected the close alliance between them and the King of Spain, and had experienced Philip's constant hostility. Catherine de Médicis hoped that her usual arts would avail to remove this hostility, at least for a time, but she was ill, troubled with gout, racked with a constant cough. The time of her influence on public affairs was passing.

Henry III knew that the presence of Henry of Guise in Paris might be dangerous, and he commanded him therefore not to enter the city. But Guise set the King's command at defiance, and on May 9, 1588, he rode with a very small escort into the city and visited Catherine de Médicis. He had come, he said, to defend the Catholics, against whom he had heard plots were in progress. The King was furiously angry, and there was some thought of assassinating the Duke; but he remained outwardly calm and consented to an interview with Guise. The people meanwhile crowded round their favourite;

the admiration for him became a frenzy. Henry III (it was said) wore the crown, but Guise was the king of all hearts.

The King did not feel himself safe from attack, and doubtless meditated some blow against his enemies. On May 12, three days after the entrance of Guise into Paris, he ordered certain Swiss and French regiments stationed at Lagny, not more than 6000 men in all, to march into the city. They occupied many of the important points of Paris. The result was immediate. Paris felt itself threatened and rose in arms on every side. Barricades and chains were stretched across the streets. The Swiss troops were attacked; some surrendered and some were killed. Guise took no open part in all this, perhaps he took no direct part at all. Brissac was the chief soldier concerned; but there could be no doubt that the whole movement was in Guise's interest. The King was quite helpless; every street had become a fortress that could only be taken with great effort and much loss of blood. Henry III had to humiliate himself to the uttermost; he was forced to ask his subject and his enemy to defend him from his own capital. Guise, unarmed, rode from street to street. His ascendancy over the people was complete; the barricades were removed; the captive Swiss were released. He seemed, men said, like the God of the sea calling up tempests and allaying them with a gesture of his hand.

The danger had for the moment passed, but the King feared its return. In any case he could not endure to remain in a city where he had been thus humiliated. He determined on flight, and in the night slipped off through the Porte Neuve towards Rambouillet and Chartres. His escort was seen when it had got beyond the walls of Paris, and was fired upon, but no damage was done. "God be praised," he is reported to have said, when he found himself outside of Paris, "the yoke is off." Yet Henry of Guise and the Sixteen reigned in Paris, and it was very doubtful who reigned in France.

Those historians who have followed the career of Henry III

closely in the original documents, assert that he was not wanting at times in certain noble aspirations, that his religion was sincere, and that he had occasional glimpses of a nobler policy and a desire to pursue it. But his whole career, as it is represented in his actions, is a compound of weakness, cowardice, and cruelty. His share in the St Bartholomew Massacre is more entirely without palliation than that of any other actor in that terrible event. From that time forward he drifted aimlessly from policy to policy. His word was valueless; an oath that he would follow one course was constantly and immediately followed by the adoption of the opposite. When driven into a corner he had recourse to the statecraft that he had learnt from his mother and from Machiavelli; murder seemed to him legitimate in a King.

The States at Blois and the murder of the Guises.

He had fled from Paris in passion; but he was not strong enough to attempt revenge upon his great enemy. He determined to call the States General together—the usual expedient of a French King in distress. Meanwhile he again made terms with his enemy, and once more declared his adhesion to the League by his Edict of Union (July, 1588). By this Edict he promised never to lay down his arms until he had destroyed the Huguenots; no official was to be appointed until he had taken an oath of allegiance to Catholicism; the Government of the Sixteen in Paris was, with the exception of some details, confirmed. As crown of this extraordinary surrender he appointed the man whom he feared and hated most to command the royal forces. Henry of Guise was named *généralissimo* on August 14.

The States General met at Blois in September. The King had hoped that more moderate opinions might prevail there; but the League had attended to the elections, and had succeeded in controlling them. The whole assembly was decidedly favourable to Guise rather than to the King. The King opened the Estates with a rather striking speech, for he could usually find the right words. He welcomed the Estates. He promised that he would submit to certain limitations of the royal power, though at the same time he insisted on the importance of maintaining the royal prerogative intact.

But when the debates began it was found that the demands of the deputies would far outrun the King's concessions. The leaders of all three orders were violent leaguers. The Cardinal of Guise was president of the Clergy; Brissac, a prominent actor on the day of the Barricades, led the Nobility; the commons were led by Marteau, a prominent Parisian politician. Theories decidedly opposed to the King's prerogative were popular in the assembly. Many based the power of the monarchy on popular election and the consent of the Church. The desire was expressed that the decisions of the States should at once be valid, even without the approval of the King. The deputies demanded, too, a very large share in the control of the finances; they proposed that the taxes should be reduced to the figure at which they had stood in the reign of Louis XII, even while they urged military enterprises that could not be carried out without a great expenditure. The King bitterly disliked the tone of these debates, yet in the end he yielded on the crucial question of the finances.

But the personal question touched him more closely than the Constitutional. Henry of Guise conducted himself throughout the sittings of the assembly as though he were the King's equal or superior. The quarrels of his pages with those of the King produced confusion and bloodshed, and he would do nothing to check them. There were rumours circulated that he aimed even at the throne. Henry III was to be shut up in a monastery like the last of the Merovingians. Guise was the centre if he were not the author of all the opposition that the King experienced since he had opened the Estates. We are not surprised to find that the idea of assassination suggested itself to the King. He said himself that it was only after much thought and against his inclination that he adopted it. There were doubtless excuses to be made. If ever 'the tyrant's plea' was applicable, it was surely applicable in this case. The Duke of Guise and he could not both reign in France, and he could not now by open means overthrow the Duke. Other arguments were not wanting as salve to his conscience. He held that the authority of Kings was something separate and inviolable. They were above the laws, and what was crime in another would not be crime in them.

Whatever the excuse or the motive, the Duke's death was decided on. It was not difficult to carry it out, for Guise was over-confident and careless. Rumours reached him of the King's intention. He answered, "He dare not," and took no precautions. The King found the agents proper for his purpose. Crillon, the captain of the guards, refused to strike Guise except in a duel; but Longnac, captain of the King's immediate body-guard, was less scrupulous. He chose his men and posted them at the entrance to the King's council chamber, on the morning of December 23rd, 1588. Guise was then summoned to the Council. He came unsuspectingly, and, as he withdrew the curtain that lay across the entrance to the King's apartment, the assassins flung themselves upon him. He fought furiously with hands and teeth, but could not draw his sword, and was soon mastered and slain. The King expressed the greatest pleasure. "I am a King at last," he said, and kicked the body of his dead enemy. His brother, the Cardinal of Guise, was arrested at the same time, with some others. These were spared; but it was felt that the Cardinal must die. On the morning of the 24th, four soldiers were sent into his room, who killed him with blows from their halberds.

Catherine de Médicis heard the news with deep misgivings. "I am King of France now," Henry had cried to her, "for I have killed the King of Paris." "You have killed the Duke of Guise!" said Catherine. "God grant that you have not made yourself King of nothing." She survived the catastrophe less than a fortnight and died on January 5, 1589. With all her faults and crimes she had a wiser head than any of her sons.

Immediately after the murder of the Guises, Catherine's words seemed likely to come true. The bold stroke had not restored power to Henry III; it seemed rather as though it had struck the crown from his head. There rose against him a cry of execration from all Catholic France. All the great towns of France, except Blois and those in the possession of the Huguenots, rejected the royal authority and declared for the League. Paris of course was especially prominent in demanding vengeance for the death of the King of Paris. The pulpits rang with denunciations of the King's crime. The Sorbonne declared that Henry III was no longer King of France: the blow he had struck against the Catholic faith had absolved the people from their oath of fidelity. The Parlement of Paris, faithful to its traditions, upheld at first the royal authority with much firmness; and Parlement was so important that its opposition would materially weaken the Catholic movement. It was necessary to 'purge' it. Bussy le Clerc, governor of the Bastille, entered the Chamber and arrested some sixty members. They were imprisoned in the Bastille. The 'Rump' took the oath of the League and ratified the decision of the Sorbonne. There were strange religious ceremonials to intensify the spontaneous feeling of Paris. On January 10 there was a huge procession of children to the Abbey of St Geneviéve. All carried tapers and at a given signal extinguished them, crying, "Thus may God extinguish the race of the Valois." "The General Council of the Catholic Union" established itself at the Town Hall as the government of Paris. Mayenne, the deceased Duke's uncle, was recognised as their chief and declared Lieutenant-General of the kingdom. Heralds from the King were driven off with contumely.

Union of Henry III with Henry of Navarre. Siege of Paris. Murder of Henry III.

What could Henry III do? He had no very considerable armed following; he was entirely discredited as King and as soldier. He tried in vain to negotiate with the League: every overture was repulsed. Nor could he stand alone. The Catholics would lend him no support. He had massacred the Protestants in 1572; he had again and again, and quite recently, sworn to exterminate them, and yet necessity now drove him to their side. Henry of Navarre made the strange alliance as easy as possible for him. He published a manifesto in March full of respect for the King, demanding peace as the one supreme need of France, finding excuses for the assassination of Guise. On the 3rd of April a truce was agreed on. On the last day of the month the two surviving Henries, Henry III and Henry of Navarre, met at Plessis les Tours. Henry of Navarre went to the interview with much hesitation; but Henry III threw himself wholly into his arms and gave utterance to the most humane sentiments. Protestants, he said, "should not be called heretics; whoever confessed the Gospel was a Christian; small differences ought not to cause hostility." The memories of St Bartholomew's Day made the words sound strangely on Henry III's lips.

Henry of Navarre's seasoned troops joined to the King's forces gave him the superiority. It was increased by considerable royalist levies; for the title still counted for much. More important still, the Swiss allowed a new levy of mercenaries: it was clear that now at least they would not be fighting against the King of France. Thus strengthened, Henry III and his new ally moved against Paris; it was necessary, he said, to strike the League in the heart. Paris saw the approach of the troops with the greatest excitement and alarm. The Catholic fanaticism of the clerical demagogues grew to a white heat. They declared that the King was a tyrant, who had tried to murder, not an individual, but the general well-being of State and Church: to kill him as such would be no murder. But Paris was in no good state of defence; a large section of the population was not in hearty sympathy with the League, and desertions were frequent. The royal troops overcame all obstacles to their advance on Paris. The Parisian army was defeated at Senlis on May 17. At the end of July, Henry III with 40,000 men had taken up his quarters at St Cloud. It was arranged to assault the city on August 2, and both in the city and the camp it was believed that the assault would be successful.

But the advocacy of tyrannicide had not fallen on unfruitful ground. A Dominican friar, Jacques Clement, 22 years of age, a man of weak mind, had received the doctrine, and was prepared to act on it. He procured some letters for the King from the Comte de Brienne, a prisoner in the hands of the League. On the pretext of delivering these he made his way to the royal camp. After some difficulty he was introduced into the royal presence, presented his letters, and as the King read them, stabbed him in the stomach. The attendants at once fell upon the monk and killed him. The King's wound was not at first thought mortal: but inflammation set in and in eighteen hours he was dead (August 2, 1589).

CHAPTER VI.

KING HENRY IV.

PARIS was saved by the dagger of Jaques Clement, but the ultimate prospects of the League were made darker rather than brighter. A Protestant now possessed, without any question, the constitutional right to the throne of France: the League was driven more and more into the arms of Philip of Spain, and sealed its own doom by becoming anti-national.

But for the present the outlook was very obscure. Henry III and Henry of Navarre had been able to hold together their composite army of Catholics and Huguenots : but it would not yield the same obedience to Henry IV. The Catholics, for all their royalist sympathies, refused to serve a heretic. "Rather die a thousand deaths" was the end, says d'Aubigné, of all their debates on the subject. It was in vain that on August 4 Henry promised definitely to maintain "the Catholic, apostolic, and Roman religion" in its entirety, without innovation or change, and declared himself ready to be instructed by a national or universal council. The declaration offended the Protestants and did not satisfy the Catholics. It was impossible to maintain the blockade of Paris. On the 8th, Henry broke up from before Paris and moved into Normandy, where he hoped to get into touch with English assistance, and possibly to control the lower course of the Seine, and thus incommode the city of Paris.

After the first delirium of joy in Paris, caused by the unexpected deliverance, the Leaguers discovered that they had to face difficult and almost insoluble problems. Who was to be their candidate for the throne? How were they to satisfy the ambitions of Mayenne and Philip of Spain? How were they to satisfy those who held by the traditional and legal view of the succession? On the 5th of August, Cardinal Bourbon was declared King as Charles X. This was to postpone the consideration of the question, not to settle it. For the new King was a prisoner in the hands of the King of Navarre: he was an ecclesiastic and unable to found a new royal line: he was old, and not likely to live long. But for these very reasons his appointment was acceptable to all Catholics: it provided an interval in which the different parties might make up their own minds and develop their intrigues. But Philip II was henceforth the unacknowledged head of the party of the League, and, through his agent Mendoza, he soon made his wishes known. He wished to sweep aside the Salic Law as a fiction that no longer served any good purpose. He would have had the States General called, with authority to decide as to the succession. He hoped that their choice would fall on his eldest daughter Isabella; but he was willing to accept the Duke of Guise or the Marquis du Pont, on condition that the chosen candidate should promise not to marry without the King of Spain's consent, and should yield to Spain certain harbours on the Channel, which Philip might use for his enterprise against England. But Philip's proposal conflicted with the strong national sentiment of France, which ultimately rejected the idea of any foreign rule of whatever kind. From the very first it ran counter to the aspirations, open or secret, of Mayenne, the nominal leader of the League. He hoped to gain the crown himself, though he was little qualified for success. His corpulent person and his slow or cautious mind made any activity difficult to him. But none the less he could oppose with all his sluggish power the plans of Philip, and defeat the popular government of Paris that supported them. Paris had developed fresh organs of government as the Catholic Revolution went on. The "Council of the Sixteen" had correspondence with other similar clubs or governments all over France. As executive in Paris there was a sort of Federal "Council of Forty." But Mayenne distrusted it, as well he might, and soon abolished and replaced it by a Privy Council, attached to his own person.

Henry's successes in Normandy soon made it doubtful whether the League would in any case have been able to carry through its plans. He had marched from Paris to Dieppe. On Aug. 24 he had appeared before Rouen. But judging the siege impossible, he marched off again towards the sea-coast and established himself at Arques. His camp lay between Arques and Dieppe, and was commanded by the cannon of both places. It gave him access to the sea, and was strengthened by all the resources of the military art of the sixteenth century. But his forces did not amount to more than 9,000 men, and Mayenne soon brought against him an army of twenty-five or thirty thousand. For twelve days Mayenne tried in vain to force the lines. On the 21st Sept. the lines were actually penetrated, and, but for Henry's own ready courage and his power of inspiring it in others, all might have been lost. His German troops played him false: the heavy fog that lay over the country side made it impossible to get any general view of the action. But the fog lifted; the old Huguenot troops stood firm, and Mayenne was driven out. Henry's success produced a great impression in France. The stories of his valour and *sangfroid* passed from mouth to mouth. Men told how he had appealed at Arques for fifty men who were prepared to die with their King; how after Mayenne had abandoned the attack he had written to Crillon, "Hang yourself, my good Crillon; we have fought at Arques and you were not there." His confidence in himself rarely deserted him. When his comrades were depressed by the strength of the enemy, he said, "My allies must be reckoned

King Henry IV.

in the balance—God and my right." Such stories as these served soon to make him attractive, even to those who were not of his party, and have gained for him the name of the most French of all French rulers.

After his success at Arques he received valuable reinforcements from Queen Elizabeth. Mayenne fell back on the Somme, on October 6. Most of Normandy was in Henry's hands, and he thought it possible to take Paris itself by a sudden blow. Accordingly, on the last day in October, he suddenly appeared before Paris. The alarm was very great. The faubourgs fell into his hands without much difficulty; but the walls of Paris were not to be forced, and he called off his troops after they had plundered their fill. Yet the exploit rather heightened his prestige. Immediately afterwards Maine came over to him almost entirely. Only a few towns in Normandy held out. Most Protestant States had already recognised him as King of France; but hitherto no Catholic state had ventured to do so. In November the Republic of Venice took the step.

The early part of 1590 brought him even greater successes. Mayenne was besieging Meulan, but the arrival of Henry forced him to raise the siege. Henry then himself laid siege to Dreux: but Mayenne received help from his Spanish allies, from Flanders and Lorraine, and Henry had to leave his siege lines and face round against Mayenne. All seemed to depend on the results of a battle. The battle took place at Ivry, near Dreux, on March 14. Henry's forces were much outnumbered. He could not bring together more than 8,000 foot and 3,000 horse, while Mayenne's force amounted to 12,000 foot and 4,000 horse. The numbers, therefore, were not large, but the result was decisive and the consequences important. The battle opened with artillery fire on both sides; but it was decided by Henry's favourite arm—the cavalry. He put himself at the head of his cavaliers, at the moment when his own line seemed to be wavering, and, in words that soon rang through France told his comrades that if their standards

Ivry.

fell they should rally round his white plume, which they would always find on the path of victory and honour. The fury of the attack made up for deficiency in numbers. The army of the League was broken; Henry cried to his men to save the French, but to slay the foreign mercenaries. Mayenne escaped with some difficulty. Panic reigned in Paris. If Henry had pressed on at once, many held that Paris would have fallen into his hands. But Henry did not advance at once, for his army clamoured for arrears of pay, and seemed on the verge of mutiny. Sully, who next to the King knew most about the position of the King's affairs, says, "If we except a small number of French Protestants, whose fidelity was unquestionable, and most of the English troops, who seemed to act sincerely with us, all the rest of the King's army served him without affection, often unwillingly, and wished perhaps that he might suffer some considerable loss." There is probably some exaggeration in this, but there is doubtless enough truth in it to account for the slowness of Henry's advance on Paris. When at last he appeared before the city, it was prepared to stand a siege.

Catholic enthusiasm was still the chief characteristic of Paris. Paris seemed in 1589 to have been saved by miracle. In certain circles Jaques Clement was honoured as Saint and Martyr. Every agency of religion was put in motion against Henry. Cardinal Caietano, the new Papal Legate, had for a moment hesitated which side he should support. But in the end he threw himself decidedly on the side of the League. He became during the next few months one of the chief influences in Paris, and along with him must be reckoned the Duchess of Montpensier, a Guise by birth. On his entry into Paris, in January, 1590, Caietano had supported the declaration of the Sorbonne against a heretic King, and given money to Mayenne on behalf of the Pope. Henry appeared before Paris on May 1, 1590. As he drew near, the dictatorial Sixteen regained their old

Condition of Paris.

King Henry IV.

power. The Sorbonne, on May 10, declared that, even if Henry were to be converted, he would still be no King for France. On May 14, when already Henry's grasp on Paris was tightening, there was a huge procession through the streets of Paris. The religious orders appeared under arms: all present swore to give their lives for the defence of the Catholic religion, and never to obey a King who *had been* a heretic.

The chances of war seemed to be on Henry's side. The line of blockade was indeed incomplete, for his troops were in numbers insufficient for the task, and fell far short of the fighting men contained within the walls of Paris. But Henry occupied all the chief strong places round the city, and the short intervals which were left were constantly patrolled with cavalry. Famine was soon at work in the city. Provisions were carefully husbanded and distributed; but by the beginning of July, cats, dogs, and vermin were being doled out to the people, and the preachers were urging that no form of martyrdom was so pleasing to God as death by hunger. Horrible tales of cannibalism are told, apparently on good foundation. The Duchess of Montpensier advised the use of flour made of ground human bones. Religious enthusiasm was carefully fomented from the pulpit: "nothing was cheap but sermons." The religious orders volunteered for active military service. But in spite of all expedients the end seemed drawing near. On the 24th of July all the faubourgs of Paris fell into Henry's hands.

By the beginning of August it was clear that all depended on the action of Spain. Left to herself Paris must capitulate: for Mayenne by himself was clearly unable to raise the siege. At last he consented to the humiliation of appealing to the Prince of Parma, and on the 23rd of August that consummate general, with a splendidly equipped army, joined Mayenne at Meaux. Even Henry was not rash enough to allow himself to be caught between two enemies. On the 30th of August he abandoned the siege of Paris. The presence of his troops in various strong places

The relief of Paris.

near the city still made the Parisians feel a certain amount of scarcity, but with immense exultation they saw the extremity of their danger pass away.

Henry advanced towards Parma and offered him battle; but Parma was careful to refuse it. He could do all that he wanted to do without the risk of fighting, and quite out-manœuvred his opponent. On Oct. 16 he took Corbeil and garrisoned it and shortly afterwards re-entered Spanish territory. The year 1590 had brought to Henry the extremes of both hope and despair: Ivry had shown that the King was not to be crushed; the relief of Paris seemed to prove that Henry would never reign over a united France if he trusted only to arms.

The year 1591 is tame in comparison with its predecessor.

Papal and Spanish intrigues.

Diplomacy tried, but in vain, to find a solution of the problem that arms had failed to settle. The chief interest was now in Paris, for Henry IV undertook during this year no military enterprise of much importance. In April, Chartres surrendered to him—an important place because of its command of one of the chief routes by which provisions entered Paris. The King watched the outcome of the eager debates and intrigues which he knew to be troubling the councils of his enemies. On his side he did little more than repeat his formula that he was willing to be 'instructed' in the controversies that separated Catholics from Protestants.

Great lines of division were meanwhile showing themselves among his opponents. In Paris and France the more moderate party of Mayenne—to which the Parliament and the Middle Class were now rallying—was opposed by the extreme section of the League. This section was represented in Paris by the old Council of Sixteen and the more zealous of the clergy. They were willing to make any sacrifice of national independence or prestige if only France might keep her Catholicism undefiled by any taint of heresy or toleration. All Philip's hopes rested on this party. His various failures—the loss of his Armada, the constant drain of the war in the Netherlands—did not make him abandon his grandiose plans. If France were only added to the dominions of Spain, that would compensate for all; and there seemed now a real chance of that consummation, in fact if not in name.

King Philip's designs were revealed clearly during the year. Jeannin, President of Parlement, was despatched to Spain to learn what were Philip's intentions and what reliance might be placed upon his support. He went in the interests of the Duke of Mayenne, but he received little encouragement. Philip, through his minister, Idiaquez, rejected altogether the idea of conciliation with Henry IV, even if Henry IV were to declare himself Catholic, and at last, after much beating about the bush, Idiaquez declared his royal master's secret intention. The Infanta of Spain was declared to have the best right to the Crown. She was the daughter of the eldest sister of Henry III. The Salic Law indeed absolutely blocked her right, and the Salic Law had hitherto been regarded as an unquestionable part of the Constitution of France. But Philip waved that aside. He did not even intend her to marry the Duke of Mayenne: he had chosen his cousin the Archduke Ernest to be her husband. Jeannin returned to France in August disillusioned of his trust in Spain.

But the Sixteen of Paris and the zealots whom they represented made no opposition to these Spanish schemes. The presentation of Philip's plans varied from time to time according to the audience to which they were addressed and the varying events in France; but they always aimed under one form or another at the subordination of France to Spain. But "the Sixteen" shrunk from nothing. In September, Henry IV intercepted a letter to Philip, in which they declared that it was "the wish of all Catholics to see Philip reign over them"; they were, they said, most anxious to welcome Isabella as their Queen. It was determined to call a meeting of the States

General to decide these difficult questions. The real meeting did not take place until 1593, but Paris elected her deputies in 1591. It marks the passions of the hour and the influence of "the Sixteen" that the representatives of Paris insist in their 'cahiers' that any heretic, whether prince, noble, or commoner, shall be burnt alive.

Mayenne of course saw the development of the plans of Spain with bitter dislike, and soon the turbulence and savagery of the Paris factions gave him an excuse for intervention. For some time past the preachers had been demanding, in tones that remind us strangely of 1793, the death of their opponents. "Another Bartholomew bleeding," said one, "would cut the throat of our disease." President Brisson was murdered. The wildest theories of democratic anarchy were advanced at the same time that Philip, the very representative of absolutism, was invited to interfere. The extravagance of "the Sixteen" produced a reaction of public opinion against them. Mayenne entered Paris, reassembled the Parlement, which had not met since the death of President Brisson, and then on Dec. 4 seized four of the leading members of "the Sixteen," and had them put to death without form of trial. Under Mayenne's protection a strong reaction against the most violent sentiments soon made itself felt in the government of Paris, while the deep cleavage thus established between the Moderates and the Extremists gave great encouragement to Henry.

But though the King's enemies were divided, the next year (1592) brought with it another humiliation for his arms. He had received reinforcements from Germany and England in the autumn of 1591, and with these he had recommenced the war in earnest. He had some thoughts of striking a blow in the North-east of France, but Elizabeth insisted that the maritime provinces should be cleared of enemies; and in November he laid siege to Rouen with an army of 40,000 men, of whom only 8,000 were French troops. He intended to reduce the place by

The siege of Rouen.

blockade, and, if external help did not arrive, success was certain. But external help did arrive, and from the same quarter as in 1590. In February, Parma moved over the northern frontier. Henry left Biron in command of the army at Rouen, and himself tried to intercept Parma; but though he used the utmost energy, and constantly risked his person with more than the recklessness of a common soldier, Parma eluded or defeated all his attempts. During Henry's absence, Villars, who commanded the garrison of Rouen, had defeated Biron, and thus practically broken up the siege. Henry in vain tried to re-establish it. But Parma was not satisfied with having relieved Rouen; he wished to clear the course of the Seine, and with that view attacked and took Caudebec, which lies on the north bank of the Seine, half way between Rouen and the mouth. But though the siege was an easy task, Parma received a wound in his arm during its course, and left the command of the troops in the hands of Mayenne. Against the weaker adversary Henry nearly gained a great success, which would have compensated him for the loss of Rouen. He gathered a large army with great speed, and soon had pinned Mayenne and the Spanish army between his lines and the Seine, which is there more than a mile broad. Henry thought the surrender of the enemy inevitable. But Parma again out-manœuvred him. He collected a large number of boats in Rouen, brought them unperceived by night down the stream to Caudebec, and before Henry was aware that he was making the attempt, conveyed Mayenne and his troops across the river. They then marched by the south bank of the Seine to Paris. Parma left a garrison of 1500 troops in Paris, and with the rest of his army marched back to the Spanish Netherlands. It was an extremely brilliant campaign, but it proved his last. The wound that he had received at Caudebec was very much more serious than he had thought, and he died soon after his return to Spanish territory (Dec. 1592). His death removed from Henry's path the one man whose military reputation and capacity was greater than his own.

The year 1592, then, had been a dark one for King Henry IV. He had been out-manœuvred a second time by Parma. In May the Duke of Mercœur had defeated a royal force at Craon, with the result that the League was dominant in Brittany, Maine, and Anjou. What hope could Henry have of overthrowing his opponents? The outlook was far less encouraging now than when after the battle of Ivry he had led his forces against Paris. He had hoped then that his sword would win him the crown: he had abandoned that hope now. He had lost no important battle, and yet it was clear that he could not take Paris, and until he was master of Paris he was only King of France by title. It was clearly his religion—or rather his profession of faith—that stood in his way. Questions of creed and faith were not such powerful motives of political action in 1593 as they had been in the middle of the century, but they were still strong enough to close the gates of Paris against a heretic. And thus the question of 'instruction' and 'conversion' was forced upon Henry. His was not a deeply religious nature; his convictions were neither clear nor strong. His career had all along been governed by political and human motives, not by theological ones. No one can be imagined much less like a Calvinist after the pattern of Calvin himself or du Plessis Mornay than the jovial, amorous, chivalrous King of the French. If he felt a keen regret at abandoning the creed of his mother, it was rather because to abandon it implied a defeat, and seemed a desertion of his comrades, than because he entertained any intellectual belief in the doctrine that had been enunciated by Calvin in his *Institutes of the Christian Religion*.

The States General of the League met on January 17. The meeting was thin and far from representative. There were never more than 128 members, and the nobles had only

24 representatives: at Blois the total number had been 505. The all-important question before the Estates was their relation to Philip of Spain. On the part of the Leaguers there was a readiness to offer the Crown of France, not merely to the Infanta, but even to Philip himself; but at the same time they tried to safeguard the liberties and interests of France by restrictions that would have been useless if Philip had controlled the wealth and power of France as well as of his Spanish dominions. Philip, distrusting the effects of any direct claim to the French throne, preferred to put forward the claims of his daughter the Infanta. He tried to win Mayenne by the offer of a great position, but reserved to himself the choice of his daughter's husband. Mayenne was not conciliated.

There was little likelihood that Philip's plans would succeed; but there was a certainty that the civil struggle would be prolonged, and that the end would remain doubtful unless Henry were willing to be converted. The time had now come for Henry to yield. Some bold Huguenots—d'Aubigné, for example—urged him to trust in God and the justice of his cause; but most even of his Huguenot councillors gave him different advice. Sully's may be taken as characteristic. He gives us in the fifth book of his Memoirs the history of his opinions. He saw, he tells us, dangers on both sides, but he saw too that the greatest danger was to take no side at all. To persist in Protestantism was to prolong the war: he decided to advise the King to embrace Catholicism. The chief arguments that he used were founded on the misery of the country, the need of peace in order that the woes of France might be remedied and that she might have revenge on her great enemy. He sensibly affected the King by imploring him "to render his name immortal by restoring peace and plenty and security to a kingdom wasted with intestine divisions"; and he concluded with some platitudes about the common basis of all religions, and the many beliefs which were common to Protestants and Catholics. Even without Sully's arguments, Henry had probably made up his mind. On April 26 he told the Grand Duke of Tuscany that he had determined to become Catholic. On the 29th a conference between certain Catholics of the States General and others of Henry's own following began at Suresne. On May 15 the official announcement was made that Henry was prepared to be instructed. The news was received with very general satisfaction in France, for all felt that it meant peace. Philip was proportionately alarmed, and at once lowered his claims. Early in July the Duke of Feria, on behalf of Philip, offered to marry his daughter, if she were chosen, to the Duke of Guise. But the offer did not in the least satisfy Mayenne, and the Parlement of Paris had already declared in favour of the maintenance of the Salic Law.

Early in July the farce of "instruction" began at Mantes. Henry had already determined, as he tells Gabrielle d'Estrées in a letter, to take "the dangerous leap." But he listened carefully to the arguments of the four bishops and made some very apposite criticisms. Then he signed the formula of abjuration. He took leave of certain Calvinist ministers with much emotion; then on the 25th July he went in state to the church at St Denis. He found the doors closed. He knocked, they were opened, and the Archbishop of Bourges with seven bishops presented himself at the door and asked, "Who are you?" "I am the King." "What is your wish?" "My wish is to be received into the pale of the Catholic Apostolic and Roman Church." Then Henry knelt down and repeated his profession of faith, "I protest and swear in the presence of Almighty God to live and die in the Catholic religion, to defend and protect it against all, at the peril of my blood and life, renouncing all heresies contrary thereunto." He had taken the dangerous leap. It was the most important and the most questionable incident of his life.

Henry's conversion has long been a favourite problem with casuists, and, on its ethical side, has failed to secure the entire approbation of either Protestant

The submission of France.

or Catholic historians. But its success as a political measure was soon apparent. The sinews of resistance were cut. The League, after a fruitless effort to disguise its weakness, began to totter everywhere and soon collapsed.

Immediately after the abjuration Henry IV granted a general truce for three months. It was not possible as yet for him to enter Paris, but crowds thronged out to see him at St Denis and gave him the most enthusiastic reception. "They were wild," as Henry himself said, "to see a King." "God bless him," they cried, "and grant that he may soon hear Mass in our church of Notre Dame at Paris." Events moved rapidly towards the fulfilment of that prayer.

The States General still continued to sit at Paris, but their debates were no longer of consequence. They came to an unobserved end late in December 1593. The Pope about the same time declared that it was his intention to refuse absolution to the King. But if France were with him Henry was confident that he would be able to force the hand of the Pope. And France was rapidly coming round to his side. February 1594 was a month of bright augury. A revolution in Lyons brought that city over to the side of the King. Orléans surrendered in the same month. Meaux had already come in. Negotiations were being hotly prosecuted with Villars for the surrender of Rouen. It was no longer a question of principle but only of terms, and the surrender of Rouen would bring with it the rest of Normandy. Sully was the agent here, as in most of the negotiations of the time, and he had to offer a very high price for Villars' loyalty. In the end Villars obtained nearly a million and a quarter of livres (about £500,000) in addition to a pension of 60,000 livres, the revenues of six abbeys, and the promise of office and title. But before these negotiations were completed King Henry IV had made a greater conquest—the greatest of all—he was master of Paris.

In February the abjuration of the King had been succeeded by his consecration, though the Papal absolution had not yet been obtained. Reims was in the hands of the Leaguers, and it was impossible therefore that Henry should be consecrated as King there. The consecration was in consequence held at Chartres with all the accustomed ceremony, and the King took the usual oath, including a promise to expel from France all heretics. The irregularity in the place seems to have produced no effect on the public mind: the majority of Frenchmen assuredly now regarded Henry as their King. Yet his triumph could not be complete until he had entered Paris. Mayenne had been doing his best to maintain the League there, but the fanaticism of Paris had ebbed into indifference or given place to royalist feeling. The preachers preached in vain: it was clear that if Paris were to be kept from recognising Henry it must be by force of arms. Mayenne had made Brissac Governor of Paris in January: his action at the time of the Barricades seemed to assure his fidelity to the cause of the League. But his pretence of Catholic and Republican fanaticism covered, Sully tells us, a thoroughly self-seeking character. Henry's cause was in the ascendant, and Brissac was willing to sell himself to the winning side provided he could get a sufficiently high price. Henry made no attempt to cut down his terms. But even when Brissac had been won, a good deal of plotting was still necessary. Mayenne had indeed left Paris on March 6, but de Feria and the Spanish garrison were very likely to give trouble if they got wind of the project. All therefore was carried out in the profoundest secrecy. Troops suspected of devotion to League principles were sent out of the city on the pretext that there was a convoy to be intercepted. Then the chief strongholds of Paris were occupied by the troops of Brissac or the King, and when the city was safely in the hands of his forces Henry himself entered. At first the chief impression in Paris was amazement at the extraordinary change. But soon the royalist enthusiasm of the majority overwhelmed the discontent of a few zealots. Henry spared no pains to conciliate both high and low. The strictest order was maintained: the privileges of Paris and its exclusive Catholicism were guaranteed. There were few probably who did not see with relief or exultation the Spanish troops defile out through the gate of St Denis. Henry won many hearts too by his *bonhomie* and his entire absence of vindictiveness. He visited the Duchess of Nemours, the mother of Mayenne, and played cards with the Duchess of Montpensier, the sister of Guise and the patron of Jaques Clément, who had recently invoked the dagger of the assassin against Henry himself.

Victory seemed now well in sight. The Sorbonne withdrew its opposition to Henry. But much yet remained to be done. The League and the Spaniards were still strong in the North. Mayenne, the Duke of Aumale, and the Duke of Guise maintained with Spanish assistance their hold on Laon, Amiens, Soissons, Noyon, Reims, Rocroi, Rethel, and many other strong places. Brittany was in the hands of Mercœur. Marseilles, Toulouse, and a great portion of Languedoc, were still faithful to the League.

But before the end of the year much progress had been made. In July Laon, after a stubborn siege, surrendered to the King, in spite of the attempts of Mayenne and the Spaniards to relieve it. Amiens yielded in August, and all Picardy with it. St Malo followed in September. But the greatest acquisitions were made at the end of the year. The Duke of Guise, the son of the murdered Duke Henry le Balafré, quarrelled with his troops, and, as these surrendered some of his strong places to the King, thought it best to accept the King's offer for the rest. The King paid his debts and lavished on him pensions and benefices. He surrendered the Governorship of Champagne, but was promised that of Provence in its place, where he would be unsupported by associations and less capable of intrigue with an enemy. Soon after the Duke of Lorraine came in and handed over Toul and Verdun to Henry. The North of France therefore was almost entirely in the King's hands. Moreover, nearly the whole house of Guise had now come over to the King; there remained in opposition only the Duke of Mayenne and the Duke of Aumale, and the time of their surrender was drawing near.

At the end of the year 1594 Henry was reminded that there were other weapons in the armoury of Spain and Rome besides those of open warfare. It was believed that more than once already assassins had aimed at his life. On November 27, while the King was at Amiens, a young man called Jean Chastel, only eighteen years of age, attempted to stab the King as he was entering the apartments of his mistress, Gabrielle d'Estrées. Henry stooped just as the blow was delivered. It struck him therefore not on the throat, as had been intended, but on the lip and gum. The wound was quite a trivial one, but it had some important consequences. Jean Chastel had, it turned out, been a pupil of the Jesuits, and maintained upon his trial that he had been encouraged in his attempt by the theories of Jesuit teachers. Consequently, after he had been put to death with the most shocking tortures, the blow fell upon the whole order. Their constant hostility to the King needed no proof. They were expelled from France by order of the Parlement of Paris, and the decree of Paris was followed by similar orders from the Parlements of Rouen and Grenoble. But these decrees were ineffective. The Parlements of Aix, Rennes and Bordeaux refused to follow the example of Paris, and the Jesuits found therefore a refuge within their jurisdiction.

The League then seemed clearly defeated in France. Yet Mercœur still held Brittany, and Mayenne was still strong on the Eastern frontier. Henry's difficulties were increased by social disturbances. The troubles began before 1594, but came to a head in the spring of that year. The condition of the peasantry must have been desperate. The perpetual unrest had in some cases prevented the peasants from tilling the fields; the taxes were heavy; both sides took what they could from the districts through which their armies passed: there were parts of France

War with Spain.

where the fields went quite out of cultivation. It was not until
1595 that these blind efforts of famine were repressed. And
yet at this moment Henry determined to add a foreign war
to his domestic troubles. Sully protested the poverty of the
exchequer and the needs of France, and yet the King was
probably right. The League was nothing now without the
support of Spain. If once Spain's incapacity were demon-
strated the League would fall through very weakness. It was
time to throw off the mask and force Spain to throw it off too.
In January 1595 war was declared against King Philip. The
situation was not much altered, for war with Spain had been
in progress for years. The chief result of the declaration was
perhaps this—it made the League a more distinctly anti-
national party.

The war lasted for three and a half years and was devoid of
any very striking incidents. Before the end of the year 1595
the King had strengthened his hands by a reconciliation with
the Papacy. Clement VIII saw that the star of France was
rising and that of Spain was setting. It was too late for the
Roman bishop to maintain the pretensions of Innocent III.
There were rumours at Rome that if Henry IV were pushed
too far he might try to play the *rôle* of Henry VIII of England
and set up a separate national Church. The Pope consented
to receive a representative of France, and du Perron reached
Rome in July. Much debate and intrigue were necessary before
the terms of the absolution could be agreed upon. On the
whole Henry IV got the best in this diplomatic encounter.
The Pope was not to insist on any "temporal rehabilitation":
Henry IV refused to owe his crown to the fiat of the Pope.
Nor would he consent to the unconditional introduction into
France of the decrees of the Council of Trent. He drew
a distinction between those decrees which concerned doctrine
and those which dealt with discipline. The former he was
willing to accept. The latter he regarded as conflicting with
the liberties of the Gallican Church. He promised to observe

the decrees of the Council, but only so far as they were consistent with public tranquillity—an all-important limitation. It was not much of a counterweight that Henry undertook to introduce the Roman Catholic religion into Béarn; that du Perron consented to receive light blows upon his shoulders as he knelt, representing his royal master at the Pope's feet; that Henry promised to confess and communicate four times a year, and to take the Virgin as his advocate and patroness.

The war with Spain had meanwhile begun. In May 1595, the King's troops entered Burgundy, under the younger Biron, and when the King joined his forces he was drawn into the sharp cavalry skirmish of Fontaine Française, noteworthy for the almost foolhardy courage of Henry. The Spaniards might have crushed and captured him if they had used their opportunities, but they let them pass and only added another day of glory to the King's record. All Burgundy was left in the power of Henry and he ravaged Franche Comté. Immediately afterwards Mayenne wearied of his position of dependence upon the Spanish, and began secretly to negotiate with the King. The terms were not definitely arranged until the beginning of the next year, but a truce was made in September, 1595. Mayenne received the government of the Isle of France, the payment of his debts and sundry other favours.

No such good fortune had attended the King's arms on the northern frontier. The Spaniards, under the Count of Fuentes, laid siege to Doullens. The Duke of Bouillon and Admiral Villars attempted to relieve it; but they quarrelled and were decisively beaten with a loss of 3000. Villars was taken and put to death as a traitor on account of his surrender of Rouen. In October came another disaster. The Count of Fuentes took Cambrai; and though Henry laid siege to La Fère and subsequently, after a long blockade, took it, it was only a small set-off against all these losses. The spring of 1596 was again disastrous. In April the Spaniards took Calais; in

King Henry IV.

May, Ham, Guisnes and Ardres fell into their hands. Yet Henry could still face the war with good hope. In January he concluded his negotiations with Mayenne: in February an internal revolution gave him possession of Marseilles; and Épernon soon surrendered, leaving Mercœur the only prominent Leaguer still a rebel. Best of all, in May he made a new treaty of alliance with Elizabeth, by which each party promised to make no peace without the consent of the other. The Netherlands shortly afterwards entered the compact.

Nevertheless, the spring of 1597 brought upon the King the heaviest disaster he had yet suffered. The Spanish Governor of Doullens, Porto Carrero, captured Amiens by a stratagem that might have come direct from the pages of a romance. A party of Spanish soldiers disguised as peasants carrying sacks entered the gate of Amiens at eight in the morning. As if by accident one of them let some nuts escape from one of the sacks. The guards scrambled for them, and at the same time a carriage pulled up under the portcullis. The unsuspicious guards were cut down—the carriage prevented the fall of the portcullis—Spanish soldiers lying in ambuscade in the neighbourhood rushed up, and before the city knew that it was attacked it was in the hands of the Spaniards. The consternation at Paris was extreme: Paris could never feel itself safe if Amiens remained permanently in the hands of the Spaniards. The King determined to use every effort for its recapture: he had played the King of France long enough, he said; it was time once more to be the King of Navarre. Sully, who had recently (May 1596) entered the King's Council, used every effort to procure supplies, and the King was soon able to march against Amiens with a considerable force. The position was a strange one. His old enemies, the Leaguers, readily took service under him, and many of their leaders fought at Amiens against the Spaniards with whom they had so recently been in alliance. But the King's lifelong friends, on whose shoulders he had risen to power, stood for the most part sullenly aloof.

The siege was certain to be a long one, but it was hotly pressed, and in the autumn success came. The besieged suffered a great loss in the death of Porto Carrero, who was killed on Sept. 3. The garrison offered to capitulate if help did not reach them within a certain time. The efforts of the Spaniards failed: the Archduke Albert was beaten off: the garrison capitulated and marched out of the town (Sept. 25). Their stubborn defence allowed them to secure full military honours at their departure; but none the less the blow was a severe one to the hopes of Spain. The French King had indeed to abandon the siege of Doullens in consequence of the heavy rains; but the north of France was nearly swept clear of Spanish troops.

Spain then had gained no permanent, no decisive advantage. Philip II felt himself and his country incapable of continuing the struggle. During his long reign he had been in bitter conflict with more victorious and progressive causes and nations than perhaps any other well-known name in history. He had entirely failed to crush Protestantism: the Dutch had established the independence of what had been some of the richest of the Spanish Provinces: England had begun her great maritime and commercial career: the stubborn resistance of France discovered in her a vigour which it was quite beyond the power of Spain to crush. Spain was exhausted and her King was dying. But France on her side too was suffering severely, her finances strained to breaking point, her peasantry driven by hunger into rebellion. Negotiations for peace came as a matter of course under such circumstances. The only reason that could have kept Henry from such a step was the promise that he had given to England's Queen not to make terms with Spain without her approval. But the need of France was great, and diplomatic promises were not so binding as those between men of honour in ordinary affairs of life. In February 1598 the French plenipotentiaries, Pomponne de Bellièvre and Sillery, met the representatives of Philip of Spain at Vervins, and on

King Henry IV.

the 2nd of May the Treaty of Vervins was signed. It did not settle the essential question at issue—the rival claims of France and Spain to supremacy in Europe. It was rather a truce dictated by the temporary exhaustion of both sides. The Spaniards gave back all their conquests, except Cambrai, which was a recent acquisition of the French Crown. The French thus regained possession of Calais. The most difficult question was the future of the United Provinces. The French induced the Spaniards to consent to a truce, but it was rejected by the Dutch, and France therefore made peace without respecting her promises to either of her allies. Four months later (Sept. 15) Philip II died.

Peace with Spain brought with it the complete restoration of order in France herself. The Spaniards had in vain tried to include Mercœur—who still held out for the League in Brittany—in the terms of the Treaty of Vervins. Henry insisted on maintaining entire freedom in the settlement of the internal affairs of his kingdom. Mercœur saw that he would be deserted by Spain, and hastened to make terms on his own account: Henry might have imposed very hard conditions, for with or without Mercœur's permission most of the towns of Brittany offered themselves to the French Crown. But Mercœur gained an ally in the King's mistress, Gabrielle, by proposing that her son should marry his daughter, the only heir of his immense wealth. The King at last consented to shower on him pensions and indemnities as upon the other leaders of the League. And thus the League disappears from French History.

The Pacification of France: the Edict of Nantes.

A more serious question remained. The Huguenots, "who had guarded Henry's cradle and borne him to power on their shoulders" (to quote his own words), were bitterly and reasonably discontented. The King showered favours upon his new friends, who had been but lately his foes: he seemed to be entirely neglecting his old comrades of a hundred fights. They had heard with alarm his promise at his consecration "to drive all heretics from his dominions": they distrusted his promise of defence and protection, and could not enter into the reasons of statesmanship which forced him to follow this course. During the siege of Amiens they remained sullenly aloof: Henry's entreaties were not sufficient to induce them to leave their conference at Saumur to come to his relief. Yet Henry's intentions had always been honourable. The pressure of other dangers, the struggle with Spain, the fear lest any concession that he might make during the course of the war should seem dictated by fear had kept him hitherto from taking any measures for their relief. But no sooner was the Treaty of Vervins in assured prospect than he began to consider the case of his Protestant subjects more seriously, and on April 15, 1598, while he was in the West dealing with the recent submission of Brittany, he signed the great Edict of Nantes—by far the greatest act of religious toleration that Europe had seen or for a long time was destined to see.

Henry explains the motives for his delay in the preamble, "The fury of war did not allow the making of laws. But now that God has been pleased to give us the enjoyment of greater peace, it has seemed to us that we could not better employ it than in providing for His worship by all our subjects, so that, since He has not yet granted that we may worship Him in one form of religion, at least we may do so with one intention and in such a fashion that there may be no tumult or riot in our midst." And therefore, he goes on, it has seemed well to him to publish this "perpetual and irrevocable edict." The chief provisions of this Edict are the following:

1. Freedom of worship to the adherents of the "so-called reformed religion" in all places where it had been established in certain previous years (1596, 1597) and by the Edict of 1577. Further there was to be freedom of worship in one town of every bailiwick or *sénéchaussée*, and on the domains of the great nobles.

2. Protestant opinions were to bar no man from a career,

King Henry IV.

either in State or army, in spite of all treaties or edicts to the contrary.

3. A double security was given for the maintenance of the Edict. For, first, the Protestants were to continue to garrison certain strong places—some seventy-five in all—Saumur, La Rochelle, Montauban, Nîmes and others. Secondly, equal justice was to be secured to them by the creation of 'Chambers of the Edict' in the Parlements of Paris, Rouen and Rennes, in which at least one Protestant was to have a seat; and in the South by courts or judges half Protestant and half Catholic (*chambres mi-parties*).

4. There were other regulations concerning freedom of teaching, the position of Ministers, the rights of burial, &c.

Such was the famous Edict which reflects equal credit upon Henry's head and heart. In the granting of favours he leaned perhaps unfairly to his new rather than to his old co-religionists. Yet in one matter he went beyond what the Edict had promised to the Huguenots. He had made a promise to the Parisians on his entry into the city that no Protestant 'temple' should be established within five leagues of Paris: yet in 1606 he allowed them to build a great temple at Charenton, barely five miles outside the city.

The Edict was not the result of the religious movement of the time, for Catholics and Protestants alike would have supported the Calvinist axiom, "The liberty of conscience is a devilish doctrine." Rather it sprang from statesmanship and the general humanity of Henry IV. It was a glorious achievement: well would it have been for France if it had really been 'perpetual and irrevocable.' But while toleration was to Henry as welcome as it was expedient, to the majority of Frenchmen it was a hateful concession made under hard necessity. The Huguenots, in spite of their wealth, their culture, their energy (perhaps partly by reason of these qualities), were disliked and despised. They were a small minority of the people of France, at the outside not more than 1,250,000. It required all the force of the King to procure the acceptance of the Edict from the Parlements of France, and this is one argument the more to prove how well it was for France at this time that her government was concentrated in a single man rather than weakened by some form of representation. Unfortunately before a hundred years were over the King of France would side with his people in their repudiation of one of the noblest acts of his great predecessor.

After the Peace of Vervins, Henry reigned without dispute in France; and he reigned, if ever king did, in the hearts of his people. There were nobles still who resented the growth of the Monarchy; there were districts in France where the poverty was still very great, and gave rise to disturbance. But the great majority of the people of France welcomed the rule of this courageous, frank, humorous King, who had given them peace for war, unity for savage faction fights, and had restored the nation to a distinguished position in Europe. Most men were weary of the theological struggles of the last generation: their enthusiasm and their fanaticism were dead: they craved for order, prosperity, and success. Henry had much that attracted all who came in contact with him, a free and genial manner that was rarely concealed under the etiquette of the court, a persuasive faculty of speech that had nothing of the trained orator about it, a ready interest in every side of life. Stories true or invented passed from mouth to mouth, how he had let the starving people through his lines at the siege of Paris; how on Mayenne's surrender he had walked with him at a rapid pace about his grounds until the corpulent champion of the League panted for breath, and then, clapping him on the back, assured him that it was the only revenge he would ever exact; how he had expressed a wish that soon there would be a fowl in the pot of every peasant on Sunday.

The Duke of Sully and the reorganization of France.

The internal administration of France was no easy problem, for the King and his statesmen had to face the accumulations

of the disorder and dishonesty of many years. Fortunately the
King had at his side a statesman admirably qualified to assist
him in the task. Rosny, Duke of Sully, had fought for the
King in his Protestant days, and though he acquiesced and
even advised the King's change of religion, he had refused to
follow his example. In 1598 he had been given the administration of the finances with the title of superintendent. He
was hard-working, honest, a master of detail, quite careless of
unpopularity; and these qualities perhaps fitted him for the
work in hand even better than higher statesmanship would have
done. For what was immediately wanted was the unsparing
punishment of financial abuses and the rigid enforcement of
a better system. The abuses were obvious. The public debt
was, for that age, enormous. It was estimated at about
forty-three millions and a half (livres) in 1560, a hundred and
one millions in 1576; but now it had become a sea whose
bottom and whose shores no one knew. Sully reckoned it at
nearly three hundred millions. It is not difficult to enumerate
the chief causes of this disastrous condition of things. The
war had discouraged the industry and ruined the commerce of
France. The interest paid on the debt was very high; in some
cases as high as 10 per cent. Corruption in the Court and
dishonesty in its instruments made the expenses of collecting
taxes incredibly large. The revenue of future years had been
anticipated. It is reckoned that the people paid 200 million
livres while the State only received fifty.

Sully set himself, with stubborn zeal, to remedy this
condition of things. No new system and not more than
one new tax of importance was introduced. But he did
his utmost to make the old machine work with less friction
and less waste. He insisted that there should be no antici-
pations of income, no sub-farming of the revenues (a
constant and most ruinous practice), and no independent
taxation by Provincial governors. Where the collection of
taxes was 'farmed,' the right of farming them should be sold to

the highest bidder, not given to a courtier as a favour. He introduced a much more strict and regular method of keeping accounts, so that he knew the real financial position and could trace and punish fraud. He saw, as every financier down to the time of the Revolution was to see, that the unjust distribution of the *taille* was one of the chief financial wrongs in France. But he made no attempt to alter the principle: only he scrutinized all claims of privilege and rejected a very large number as invalid. His rigid economy produced its effect. At the end of twelve years the debts of the State had been paid, the administration was well provided for, and there was in the cellars of the Bastille a reserve of 30 million livres.

Two new taxes appear during Sully's administration, of which one was permanent and the other soon disappeared. The King had called a meeting of the Notables in Nov. 1596, the same year in which Sully was made Minister of Finance. The King was careful not to call the States General, yet he treated the Notables as if they were the real representatives of France, and even spoke of placing himself under their 'guardianship,' doubtless without meaning anything of the sort. There was much debate but only one permanent result. The Notables suggested a tax of five per cent. on the value of all goods brought for sale into towns, villages, and markets. This tax (the so-called *pancarte*) was levied for a time, but produced great discontent and was soon withdrawn. The other novelty in taxation (the *Paulette*) is far more important. By this the membership of Parlements and other courts of law was made hereditary on condition that the occupants of such posts paid annually to the State one-sixtieth of the value of their office (1604). It was obviously a momentous step, and the evil consequences of making the judges into an hereditary caste were what would naturally be expected. Yet there was much to be said for the new tax. The judgeships, it should be remembered, were already venal, while many of the offices of the Parlement had already become hereditary in practice.

King Henry IV.

The Edict of 1604 did but regularise and give legal sanction to an already marked tendency. And if the venality of such offices be once admitted, it was but a natural corollary to give them a hereditary character. Richelieu, in his *Testament Politique*, defends both the venality and the heredity: he recognises the abuse but considers it necessary in order to prevent greater abuses. The character of the judges improved after the Edict of 1604. The honourable traditions of the Bench were handed on from generation to generation, and most impartial critics have admitted the high character of the members of the French Parlements during the 17th and 18th centuries.

The most important consequence of the new arrangement—one perhaps which neither the King nor Sully foresaw—was to give the judicial bench a position of remarkable independence in face of the Crown. In the 18th century the Parlements were the only channel through which resistance could be offered to the descendants of Henry IV, and the resistance could not have been made had it not been for the *Paulette*.

Sully was anxious to help agriculture in every possible way—by the building of roads, the making of canals, the introduction of improved methods of culture. But he had no anxiety to see manufactures introduced into France, as they did not tend in his opinion to produce men fit for soldiers' work: the tilling of the fields and the rearing of cattle he declared to be the real mines and treasures of Peru. But here he came into conflict with the King. Henry indeed was deeply interested in agriculture. The treatises of Olivier de Serres, the father of French agriculture, were the only books, it was said, that the King ever had patience to read. But he was also anxious to make France independent of the industrial products of her neighbours. It was due to him that silk-culture was introduced into France, and this soon developed into a very important source of wealth.

The King was specially interested in Paris and did much to inaugurate the transformation from its former condition—a sea of squalid houses round a few isolated palaces or churches of superb architecture—into the most refined capital of Europe. It is especially remembered that the gallery of the Louvre was built by him.

Considerations of space make it impossible to go further into the details of the new *régime*. In its essentials it was merely a more honest and capable copy of the old one conducted by stronger hands. When the King and his Minister were removed, the old abuses soon crept back again. It was left for Richelieu and Colbert to give to France not merely a better and honester administration, but a better organisation of government, which would continue to work after the death of its originators.

The condition of France grew rapidly more prosperous during the years that succeeded the Peace of Vervins. Yet all rested on the life of the King. The King was then only forty-three years of age, but the hardships and anxieties of his life had told even upon his elastic spirit, and moreover Jean Chastel might at any time find a more fortunate imitator. And if Henry died, into whose hands would the government of France fall? Apparently into those of the young Condé, though there were doubts cast upon his birth: for Margaret of Valois, the King's wife, had borne him no child and had lived for some time past apart from her husband. The idea of a divorce and a new marriage was thus inevitably suggested, and Margaret was as eager to obtain it as the King himself, for divorce would be likely to give her a position of assured dignity and a settled income. While the King was at variance with the Pope it was impossible to procure a divorce in regular form. But the absolution of the King changed the situation. Now there would be little difficulty in annulling his marriage with Margaret of Valois, on the ground, so often alleged by sovereigns, that the contracting parties had been within the prohibited degrees. The King had a special reason for a divorce just at this moment, for he had made up his mind to advance his mistress, Gabrielle

King Henry IV.

d'Estrées (recently created Duchess of Beaufort), to share the throne with him. Few 'Queens of the Left Hand' have gained or deserved so much respect from posterity as the beautiful Gabrielle. The connection was excused by the evil character of the Queen, and dignified by Gabrielle's genuine affection for the King. She never used her position for public evil, and occasionally used it very markedly for the public good. And yet her elevation to the throne could hardly have been satisfactory: any children she bore the King would hardly be recognised without dispute as heirs to the French throne. Yet there can be little doubt that the King would have persisted in his project if his mistress had not suddenly died (Easter, 1599). With her one of the best influences passed out of the King's private life. Henceforth his Court shows little more respect for monogamy than that of the Sultan of Turkey. He proceeded with his marriage project and scanned the Catholic courts of Europe for a suitable consort. He fixed at last upon Marie de Médicis, niece of the Grand Duke of Tuscany, and grand-daughter of the Emperor Ferdinand. The Pope declared Henry's marriage null and void in Dec. 1599. In Oct. 1600 Henry married Marie de Médicis. On Sept. 27, 1600, she bore him a son, who afterwards reigned as Louis XIII. The new Queen of France was a heavy and lethargic woman, who soon fell under the influence of Leonora Galigai, an Italian lady-in-waiting. Between King and Queen the relations were never of the best. The King had no love for his wife, and after marriage pretended to none. He insulted her by installing in the palace Henriette d'Entragues, Duchess of Verneuil, as his avowed mistress.

After the Peace of Vervins Henry was soon engaged in another war; but it was one of small duration and little difficulty. The position of the territories of the Duke of Savoy gave him an importance in European affairs that neither the wealth nor the extent of his dominions could have brought him. For he

The revolts of the Nobles and their punishment.

commanded important passes over the Alps, and had a foothold in Germany, France, and Italy. Charles Emmanuel, the present Duke of Savoy, had seized in 1588, as an ally of Spain, the Marquisate of Saluzzo, and no decision as to the ownership of this important place had been reached by the Peace of Vervins. Yet the Duke realised that he was not strong enough to face an united France, and tried to make terms. He actually visited the French Court in 1599, but found that Henry was firm: the Duke must either surrender Saluzzo or yield in exchange Bresse, Bugey, and Valromey. The Duke, trusting to his strong fortifications and the difficulties which his mountainous country would present, refused, and the war was renewed. But the French forces were admirably equipped; their artillery especially had been much improved by Sully; and the French generals, the Dukes of Biron and Lesdiguières, took place after place. Bourg and Chambéry fell, and the French laid siege to Montmélian, a fortress that the Duke of Savoy had believed inaccessible. But the French artillery soon forced it to surrender (Oct. 1600), and in Jan. 1601 the Duke of Savoy sought and found peace. Saluzzo remained in the hands of Savoy, but the French frontiers were advanced by the acquisition of Bresse, Bugey, Valromey, and Gex.

The Duke of Savoy, during his expedition to the French Court in 1599, had tried to find allies among the French nobles. He had not succeeded in raising any revolt, but he had found some of them willing to enter into compromising negotiations. No one had gone further in this direction than Biron, who had actually commanded the French armies in the war against Savoy. The Duke of Savoy had proposed that Biron should marry his daughter, as a reward for his support, and the assassination of the King was considered. Henry had become aware that some intrigue was in progress, and Biron, afraid of detection, had admitted some part of it, and implored and gained the King's pardon. But the intrigue was no sooner pardoned than it recommenced. Biron's ambition had no limits. Astrology seemed to promise him boundless power, and alchemy boundless wealth. Something of his scheme was betrayed to the King by a confederate, La Fin. The King summoned him to Fontainebleau. He wished to save Biron's life, for they had been for many years comrades in arms, and more than once the King had saved Biron's life at the risk of his own. He promised to save it again if he would confess all. But Biron stubbornly maintained that he had nothing to confess; and the King therefore allowed the law to take its course. He was tried before the Parlement of Paris and declared guilty by an unanimous vote. Even so he could not believe that the King would allow him to be executed. He appealed to the memory of his father's services and his own, to the long list of campaigns that he had fought for the King, to his thirty-two wounds. But his importance only made his intrigues more dangerous, and the example of his execution more necessary. The King spared him the ignominy of a public execution. He was beheaded in an inner court of the Bastille (July, 1602).

In spite of this warning to traitors, all the rest of Henry's life was passed in an atmosphere of intrigue and suspicion. He thought to conciliate one body of his opponents by recalling the Jesuits (Sept. 1603)[1]. But his enemies were now political rather than religious. The Treaty of Vervins had not ended for a moment the hostility between France and Spain, and the situation in Europe seemed to show that the renewal of actual hostilities was far from improbable. Thus the Spaniards would be ready enough to lend a hand to any conspirator who would

[1] He gives the following account of his motives in a letter to James I. "To persecute so powerful a company would be to drive many superstitious spirits into plots against myself, to disappoint a great number of Catholics, and to give them a pretext for causing new trouble in my kingdom....I thought too that if I left the Jesuits some hope of being recalled, I should divert and prevent them from yielding themselves entirely to the ambitious plans of the King of Spain, and in this I did not miscalculate."

weaken the government of the King of France. It is impossible to trace the rumours and events of the time in any detail. The chief centre of intrigue was the King's new mistress, Henriette d'Entragues, Duchess de Verneuil. Her half-brother, the Count of Auvergne, relied upon the King's conditional promise to make her his wife, and claimed for her son the right to succeed to the French throne before the son of Marie de Médicis. Spain joined in the project and promised help. But all came to the ears of the King. The leaders would have been put to death, but the King could not tear himself from Henriette, and, to keep her, pardoned those whose heads were forfeit (1605). The King too had had his suspicions of the Duke of Bouillon in 1602. His influence as one of the leaders of the Protestants, and his position at Sedan, made him particularly dangerous. The evidence against him seems to have been insufficient, but when he was summoned to Court he took flight to Geneva. Henry at once occupied Sedan. But, as in 1595, the King may well have thought that open war against the foreign enemy was the best way of crushing his domestic opponents.

Since the Peace of Vervins the power of France in the international complications of Europe had considerably increased. Twice already France, under King Henry, had thrown a decisive weight into the scales. In 1606 the relations between the Republic of Venice and the Papacy were so strained that war seemed probable. The Republic had cancelled certain privileges of the Church; the Pope demanded their reestablishment. King Henry IV was the ally of both the disputants: he wished to avoid any complications in Italy that would probably end in the profit of the Spaniards. Through his mediation each side consented to abate something of its demands, and peace was maintained. A much more serious question was presented by the continuation of the war between the Netherlands and Spain. It had already lasted forty years.

Foreign affairs. The last Projects of the King, and Death.

Spain had exhausted in that war her armies, her navies, and her treasures. The country which had once been her chief financial support was now a constant drain upon her. The war probably had done more to hasten the decline of her power than the loss of the Armada which she had sent against England, and all the depredations of English sailors. And yet Spanish pride refused to accept defeat, and insisted on maintaining a now hopeless struggle. But in 1607 the exhaustion of both sides resulted in a suspension of arms for eight months. The relations between Holland and France had for long been of the closest, and King Henry, through his representative Jeannin, did his utmost to turn this breathing space into an assured peace. At first the Spaniards altogether declined the intervention of France, but at last yielded on this point. A middle point was found between a mere suspension of arms and a permanent peace. Spain accepted in Jan. 1609 a truce for twelve years. It was not very likely that the war would be renewed, or at least not on the same grounds; but the name of "*truce*" and its limitation in point of time seemed to save the honour of Spain.

This settled, another and more difficult question soon rose to view. In Germany all the elements of the Thirty Years' War were accumulating. The Catholic reaction had made rapid headway, and the Catholics now felt that the time was come to take back some of the concessions that had been made to the Protestants. The Empire saw a chance of establishing its authority over the German princes and electors on a safer and sounder basis. The strength of the Protestants was much diminished by the bitter feuds between Lutherans and Calvinists. At this moment a controversy arose on the Rhine frontier that seemed quite likely to put a match to the inflammable elements that lay all around.

In March, 1609, William, Duke of Juliers, Clèves and Berg died without direct heirs. The territory of the late Duke was valuable in itself, trebly valuable because of its position. If it fell into Catholic hands, still more if it fell into the hands of the Empire, it would open a gate of attack for the Austrian house against Holland.

The claimants were many. The most important and the best supported were the Elector of Brandenburg and the Duke of Neuburg. But the territories were too valuable to the Emperor to allow the matter to be settled as a mere process at law. He placed the estate in question under sequestration, put his cousin the Archduke Leopold into possession, and declared his intention of safeguarding the interests of the Catholics in those states where the claimants were all Protestants.

It was not a matter that Henry could possibly overlook. The closest union and relationship existed between the royal houses of Austria and Spain; and France could not but regard with the greatest jealousy any increase in the power of either. Henry prepared to interfere with arms. At this moment, too, he had other and less honourable reasons for animosity against Spain. The domestic life of Henry had gained neither in purity nor dignity since the death of Gabrielle. The Queen was insulted by the installation of three publicly-acknowledged mistresses. And now Charlotte, the daughter of the Constable Montmorency, had inspired him with a last violent passion. The King had procured her marriage to the young Condé, who was, after Henry's children, the next heir to the French throne. But Condé, to the surprise of all—for he was considered weak in will and mind, and not likely to be sensitive on the point of honour—resented the King's attentions to his wife, and, to remove her from Henry's reach, fled with her to Brussels. The King demanded their surrender from the Spanish governor of the Netherlands, and was constantly refused.

It would be a mistake to regard this indecent quarrel as the cause of Henry's preparations for war, for these were in entire harmony with the arrangements and diplomacy of many previous years. But so violent was his passion and the means by which he was prepared to gratify it, that it threw him open to dishonouring comments from his many enemies; it has even made it possible for some serious historians to believe that if Spain had yielded to his clamour for the restoration of the Princess of Condé, the preparations for European warfare would have been dropped. Henry prepared for war on a great scale. He entered into alliance with the Protestant princes of the Rhine (Union of Hall, Feb. 1610), with the Duke of Savoy and the Duke of Milan. He prepared to attack the twin powers of Spain and Austria at three points. While he himself with the main army struck for Juliers and the Rhine, other armies were to invade Italy, and even Spain itself.

A great crisis in the affairs of Europe seemed approaching. Sully in his Memoirs speaks constantly of the King's 'Great Design,' and traces for us the outlines of a scheme whereby the Turk was to be expelled from Europe, the power of the Austro-Spanish House broken, the religious controversy settled by the French system of religious toleration, while finally, as sum and crown of all, Europe was to be built up into a huge federal Union, under the presidency of France. This grandiose and yet noble plan seems to be rather the product of Sully's imagination than of Henry's practical and rather selfish statesmanship. But, putting the 'Great Design' quite on one side, much might have been changed, and changed for the better, by the campaign that Henry contemplated. The long agony of the Thirty Years' War might quite possibly have been avoided: a large measure of toleration might have been reached, and Germany saved from the dominion of Austria, without the terrible loss of life and the profound demoralisation which came upon the whole Empire between 1618 and 1648.

The Queen was to be regent during Henry's absence. She had long desired to be crowned, and the King now granted her request. The ceremony took place on May 13, 1610, at St Denis. He had arranged to leave for the front on the 19th. He was, we are

The murder of Henry IV.

told, uneasy in his mind, full of forebodings and yet anxious to get away. The Queen was to make her solemn entry into Paris on the 17th. On the 14th the King determined to visit Sully in his rooms at the Arsenal. He set off in his carriage, "one of the clumsy conveyances then used, something between a cart and a four-post bed, with leather curtains, on wheels." In the Rue de la Ferronerie a block in the road made the King's carriage halt. As it stopped a man stepped on to one of the hind wheels, and reaching forward into the carriage stabbed the King twice. He was carried back dying to the Louvre.

Ravaillac, for that was the assassin's name, does not seem to have had any confederates. The King, he said, was going to make war on the Pope, and to slay him was therefore a good deed. He was of course executed with every barbarity that ingenuity could suggest.

The death of the King produced a profound sensation throughout Europe. We shall see how much France suffered from his loss. "When I am gone," he had said to the Duke of Guise shortly before his death, "you will know what you have lost." France had to wait twelve years before she found anyone to take up his work. And yet so necessary was that work, so impossible was it for France to find political rest except in the strong centralised monarchy, that when Henry's greater successor, Richelieu, appeared, he followed in most points both of foreign and domestic policy the lines that Henry's action had suggested.

CHAPTER VII.

FROM THE DEATH OF HENRY IV TO THE PEACE OF ALAIS.

The murder of Henry IV seemed likely to change the whole course of European history. All his great schemes were thrown aside. For fourteen years the current of French affairs flows dismally through marsh and bog, but then it finds its old channel and resumes its course in the old direction. The history of these fourteen years is somewhat tedious. Its chief interest is that it serves to convince us that if order and progress were to be maintained in France there was no alternative to the strong centralised monarchy. During these years no new or fruitful idea emerges, and the action of the old parties is seen to be more petty, egotistic and impossible than ever.

"France will fall into strange hands," said Sully, when the news of the assassination was brought to him; and so it proved. Marie de Médicis showed considerable energy in putting forward her claims to the Regency, and the Parlement of Paris took upon itself to ratify them. The Queen had had little influence on public affairs during the life of her husband, and she thought that her time had come at last. But she showed no capacity for policy or statesmanship; her likes and dislikes were personal rather than political, and the chief influence on France was at once not the Queen, but the Queen's favourite, Leonora Galigai, and her husband, Concini. Their nationality and their attachment to her in her less powerful days gave them influence now. Leonora Galigai's power over the Queen was so great that, later, a charge of sorcery was founded on it. It was through his wife that Concini managed the Queen. The youth of Louis XIII, for he was only nine, seemed to secure to the Queen a long tenure of power. Sully withdrew from the Court almost immediately. New men and a new policy were to reign for the future. The Queen hoped to reverse the policy of Henry IV, to enter into an alliance with Spain, and to support the policy of Spain in Europe.

But the Queen's position was in the highest degree unstable. The old feudal nobility which had submitted with reluctance to the rule of Henry, was not at all prepared to bend to a new and weaker hand. The spirit of provincial independence showed itself on all sides. Above all, Condé in Guienne, and Épernon in Angoulême, seemed barely to recognise the supremacy of the Crown. Henri de Bourbon, Prince of Condé, is for the early years of this reign the most important figure in French history. His birth was doubtful, his courage was questioned, and his abilities were not more than second-rate, but his avarice and his ambition were inexhaustible. He aspired to play over again the part of the Guises, and aimed at the Regency, if not at the Crown itself: and his birth assured him an influence far greater than his talents warranted. He was the son of the King's cousin, and, after Gaston the King's brother, the nearest Prince of the royal blood. Those nobles who remained at Court filled it with their rivalries, their dissensions and their duels. An Italian ambassador notices the astonishing change in the behaviour of the nobles; "they behave," he says, "like so many kings." There were some who so far misinterpreted the signs of the times as to think that the time of kings was over and the time of the great nobles about to begin. The Queen barely attempted to resist their claims. She showed her weakness by granting additional pensions and powers to Condé, Guise, Épernon, and others, without in the least satisfying their ambitions. The Protestants too began to think of stirring. They held their assembly at Saumur, in May 1611. They had been offended during the late reign by encroachments on their privileges, and the assembly showed a spirit of discontent and protest. Henri, Duke of Rohan, was the leading figure. He was the son-in-law of Sully, and eventually induced that statesman to embark in the Protestant cause. Lesdiguières, meanwhile, was separating himself from his co-religionists. We shall soon find him fighting against them and even abjuring their faith.

In 1612 the policy of the new Government was unmistakeably proclaimed. In June a double marriage was arranged that was to bind France to Spain. Louis XIII was to marry Anne of Austria, daughter of Philip III, King of Spain, and at the same time his son was to marry Elizabeth of France. There could not possibly be a more open avowal that the policy of Henry IV was abandoned. The project called out protests from many quarters. The Protestant party was of course alarmed by the proposed alliance of France with the zealous supporter of the Counter-Reformation. The nobles objected to a marriage which was likely to strengthen the hands of the Crown. But for the present there was no open outbreak. The Protestants indeed, on the suggestion of the Duke of Rohan, called an assembly at Rochelle, and held it in spite of the protests of the Government. In the end the Queen gave way. She granted them some of their demands; Protestantism was no longer to be styled the "so-called Reformed Religion" (*la religion prétendue réformée*); Protestant ministers were to be exempted from the *taille*. Such attempts to buy off Protestant opposition were doomed to failure in the end, but the Queen gained a breathing space. Concini meanwhile advanced in power and favour. In Nov. 1613 he who had never commanded an army or seen war on a great scale was created Marshal, and is henceforth known to history as Marshal D'Ancre. His wife at the same time was receiving great grants of money which the country could ill spare.

Meanwhile the unruliness of the nobles was constantly increasing, and with the beginning of the year 1614 the long-prepared revolt broke out. Nothing can be more contemptible than the action of the nobles during this period. Their motives were purely selfish, and were not even associated with any high object, for they hardly even alleged the pretext of religious freedom, local liberty, or the welfare of the people. They fought in order that they might be bribed to lay down their arms: if the leaders of the League had forced open the treasury of Henry IV, they made sure that Marie de Médicis would not be able to resist their demands. Condé seized Mezières in January, and, as the spokesman of his class, issued a manifesto in which an attempt was made to give a patriotic colouring to the movement. He complained of the unworthy influences that worked upon the King, and demanded the postponement of the Spanish marriages and the calling of the States General. The insult to the Royal authority was manifest, but the Queen was afraid to try to crush her opponents. She preferred to buy off their resistance. On May 15, 1614, she concluded with them the Peace of St Menehould. Pensions and places were poured into the hands of Condé, Nevers and Mayenne, and their adherents. Marie de Médicis promised at the same time to convoke the States General as soon as possible. Thus an interval of quiet was gained. She visited Paris in September for the ceremonies that proclaimed the legal majority of the King; but as he only then entered on his fourteenth year, Marie de Médicis continued to be Regent as before.

The States General came together at Paris in the next month (Oct. 1614). The Clergy were represented by a hundred and forty-four members, the Nobility by a hundred and thirty, and the third estate by a hundred and ninety-two. Richelieu, bishop of Luçon, though only 29 years old, was chosen to be spokesman of the clergy, and played a fairly prominent part during the meeting. But the deliberations of the assembly—which gains a factitious importance from the fact that no other was held before the great Revolution—were really of very little effect. They are chiefly of interest as showing what were the chief currents of opinion and feeling among the upper classes in France. We find the Nobility demanding the abolition of the paulette, whereby the judicial authority of the Parlements had been so much increased, and insisting on the complete subordination of the third estate: the relation between nobles and commons, one speaker said, was not that of elder and younger brother, but that of master and servant. The third estate retorted with a demand for the abolition of the pensions which were draining away the strength of France. The third estate also protested against the Papal claims on political power and against the introduction of the decrees of the Council of Trent into France, especially those which declared the superiority of the spiritual over the temporal power. Sometimes a bolder note was struck, as when Savaron, a member of the third estate, told the nobles that if they persisted in their monstrous financial exactions a revolt of the people would be the consequence. He informed the King that there were districts in Guienne and Auvergne where the peasantry were reduced to eating grass (it is a statement which we hear again and again down to the Revolution), and he called on the King to confiscate the pensions of the nobles and apply the money to the relief of the people. In Feb. 1615 the three orders presented their demands (*cahiers*) to the King, and then they were dismissed. Richelieu has passed a severe verdict on these estates. They were called together, he says, under specious pretexts; they had no intention of advancing the cause of either King or Commonwealth: and their deliberations were without fruit.

Shortly after the dismissal of the estates, the Parlement of Paris protested against the arbitrary character of the Government, the confusion of the finances, and the power of Marshal d'Ancre, and claimed for itself a share in the administration. But this protest remained ineffectual, and soon the unceasing fermentation among the nobles produced another revolt. The Spanish marriages were to be solemnised in Oct. 1615. The vague alarm that they inspired, and the bitter hatred that the nobles felt for the constantly and rapidly increasing power of Marshal d'Ancre, gave Condé another opportunity. In July he denounced the Marshal (who had received the Governments of Picardy and Amiens), and in August he issued a manifesto, complaining that the wishes of the States General had been disregarded, and demanding that the Spanish marriages should be postponed. The King thereupon declared Condé guilty of high treason. In October Condé took up arms in the north. Would the Huguenots join him? Du Plessis Mornay, the noblest and soberest of them all, dissuaded them; but the impetuous spirit of the Duke of Rohan carried all before him. The Protestants at Nîmes declared themselves ready to support him, and even Sully joined them. But the Government displayed unwonted energy. The Spanish marriages were the very pivot of the policy of the Queen and her Italian favourites, and they were prepared to carry them through at all costs. Despite the efforts of Condé and his friends the King and Court moved towards the Spanish frontier. On October 18, 1615, the marriages took place by procuration at Bordeaux and at Burgos, and on November 9 the Princesses were handed over to their future countries at the Bidassoa. And then, her one great object having been realised, the Queen began to negotiate for peace with Condé. It was bought as usual. Richelieu says in his memoirs that it cost the King six million livres. Marshal d'Ancre gave up Amiens and Picardy, and received instead the lieutenancy of Normandy. The Huguenots received a promise that they should not be disturbed in their privileges. This "Treaty of Loudun" was signed in May, 1616.

From the death of Henry IV to the Peace of Alais. 195

On the return of the Court, Condé came to Paris, and at once assumed a position and deportment that implied that he had conquered the Court. The discontented gathered round him again; he negotiated independently with foreign powers. The Marshal believed that his life was threatened and fled from Paris to Normandy. The Queen herself was alarmed; rumour said that she was to be imprisoned in a nunnery. Her alarm gave her courage for another intrigue, which seems to have been recommended to her by Richelieu. On Sept. 1, 1616, Condé was arrested, and was shortly after committed to the Bastille. There was of course a fear that the nobles would rise out of sympathy with their leader; but their slight movements were easily repressed. The fall of Condé brought into the Council a figure that was destined to be the greatest in France. Richelieu had been for some time attached to the Queen-mother in an ecclesiastical office. He was now invested with control over foreign affairs and war, and, even during his very brief tenure of the office, showed his clearness of vision, his resolution and quickness of decision: but his time had not come yet. Marshal d'Ancre had returned to Paris, and his power was greater than ever and more arrogantly displayed before nobles and people. His insolence kept the nobles in constant unrest. In Feb. 1617 Bouillon, Nevers and Vendôme were declared guilty of high treason. But it was not from that side that the blow came.

Louis had purposely been kept in the background by his mother. From the first his character was sullen and reserved. He did not readily open his heart to anyone, and his feelings were often misunderstood. He was fond of the externals of war, and of field sports, especially of hawking, and hitherto he had not seemed to resent the usurpation of power by his mother and her favourites. But much of this carelessness had been dissimulation, and at the beginning of 1617 his dislike of d'Ancre was stimulated and increased. He was not merely offended by the insolence of the Italian parvenu. He contrasted

13—2

his own scanty allowance with the luxury of the favourite, and he was alarmed by rumours that Marshal d'Ancre intended to depose and imprison him and to place his brother on the throne. Early in 1617 he was warned by Sully and Lesdiguières that there was a plot against his life. His chief adviser and confidant was Charles d'Albret, Sieur de Luynes. He had been recommended to the King in the first instance by his knowledge of all that concerned falconry, and the Queen and d'Ancre had seen with pleasure his growing influence, for they thought him incapable of ambitious designs. But it was he who persuaded the King of his danger and recommended means of escape. The means were such as the French Court was only too familiar with. Vitry was one of the captains of the guard, and was personally hostile to d'Ancre. He was told on behalf of the King to arrest the Marshal, and to kill him if he resisted. On April 24, 1617, Marshal d'Ancre was arrested as he was entering the Louvre, and a cry for help was made the excuse for shooting him down. Vitry, with his foot upon the body, called for cheers for the King. Louis XIII appeared at a window to testify his approval of the deed. "At last," he said, "I am King." The deed was very popular with the people of Paris, who hated d'Ancre as a foreigner and a waster of the public money. His body had been buried hurriedly and without ceremony. It was disinterred by the people, treated with every kind of horrible ignominy, and finally torn in pieces and scattered about the city.

D'Ancre's death brought with it a complete revolution. Marie de Médicis was kept for some time in a condition of imprisonment and was then allowed to retire to Blois. Richelieu was dismissed from power at the same time and followed his mistress: to contemporaries his career must have seemed closed. The King's vengeance was not satiated by the death of d'Ancre. His wife, who had been estranged from her husband of late, was prosecuted on various charges—sorcery among others—

Louis XIII under the influence of Luynes.

and was executed. The old ministers who had been displaced by the Queen came back to the King's side—Villeroy, Jeannin, Sillery. The nobles who had been declared by the Queen guilty of high treason came in to the King at Vincennes and were well received by him. Luynes gained a vast influence over the mind of the King. His was a sounder character and a saner mind than d'Ancre's; but he soon began to show an equally strong ambition, and his position gave as much umbrage to the turbulent and power-loving Nobility. Yet the first years of the new *régime* were fairly peaceful at home, and we may postpone an examination of the foreign problem until it comes to be treated by Richelieu's master-hand.

An assembly of Notables was called in Dec. 1617 to consider what answer should be given to the demands of the States General of 1614, but their proposals, like those of the estates, had no result. The central interest in this period of intrigue is to be found in the relations of Louis XIII to his mother. Marie feigned resignation, but had by no means given up all hopes of ruling again. In Nov. 1617 she had professed to abandon political life altogether, but at the same time she was negotiating with the discontented nobles. In 1619 she escaped through a window of her castle-prison and joined the Duke of Épernon at Angoulême. She wrote to the King, speaking of the "wretched state of affairs," and the "remedies which must be applied to them," and the King feared that he would have to face another aristocratic insurrection. But the plot was mismanaged, and the Queen showed herself willing to accept a compromise. Richelieu had been exiled to Avignon in 1618, but he came forward now to negotiate a peace between Louis XIII and Marie de Médicis, and partially succeeded in his task. There was an interview between mother and son, and then the Queen with Richelieu retired to Angers (Aug. 1619). But no real solution had been reached. The autumn saw an important move. Condé was still in prison. Luynes and the King determined to liberate him. He promised of course to abstain from intrigue for the future, but the strange thing is that he kept his promise. He was henceforth a force on the King's side, but his liberation tended still further to embitter the relations between the King and his mother. The autumn was full of intrigues and preparations. The arrogance of Luynes was growing more and more insupportable. He and his brothers plunged both hands into the royal treasury, and took to themselves every important and lucrative post. In the spring of 1620 the leading nobles withdrew in indignation from the Court. Some retired to their provinces: many gathered round Marie de Médicis. The situation was full of danger; but the Government was stronger than in the days of Concini. It was determined to decide the question by force and with all possible speed. In July the King and Luynes marched towards Normandy: Rouen and Caen fell into their hands. They then pushed southward and faced the insurgent nobles on the Loire at the important bridge known as the Pont de Cé. Vendôme and Soissons were in command on the side of the nobles. Condé urged the King to attack. The army of the nobles was mishandled throughout, and there was no real resistance. The place was captured for the King, and the army of the enemy completely broken up. The Queen-mother had begun to treat even before the battle, and, as before, Richelieu was the intermediary. Louis insisted on no hard terms: he allowed the Queen to hold the position that she had had before the troubles (Treaty of Angoulême, Aug. 1620). The power of the Crown had been asserted as it had never been since the death of Henry IV, but it was very far from having recovered all its lost ground.

After this successful assault on the pretensions of the Nobility the King turned against the Protestants of the South. They had not indeed taken any prominent part in the last rising, but before that they had again and again joined hands with the nobles. Their numbers seem to have been diminishing, but their claims were

The attack upon the Huguenots.

as high as ever, or higher. No admiration for some of their leaders, no conviction of the moral strength that they might have imparted to France, can prevent us from recognising that the continued existence of their privileges was incompatible with the unity and the national strength of France. The Catholic Church had during the last half century entirely regained the ascendancy in France which at one time had been threatened by the Protestants. The Jesuits were here, as everywhere, prominent in the reaction; but the Catholic Church in France generally was displaying a new activity. The leaders of the Church were no longer satisfied with intellectual controversy: they entered also the field of action. New orders were created, mostly with practical philanthropic ends: the chief are perhaps the Sisters of Charity of Saint Vincent de Paul; the Daughters of Calvary, founded by Father Joseph; the Priests of the Oratory, founded by Cardinal de Bérulle. In short, enthusiasm and practical energy, in which the Protestants had at first been distinctly superior, had passed over to the side of their opponents. The tone of Catholicism was everywhere aggressive, and as the French Protestants were growing weak they were in danger. Colourable excuses could be found for attacking them. Henry IV had promised to take the ecclesiastical property from the Protestants of Béarn and restore it to the Catholics. But the thing had not been done, and the Protestants had protested against it as an infringement of their rights. The Clergy urged the King to carry out the plan, and were ready to subscribe money for that object. In 1620 the King marched south with the army that had done such good service for him at the battle of the Pont de Cé. He was determined to destroy the semi-independence of Béarn and Navarre, as well as to restore Catholicism to its former position. No resistance was offered to him: he forced the Edict of Incorporation to be registered by the Parlement of Pau, and then returned in triumph to Paris (Nov. 1620).

But the trouble was by no means over; its acute phase had

not indeed begun. Bitter resentment was felt against the appropriation of the ecclesiastical revenues of Béarn and Navarre, and after a period of preparation the discontent flamed out into war. The Protestants did not shrink from the contest. They held an assembly to consider the measures to be taken to meet the attack, and spoke no word of submission to the Crown. The 722 Protestant churches of France were divided into eight circles, somewhat after the German fashion. Plans were drawn up for the appointment of officers and the management of the campaign. Their enemies said that they had taken as their model the constitution of the United Netherlands, and that they designed to declare an independent republic in the heart of France, and they themselves did not shrink from the use of the word Republic.

At the beginning of the campaign the King appointed Luynes Constable—a title out of all proportion to his military talents and experience. He was soon made Chancellor as well, and grasped at riches on every side. But all went well at first with the expedition. Saumur was occupied in May 1621, and in June St Jean d'Angely submitted after a siege of three weeks. Then in August the Royal army moved against Montauban: if that place fell the war was over. But the siege presented very great difficulties. The town was strong and well fortified, and the religious fervour of the besieged, stimulated by the fiery spirit of the Duke of Rohan, was at a very high pitch. The inhabitants refused all overtures, even when they were presented through the medium of Sully, and defended their fortifications heroically. The effective force of the King was not nearly what it appeared to be on paper, and the troops suffered heavily during the siege. In November the siege became hopeless and was abandoned. The failure of the enterprise had considerably shaken the authority of Luynes; but all speculation about his future was cut short by his death through fever in Dec. 1621. There were some voices lifted for peace. Richelieu thought that foreign affairs were too embarrassing to allow of the prosecution of this domestic quarrel, and his ideas were presented to the King by Marie de Médicis. But Condé was for war, and he induced the King to go on with it. The Protestants were unable to offer any resistance in the open field. Soubise, the brother of the Duke of Rohan, at the head of a Protestant force, was defeated in April, at the Isle de Rié (a marshy district in lower Poitou). Several small towns fell into the King's hands; the capture of Negrepelisse in July was followed by a horrible butchery of men, women and children. In July, Lesdiguières, an old Huguenot who had not approved of the recent action of the party, abjured his faith and received the post of Constable, and other Protestants soon afterwards followed his example. Rochelle itself was threatened by the building of Fort St Louis, which commanded the canal that connected the harbour with the sea. Then in October the King advanced to the siege of Montpellier. The place was a very strong one, and the Duke of Rohan was prepared to defend it with vigour, while on the King's side there was some unwillingness on the part of the nobles to win a victory which would so largely increase his power. Lesdiguières negotiated a treaty with the rebellious Protestants, and the King accepted it in spite of the opposition of Condé. The treaty of Montpellier was signed on Oct. 19. The King promised to observe the Edict of Nantes, but the Protestants on their side were to hold no more political assemblies and to evacuate all their strong places, with the exception of Montauban and La Rochelle. The fortifications of Montpellier were destroyed, and the King entered the city. But it is clear that on this occasion, as on others during this period of intrigue, no final solution had been reached.

While the monarchy and the aristocracy, Catholicism and Protestantism were in France engaged in an indecisive contest, events of a more important kind were bringing on a great European struggle. In Germany the first movement of the Thirty

Richelieu enters the Council of the King.

Years' War had begun. The position there was such that war in the long run was inevitable. Religious, social, and dynastic questions pressed for a solution, and yet refused any other treatment than that of the sword. When Ferdinand, the head of the Catholic League, was elected Emperor in Aug. 1619, and when immediately afterwards Frederick, the Elector Palatine and son-in-law of James I of England, was chosen by the Protestants to be King of Bohemia, hostilities at once broke out. The real questions in this war—the most terrible that Europe has known in modern times—were first whether Protestantism in the country of its birth should be crushed out by the Catholic reaction; and, secondly, whether the House of Austria should succeed in converting the elective Empire from its old weak and inorganic condition into a vigorous and centralised monarchy, resting upon heredity. The Government of France might be pleased to see the weakening of Protestantism in Germany, but the most prominent characteristic of this last phase of the Reformation struggle is the subordination of theological and religious to political and dynastic objects. France was sure to regard with alarm the possibility of the establishment on her eastern frontier of a consolidated and energetic Empire, especially as it implied that Spain, the close ally of the Austrian House and the even more dangerous enemy of France, might again hope to become an overwhelming power in Europe. It seemed possible that Philip IV of Spain, who came to the throne in 1621, might be able to re-establish his kingdom in the position that she had held under Charles V. She was active everywhere. The interests of the House of Austria were identical with her own. A marriage between Charles, afterwards Charles I of England, and a Spanish Princess, seemed possible, and if accomplished would perhaps convert her most dangerous enemy into a useful ally.

At this moment the chief attention of Spain was directed to Italy. A single route—by the valley of the Valtelline—

From the death of Henry IV to the Peace of Alais. 203

connected her Italian possessions with the Empire. The position of Spain in the Valtelline was very unstable, for though the inhabitants of the valley were Catholics, yet their country belonged to the Protestant Grisons. A struggle between the two religions had resulted in a valuable gain to Spain. The Governor of Milan had induced the Grisons and the other claimants of the disputed territory to surrender their rights for a money payment, to allow the free passage of Spanish troops into and out of the Empire, and to admit Spanish garrisons into the chief towns of the Valtelline (1622). If this arrangement were made permanent, the situation of France would be very dangerous. The power of the Austro-Spanish House would surround her on all sides. The allies would command the whole course of the Rhine, and if the marriage of Charles of England with the Spanish Princess were carried out, would be superior to France on sea as well. But at first France seemed unable to resist. After the death of Luynes, power had passed into the hands of Sillery, an amiable but weak man, more energetic for the interests of his own family than for those of France. In Feb. 1623, a treaty was made between France, Venice and Savoy, for the restoration of the Valtelline to its former condition and ownership; but with Sillery in office and in power there was little chance of any effective action. The Pope was called in as arbitrator. His sympathies were of course with Spain. He induced the Spaniards to surrender their other claims, but granted them free passage from Italy into the Empire: it was the very thing most opposed to the interests of France. Little resistance was made to such a surrender to Spain, while Sillery was in office; but that minister soon fell. The Queen-mother, following, as usual, merely personal objects, was anxious to secure the hand of the English Prince for her own daughter, and Richelieu supported her while Sillery opposed. The King was not yet a serious force in politics, and consequently Sillery was dismissed in Jan. 1624. His fall gave power at first into the hands of

La Vieuville, the superintendent of finances. But he had not the talents that the critical situation of France demanded. The Queen had meanwhile been reconciled to the King, and regained something of her former influence over him. Thus it came about that in April 1624, Richelieu, then thirty-eight years of age and the Queen's chief adviser, entered the King's Council. La Vieuville's influence was at once weakened by contrast with Richelieu's energy and decision of character. There were rumours, too, that La Vieuville's hands were not clean in matters of finance. He was arrested in August, and imprisoned at Amboise. Richelieu became at once the chief of the Council. Henceforth until the time of his death he is the protagonist on the European stage.

Jean Armand du Plessis, Cardinal de Richelieu, was the son of a nobleman, who, though a Catholic, had attached himself to the fortunes of Henry of Navarre. The young Armand had at first been intended for the army, and had gone through some training with that end in view; but his weak health and the prospect of the bishopric of Luçon, an unimportant diocese in lower Poitou, brought about a change in his career. He took orders, and in December, 1608, became Bishop. He busied himself during his early tenure of office with the ordering of his diocese and with religious controversy. In 1614 he was one of the representatives of the Clergy at the States General, and was chosen to present their views to the Queen-mother. He had attached himself to her party, and had been introduced by Marshal d'Ancre into the ministry. D'Ancre's fall brought about Richelieu's retirement. The new Government suspected him, and he was at one time banished to Avignon. But he attached himself again to the fortunes of the Queen, and was the chief instrument in bringing about a reconciliation between mother and son at the time of the battle of Pont de Cé. His energy and decision of character impressed all who approached him. One writer had already called him "an intellect (*esprit*) to which God had set no limits." And Sully declared that the King had been guided by God in choosing Richelieu for his minister. But his accession to office in 1624 alarmed no one. It was even thought by some that the appointment was rather in the interests of the Nobility. Richelieu himself seems to have been in some doubt as to the line that he should follow. He thought of social and domestic reforms—the abolition of the purchase and heredity of offices, the diminution of taxation, the abolition of privilege. But foreign affairs were too pressing. It was to them that he first applied his unsurpassed energy and genius.

The career that now begins is not only one of the most important in French and European history, it is also one of the most paradoxical. Richelieu was always weak in health and often reported to be dying, and yet he dominated Europe at an epoch of great confusion and violence, when every question, political or religious, seemed to be settled by an appeal to physical force. He was a Cardinal of the Church of Rome and unquestionably loyal to its doctrines; but this ecclesiastic conducted campaigns and sieges in person, while subordinate commands were entrusted to other ecclesiastics, to Cardinals, Archbishops and Bishops, and his most trusted diplomatic agents were friars and priests. Not only did he thus engage in military operations that seemed unsuitable to his calling, but further, outside of France, he was usually engaged on the side of Protestantism and in opposition to the forces of the Catholic reaction. It was he who interfered in Germany when the cause of Protestantism seemed lost and all the country seemed likely to fall before the Catholic reaction guided by the Jesuits; he who first by diplomacy, and then by open military action succeeded in giving the Protestant States a dominant position over a great part of Germany. No wonder that his enemies called him the "Pope of the Huguenots and the Patriarch of atheists." If we look from Richelieu's foreign to his domestic policy the paradox is hardly less striking. His one great effort was to build up the power of the monarchy; but we find him in constant conflict with the chief members of the royal house. The King did indeed in the end support him loyally, and his personal dislike for his great minister has no doubt been exaggerated; but it is certain that he felt no real affection for Richelieu, and yielded reluctantly to his influence. With all the other members of the royal household he was in constant and bitter opposition. The King's brother—the despicable and vicious Gaston of Orléans—passed his life in fruitless intrigues against the Cardinal's power and person. The Queen-mother—the Cardinal's first patron—passed into bitter hostility to him when she found that his loyalty had been to the institution of Monarchy, not to herself as its personal occupant, and she ended her days in exile as the penalty of failure in her plots against him. The Queen herself hardly concealed her hatred of him and was willing to join in plots against his life.

The ready explanation of these paradoxes is to be found in the fact that, though a Cardinal of the Church of Rome, he was a politician before he was a churchman. Though he strained every nerve to strengthen the Monarchy, he had none of the personal feeling for the King that the English cavaliers had for their sovereign; it was rather the Crown that he regarded as the symbol of national unity and national strength. Two extracts from writings that were drawn up, either by himself or under his direction, give us in the direct and definite way that he loved, the key to his career. The first is from the beginning of his *Succinct Narration of the great actions of the King*, which is the first part of his political testament.

"When your Majesty determined to grant me admission to your councils and a great part in your confidence, and in the direction of affairs, I can say with truth that the Huguenots shared the State with you, the nobles conducted themselves as if they had not been subjects, and the most powerful provincial governors as if they had been absolute in authority. The wisest thought that it was impossible to pass without shipwreck all the dangers that threatened in that troubled time,... but in spite of all the difficulties, knowing how great the power of Kings is when they make a proper use of their power, I ventured to promise you that you would find a remedy for the disorders of the state....I promised to employ all the authority that you were pleased to give me to ruin the Huguenot party, to bring down the pride of the nobles, to bring back all your subjects to their duty and to raise your name among foreign nations to the honour that ought of right to belong to it." By the side of this we may put a few sentences drawn from the preface to the political testament. "This was the aim of my ministry—to restore to France the limits which nature has fixed, to place a French King over all Frenchmen, to identify Gaul with France, and wherever there had been the ancient Gaul there to establish the new. Three things opposed my wishes. France resisted, herself her own enemy; Spain resisted, for she thought that she could bring the whole world under one house if she could make France a part of that house; the neighbouring peoples resisted, friendly to Spain because they dared not be her enemies. To break through these obstacles I reconciled France to herself, in order that she might be an enemy to those that were without; I gave Spain occupation at home that she might cease to be troublesome abroad; I showed her allies the way to freedom and forced some to be free against their will. Gaul was possessed by two evils—heresy and liberty—and both were set right by the arms of Louis and my councils[1]."

[1] It may be well to notice here that Richelieu was already connected with the Capucin Friar, Father Joseph (Francois Le Clerc du Tremblay), who becomes subsequently his chief agent in all his most important diplomatic missions. Father Joseph's character, though the chief facts of his career are now well known (thanks mainly to M. Fagniez' *le Père Joseph et Richelieu*) remains something of a puzzle. The two parts of his life, the religious and the political, are so difficult to harmonise that his first biographer wrote of them separately. He was on the one hand a devout and enthusiastic friar, devout even to fanaticism. He founded a new

Richelieu hardly felt himself secure in his office, before he began his attack upon Spain. He strongly supported the marriage of Charles I with Henrietta Maria, the King's sister, which took place in May, 1625. Before that he had already interfered in the Valtelline question. The Marquis of Cœuvres was sent to Switzerland, and as an ally of the Grisons League he invaded the Valtelline with a force of a thousand troops (Nov. 1624). The papal garrisons were everywhere driven out and the whole valley was occupied by French troops. This important channel of communication was thus decisively blocked against the Spaniards and Imperialists. Spain was not prepared to submit to such an arrangement, and everything seemed to point to a war. But while Richelieu was fighting for Protestants in Italy he found his position endangered by a rising of Protestants at home. The same position meets us on several occasions during his career. The Protestant leaders of France were sincere in their faith for the most part, but they were aristocrats as well, and many of them were chiefly attracted to Protestantism by the cloak it afforded for political resistance to the Crown. Richelieu's triumphs might benefit Protestantism, but they would also strengthen the Crown, and thus tend to curb the power of the aristocracy. The nobles were ready therefore to use every opportunity afforded by the great minister's complications abroad to stir up resistance at home, and did not

religious order (the Calvairiennes) and devoted to its direction all the time that he could spare from politics; he worked hard and with some success at the conversion of the Protestants of France, and to the last he prayed and hoped for the union of Christendom in a quite impossible crusade against the Turk. But at the same time he supported and sometimes even suggested Richelieu's foreign policy of Protestant alliance against the Catholic power of Austria and Spain. The union between the two statesmen was of the closest, and some have even imagined that Richelieu was little more than the agent of his unseen adviser. M. Fagniez' book lends no support to such a view. Richelieu was incomparably the saner and more comprehensive statesman, and Father Joseph's death did not interrupt for a moment the course of Richelieu's policy.

even shrink from asking the assistance of Spain. Such a use they made of the present opportunity. Soubise attacked the harbour of Blavet in Normandy (Jan. 1625), and though he was driven out he found himself still master of a considerable squadron that gave him the command of the seas, and allowed him to occupy the island of Rhé. Not only the aristocratic leaders of Protestantism, but even their humble followers felt that they had a grievance against the Government of France. The fort of St Louis had not been demolished; many promises made at the treaty of Montpellier had not been kept. The city of La Rochelle joined Soubise; Languedoc rose; the whole of the south was in commotion. There were some at court who urged the opportunity of a religious war and the entire extirpation of Protestantism. But Richelieu gave no ear to these. His one desire was to settle the question at home, in order that he might pursue his anti-Spanish schemes, and he thought that the question might be settled by a compromise. Therefore he fought against the Huguenots and offered them terms at the same time. Ships were borrowed from England and Holland, and against the real desires of these Protestant States, were used to crush the rebellion of the French Protestants. Soubise was beaten and the island of Rhé occupied. La Rochelle itself was hard pressed. At last the Huguenots listened to the overtures that were made to them through the English ambassador. In Feb. 1626, peace was made: Fort St Louis and the Islands of Oléron and Rhé remained in the hands of the King. The terms of the treaty of Montpellier were accepted on both sides. But the diplomatic world was astonished to find that this treaty was not the only one that had been made. While many thought that Richelieu's only object in making peace with the Huguenots was to get his arms free to strike a blow against Spain, it was discovered that an arrangement had been come to about the Valtelline, and peace had been made. The circumstances under which the treaty was signed are still to some extent obscure.

Richelieu, in his memoirs and in the "Succinct Narration," states in the most positive terms that the negotiations were carried on behind his back and against his will[1]; but there is considerable doubt whether this is exactly true. In any case it is clear that Richelieu was not yet as fully master of the Court and the Throne as he subsequently became. A personal danger of the gravest kind was hanging over him, and this may have induced him to accept the treaty. It was signed in its final form at Barcelona on May 10. The sovereignty of the Valtelline was to be restored to the Grisons and the forts were to be destroyed.

Besides the open enemies that Richelieu had to struggle against throughout his career, besides the power of Spain and Austria, the discontented nobles and the recalcitrant Huguenots, he had also to be continually on his guard against intrigues of the Court. And these intrigues aimed not only at his expulsion from power; assassination had been used so frequently against political opponents, and with such striking success, that it naturally suggested itself to the opponents of the cardinal-minister, and they were not too scrupulous to harbour the idea.

The fall of Rochelle and the destruction of the political privileges of the Protestants.

No one saw the increase in the power of the Crown with more jealousy than those who stood nearest to the throne. They had been accustomed to regard some participation in public affairs as their right, and saw with indignation the monopoly of all power by the Cardinal. The centre of all these discontents was Gaston of Orléans, the King's brother. He was only seventeen years of age, and the first intrigue might

---

[1] Richelieu's words in the "Succinct Narration" are: "Your majesty would have freed for ever the Grisons from the tyranny of the House of Austria if Fargis, your ambassador in Spain, had not, upon the solicitation of Cardinal de Berulle, without your knowledge and against your express orders concluded a very disadvantageous treaty to which your majesty adhered from a wish to please the Pope."

be pardoned as an indiscretion of youth, had it not been followed by a long series of similar escapades. He was much under the influence of Ornano, his tutor, a Corsican by birth, who thought to win a place for Gaston in the Council, and thereby great influence for himself. The King wished Gaston to marry Mdlle de Montpensier, the richest heiress of France, and Ornano tried to turn him away from this project by suggesting the great advantage which would come to him by marriage with some foreign princess. Gaston was admitted to the Council, but Ornano was not satisfied. He began to form a party of opponents to the Cardinal, and negotiated with the King's natural brothers, with the Duke of Vendôme and the Grand Prior[1]. Richelieu was well served by spies, and the matter soon reached his ears. He persuaded the King that prompt action was necessary, and arrested Ornano at Fontainebleau on May 4. He was sent to the Bastille, where he subsequently died. The suddenness of the blow disconcerted the confederates; Vendôme hastened to submit; Gaston humiliated himself before the King, promised to reveal all plots that were made against the throne, and on that condition received an amnesty. But he could not live without intrigue, and soon a more dangerous plot was preparing. The Comte de Chalais had taken the place of Ornano, and, if at first faithful to Richelieu, was soon won over to the malcontents. The Duchess of Chevreuse, the widow of the Duke of Luynes, had been especially active in seducing Chalais from his allegiance to the King. It was asserted at his trial that he had planned to kill the King, and proposed that Gaston should then marry Anne of Austria. But Richelieu again received information in time. Chalais was seized and executed. Once more and by no means for the last time Gaston had to throw himself upon the King's mercy. Forgiveness was promised him, and he was made Duke of Orléans; but he had to consent to marry Mdlle de Montpensier. The most important result of these

[1] Both of them children of Henry IV and Gabrielle d'Estrées.

events was to increase still further the power of Richelieu over the King. The King wrote his minister a letter, which amounts almost to an oath of fidelity. He promised to have no secrets from his minister: "I will protect you against all enemies. Be sure that, whoever attacks you, you may rely on my support."

In Dec. 1626 Richelieu called an assembly of Notables to give his policy an appearance of popularity. He never appealed to the States General, and he set his face against the pretensions of the Parlement, but at many critical points in his career he called to his side the Notables—nominees of the Crown, but perhaps as fairly representative of public opinion as the States General had been. The assembly of 1626 consisted of 12 members of the lower Nobility and 29 officers of justice and finance. No duke or peer or Governor of a Province was admitted. This assembly seconded the policy of Richelieu on every important point. The members supported the creation of a standing army and of a strong navy, and the abolition of the titles of admiral and constable, which seemed to limit the authority of the King in military matters. They urged that vigorous measures should be taken against the rebels, and that the pensions given to nobles should be diminished. Above all they urged the destruction of such castles as could offer resistance to the royal troops, and they drew up a list of such fortresses. Throughout France the work of demolition began. The common people rejoiced to see the noble strongholds reduced; a French proverb had long connected the poverty of the country with the number of the nobles' castles.

Richelieu had gained for his policy a certain measure of popular support, but a struggle was now impending in which he would need support of every kind; for it was clear that another and more decisive contest would have to be waged with the Huguenots. Their relations with the Government could not permanently subsist on their present footing. Religious feeling in France was extremely bitter; more bitter among the masses than among the leaders of France. Catholic preachers, usually of an obscure and vulgar kind, stirred the fires of fanaticism, and pointed to the Huguenots as the cause of all public disasters. The Government found it difficult and sometimes impossible to repress the disturbances that inevitably sprung from such preaching. If the Huguenots were less violent it was from lack of power rather than of will. The doctrines of Catholicism were constantly insulted in their sermons, and in the towns where they were masters, Catholic worship was either entirely forbidden or only allowed under humiliating limitations. But the actual outbreak of hostilities came through foreign interference. The marriage of Charles I with the King's sister, Henrietta Maria, had entirely failed to bring about any firm alliance between the two countries: rather it had become a ground of quarrel. According to the first arrangements, the Queen had been allowed a Roman Catholic service for herself and her suite; but the Puritan susceptibilities of England were offended, and in June, 1626, the whole of the Queen's French attendants were dismissed to France. To this cause of friction was added another, for England feared the rivalry of the French navy which Richelieu was now so industriously building up. The Duke of Buckingham had his own personal grievances against the French Court, and was eager for a war in which he might play a leading part. To declare war against the French King on behalf of his Protestant subjects might moreover do something to abate the determined hostility of the English Parliament.

At the same time the Huguenots were restless and suspicious of the Government. Fort St Louis in the hands of the King was a standing threat to La Rochelle, their capital. Their privileges were constantly neglected or trampled on. There was all the material for a dangerous insurrection, and the English Government determined to take advantage of it. No definite arrangement was come to with La Rochelle, but the support of the city was held to be certain, and in July, 1627, Buckingham, with nearly 100 ships, appeared off the coast of France Richelieu's position was a very dangerous one. Fort St Louis was scantily garrisoned: if Buckingham had attacked it at once it would almost certainly have fallen. In March a treaty had been made between France and Spain for resistance to England; but Richelieu more than suspected the intentions of the Spaniards, and feared more than he hoped from their intervention. Worst of all the King was at this time seriously ill, and Richelieu could not leave his side lest he should fall under dangerous influences: yet he could not so much as speak to his master of the great danger that was threatening the State.

Had Buckingham acted with insight and vigour, a large measure of success was assured to him. But he seems to have made mistake after mistake. Instead of attacking Fort St Louis he preferred to secure his footing first in one of the islands off the coast. He landed in the island of Rhé, though Oléron is judged to have offered greater advantages, and even after he had landed he seems to have conducted his operations against Fort St Martin with little skill or vigour. These delays gave Richelieu time for preparations; the King recovered from his illness. Cardinal and King came down to the theatre of war at the beginning of October. Buckingham was then pressing Fort St Martin very closely. Richelieu determined to relieve it at all risks, and, in spite of the superiority of the English fleet, it was relieved. Buckingham thereupon abandoned the siege, and on November 17, 1627, set sail for England, having lost half his men in this miserably conducted expedition. He left behind him the Protestants exposed to the anger of the King and the Cardinal. Though there were Protestants under arms in the Cevennes and in Languedoc, La Rochelle was still, as it had always been, the real centre of French Protestantism, and therefore, while Condé was sent against the insurgents of Languedoc, Richelieu went with the King and the greater portion of the army against La Rochelle. The siege presented very great difficulties. The King's forces were indeed able to blockade the place on the land side; but the sea was open, and so long as the sea remained open the population, consisting largely of sailors, would be able to secure a supply of provisions and prolong the siege indefinitely. Relying on this the inhabitants faced the siege hopefully. To frustrate such hopes, Richelieu determined to close the entrance of the harbour against them. Modern engineering might make light of the task, but it seemed a gigantic undertaking to the 17th century, and Richelieu compares it in his memoirs to the mole whereby Alexander the Great captured Tyre. The idea had been suggested years before by an Italian engineer; it was now carried out on a more elaborate scale by the French architects Métézeau and Tiriot. A mole of masonry was run out on either side of the estuary; some 1700 yards in all had to be guarded. A wide space had to be left in the centre to admit of the movement of the tides. This opening was guarded by a stockade and a line of sunken ships. When the mole was completed, Richelieu abandoned all attempts at storming La Rochelle, and simply waited for famine to do its work upon the inhabitants. His own situation was a very critical one; victory would secure his position with the King, but failure would probably ruin his influence entirely. He could rely on the courage and fidelity of his soldiers, but not on his officers or on the nobles, who knew that the cause of La Rochelle was identical with their own. There were many of them who would have welcomed a failure that would have undermined their great opponent's position. As he dared not trust the nobles, he employed churchmen for the chief commands. Among his chief supporters were Sourdis, Bishop of Maillezais, the Bishop of Mende, and the Abbé of Marcillac. But Richelieu had to superintend everything himself, and under his superintendence nothing went amiss. The most perfect discipline was maintained in his army, and his plans and the character of his works called forth the admiration of Ambrose Spinola, the great Spanish commander.

But the stubbornness of the defence corresponded to the skill of the attack. The danger and distress roused the religious fanaticism of the inhabitants to the highest pitch. The mayor, Guiton, was the soul of the resistance. His naked dagger lay permanently on the council table as a warning against all proposals of surrender. So long as there were hands left to close the gates he said the siege should continue. He was powerfully supported by Salbert, a Huguenot minister, and by the aged Duchess of Rohan, who inspired the inhabitants with patience, by herself submitting to all the rigours of the siege. But the heroic courage of the besieged could not hold out in the long run against the deadly pressure of famine. The only hope was in English help. In May, 1628, English ships appeared, inspected and cannonaded the mole, but judged it too strong to be forced and sailed away again. The feelings of England were deeply stirred by the sufferings of the Protestants of La Rochelle, and another fleet was equipped. Buckingham was to command it, but he was assassinated on August 23, just as he was about to set out, and the fleet sailed under Lord Lindsay. Fire ships were sent against the mole, and there was an engagement between the fleets; but the English were in the end driven off, and the people of La Rochelle saw with despair their last hope disappear. And yet they refused to yield. More than three weeks passed, bringing famine fiercer than before, and disease in its train, before the stubborn city consented to surrender. More than half of the population had died of hunger, the rest had suffered terribly. On October 30, the gates were thrown open and Richelieu entered on horseback. Two days later he celebrated mass in the chief church of the place. A little later, when the King made his triumphant entry, the honours bestowed on the Cardinal seemed to rival his own. The fortifications of La Rochelle were destroyed, and its political privileges were taken away.

There were Protestant rebels still under arms, but the fall of La Rochelle made their overthrow a certainty, if Richelieu persisted in his attack upon them. His attention, however, was again turned to Italy. No sooner had the Valtelline question been settled than another rose of equal or greater importance. For the succession to the Dukedom of Mantua and the Marquisate of Montferrat was vacant. The situation of these territories, quite apart from their intrinsic value, made them much coveted, and now it was uncertain whether they would fall to France or Spain. Vincenzo di Gonzaga, the last Duke, had died on Dec. 26, 1627. His next heir was unquestionably a French subject, the Duke of Nevers, who had strengthened his own right by marrying his son to the niece of the deceased Duke. The legal point seems to have been clear, but Spain could not allow these important territories to pass without a struggle into the hands of France. The Duke of Guastalla, a more distant relative of the late Duke, was put forward as the Spanish candidate for Mantua; and the Duke of Nevers was declared to have forfeited his rights by bearing arms against the Emperor. At the same time the Duke of Savoy claimed Montferrat. Spain had already taken up arms to enforce this claim, and Spanish troops under Don Gonzales laid siege to Casale, a fortress whose position on the Po gave it very great military importance. Casale was defended by French volunteers, but without direct assistance could not hope to hold out for long. If it was to be saved it must be relieved at once, and Richelieu determined to relieve it at once. He put his plans before the King: the embers of the Protestant revolt were to be left to smoulder until the King had time to extinguish them; meanwhile the victorious French army was to cross the Alps in winter and descend upon the Spaniards. He won the King to the side of his grandiose projects, and in Feb. 1629 the King and Cardinal joined the army at Grenoble. The army was not properly ready; the King was inclined at the last moment to shrink from the danger of the enterprise; Charles Emmanuel negotiated and wasted time, and seemed inclined to refuse a passage to the French troops. But Richelieu's energy triumphed over all. The preparations were pushed on and the King was convinced of the feasibility of the enterprise; if the Duke would not grant them a passage, it was determined to force one. On March 6 the French army entered the pass of Susa. It was for a mile or so a narrow gorge defended by barricades and fortifications; but the defence was weakly conducted, and the French attack carried all before it. The Duke of Savoy himself nearly fell into the hands of the French, and soon after signed a treaty whereby he surrendered Susa to the French garrison, granted free passage to the French troops through his territories, and promised to send provisions to the garrison at Casale. The Spaniards at once abandoned the siege of that fortress. The French expedition had been a very brilliant success, and Richelieu, who knew not only when to advance but also when to stop, refused to push the Spaniards further, and turned back to administer the *coup de grâce* to the Huguenot rebellion which was assuming a somewhat dangerous phase.

The fiery Duke of Rohan was commander in Languedoc. He was consumed with a desire to be revenged on the Government, and was willing to use any means that would bring him to that end. In April, 1629, his chief hope disappeared, for in that month France concluded a peace with England. The English Queen's French household was not recalled, but Charles consented to abandon the Huguenots. Thereupon Rohan, disappointed in London, turned to Madrid. It was a strange expedient, and Philip's acceptance of the overture shows us how, during this last phase of the Reformation struggle, political and dynastic ambition overpowered religious sympathies and dislikes. Philip IV promised to assist the Huguenots with men and money, and the Duke of Rohan undertook on his side to prolong the war according to the pleasure of Spain. The only religious stipulation was that if the Protestants of France succeeded in founding a separate republic, Roman Catholicism should be tolerated in it. It is a stipulation which reveals the aims of the Protestants, and in a large measure justifies the action of Richelieu against them. But Richelieu was upon them before Spanish help could arrive. Privas, the chief Protestant stronghold of the Vivarais, was captured, and suffered murder, pillage and outrage of the most terrible kind. Richelieu tells us in his memoirs that the perpetration of these cruelties was against his desire and his orders; but at least it assisted his plans. For while Privas afforded an example of what stubborn resistance might expect, he was offering at the same time reasonable terms to those who submitted. Alais, in the Cevennes, was the next place attacked: though Rohan attempted to relieve it, it capitulated on June 15. Rohan had the sense to see that further resistance could only bring more disasters on his co-religionists. He counselled them to accept the terms that were offered, and himself withdrew into exile. By the treaty of Alais, published on June 28, 1629, the toleration accorded by the treaty of Nantes was reaffirmed. Richelieu advised the Huguenots to trust rather to the word of a King than to walls and bastions. All places of security were given up; all separate political privileges were to be abolished; but the King granted freedom of worship and an open career for Protestants, and complete amnesty for the past. Upon these terms even Montauban surrendered (Aug. 1629).

The treaty of Alais is remarkable. No nation in Europe at this moment gave such freedom and protection to religious dissidents. The Roman Catholics in England were in an immeasurably worse position than the Protestants of France, and for more than two centuries were to struggle in vain to acquire the liberty and the open career that were accorded to the Huguenots by the peace of Alais. This part of Richelieu's work has not received sufficient recognition, and yet no part of it is more remarkable. His victory at Rochelle gives us the measure of his energy and skill in organisation and in war; but the use which he made of that victory marks him as the greatest statesman of the period.

Here the separate history of French Protestantism ends. Henceforth, for good or evil, the Protestants are merged in the national existence and never again threaten the Government. We are obliged to confess that what had happened to them had been rendered necessary by the attitude that they had taken up. They were a serious hindrance to the consolidation of France and the strengthening of the monarchy; a hindrance therefore to the progress of Europe and the establishment of that religious equilibrium from which Protestantism was to gain so much. Richelieu stands acquitted of unnecessary harshness in his relations with them. It was, he insisted, only against a dangerous faction that he fought, not against their faith: for that, he said (and the words are very remarkable), "we must trust to Providence, and bring no force to bear against it except the force of a good life and a good example." If only his solution had been made permanent! But if Richelieu had the great man's power of stopping in his advance when the right point had been reached, the Catholics of France were not prepared to accept the treaty of 1629 as final. The Church clamoured again and again for more persecution, and the Catholic feeling of France responded to that cry. It is noticeable that Richelieu, in his writings, nowhere takes credit to himself or the Government for having left to the Protestants the measure of religious liberty that they enjoyed after the Peace of Alais. In his "Succinct Narration" he does not mention it. He nowhere prides himself on his superiority to religious fanaticism, and his alliance with Protestant powers is a thing that he apologises for, on the ground of necessity, instead of claiming as a virtue. Public opinion and the opinion of the Court doubtless made such a tone inevitable, even to the great Minister. And so, in the end, the Protestants of France found how little reliance there was to be placed "in the word of a King," and sixty years after the peace of Alais comes the Revocation of the Edict of Nantes.

CHAPTER VIII.

RICHELIEU SUPREME IN FRANCE.

THE fall of La Rochelle is one of the most important points in Richelieu's career. It immensely strengthened his influence with the King, for the victory was one which Louis's narrow and fanatical mind highly appreciated. And further, it removed one of the three great difficulties that Richelieu had to contend with. Hitherto he had had to watch the proceedings of the enemies of France, to follow and repress the intrigues that were constantly being formed against him at Court, and to be on his guard against the Protestant and aristocratic revolt that was always possible in the south of France. After 1629, the last danger, if it does not disappear entirely, is at least reduced to comparatively insignificant proportions. Richelieu could now give his main attention to foreign complications and dangers, hindered only by the hostility of Court circles, which showed itself again and again in dangerous but abortive plots.

The position after the fall of Rochelle.

Foreign affairs demanded the most careful scrutiny and the most vigilant and energetic statesmanship. The war in Germany seemed to be no nearer its end than before, but it was passing through a phase less favourable to the interests and pretensions of the Emperor and the Roman Catholic reaction. The questions that had caused the outbreak of hostilities were being lost sight of. The claim of Frederick, the Elector Palatine, to the throne of Bohemia, was no longer the real point at issue. Would the generals of the Emperor Ferdinand, Tilly and Wallenstein, be able to crush the Protestants in the North as they had crushed those of the South? Would the Imperial authority be raised to an absolute supremacy in Germany such as it had not possessed for centuries? These were the questions, full of importance for every State in Europe, that were now agitating European diplomacy. The Duke of Friedland, or Wallenstein, to give him the name by which he is best known to history, had in 1628 sought to secure the shores of the Baltic so as to prevent foreign succour from reaching the Protestants of the North, but his attempt to capture the harbour of Stralsund had failed. The burghers had fought with a courage that was fired by religious ardour; no blockade could be established on the side of the sea, and in the end Wallenstein had to withdraw and confess to his first check. In the next year (1629) the Emperor Ferdinand had issued his Edict of Restitution, whereby a vast amount of ecclesiastical property which had for a long time been in the undisturbed possession of the Protestants was to be given to the Catholics. The terms of the Edict were enforced by the soldiers of Wallenstein with an indiscriminate barbarity which spared neither Catholics nor Protestants. The Edict gave a new and most effective reason for Protestant resistance.

And yet the Protestants could not hope for victory without foreign assistance. No really great German had appeared on the Protestant side, either to suggest a policy or to guide armies. Their cause had been endangered by the rivalries and hostilities of Lutherans and Calvinists, and any united resistance to the Catholic reaction had thus been made very difficult if not impossible. But for foreign assistance they would probably have been in a worse plight than they actually were. Christian of Denmark had been their first champion, but he had been defeated by Tilly, at Lutter, in 1626. But now another and a far greater champion was preparing to enter the lists on their behalf. Gustavus Adolphus, King of Sweden, had viewed the misfortunes of his fellow Protestants with sympathy, and had cherished thoughts of interfering on their behalf. When Wallenstein occupied the Baltic coast and acquired Mecklenburg for himself, these thoughts became more definite. Richelieu was not ready as yet to interfere directly in the German war, even if he entertained the idea of doing so eventually. He wished rather to resist the Emperor's policy by indirect means, and the project of the Swedish King was therefore very welcome to him. No one foresaw, not even Gustavus Adolphus himself, the nature and results of his actual interference in Germany. His military genius and his decision of character were not suspected by Richelieu. He saw in him a valuable instrument for his German plans, and hoped that he would be able to curb him if he attempted to go too far. Father Joseph, the intimate friend and confidant of Richelieu, spoke of his interference in Germany as "a poison, useful up to a certain point as an antidote, fatal if used to excess." In September, 1629, the very capable French diplomatist Charnacé had negotiated a truce of six years between Sweden and Poland, so that the hands of the Swedish King were comparatively free. In March, 1630, this was followed by a proposal for a treaty between France and Sweden for six years; Gustavus was to land in Germany with 30,000 foot-soldiers, and the King of France promised on his side to contribute 400,000 crowns a year for the maintenance of the army[1]. A new and wonderful chapter of German history was about to open.

But while Richelieu thus interfered diplomatically in Germany to resist the advance of the Empire, it was necessary to strike a more direct blow in Italy against the allied and related power of Spain. The relief of Casale in March, 1629, had not settled the Mantuan question. The Huguenot movement had hardly been struck down by the peace of Alais before Richelieu found it necessary to turn to Italy, where Mantua and

[1] This is the treaty of Bärwalde, definitely signed in Jan. 1631.

Montferrat were being assaulted by an Imperial and Spanish force under Colalto and Spinola. Richelieu faced the crisis much more vigorously than he had been able to do while the Huguenots still threatened his rear. In November, 1629, he was solemnly declared principal Minister of State, and in December he passed into Italy with the title of "Lieutenant-General, representing the person of the King in his army both within and beyond the Kingdom." It was really absolute authority that he exercised in the King's name. The Duke of Savoy had fallen away from France; the greater energy shown by Spain and the Empire made him hope for better things from them. But the punishment for his vacillation fell on him very quickly. Richelieu, throwing aside all appearance of the Cardinal, turned energetically to the war. On the 20th of March, 1630, he unexpectedly attacked Pinerolo, and this place, so immensely important as a gate of entry into Italy, fell into the hands of France on the next day. It was determined then to turn the arms of France directly against Savoy, and Louis XIII, who never lost his fondness for war, joined Richelieu in order to superintend, in name at least, the military operations. They gained an easy success, culminating in the capture of Chambéry on May 16. But now Louis, frightened by an outbreak of pestilence, retired to Lyons, and Richelieu was so much afraid of the intrigues that were undermining his position that he determined to accompany him. The royal forces were placed under the command of Montmorency and d'Effiat, and they continued the course of success. The Duke of Savoy was defeated at Vegliana in a battle where the bad generalship of the French commanders was compensated for by the courage of the soldiers. But a few days later came bad news that more than counterbalanced this victory; Mantua was taken by Colalto on July 18, and was delivered over to rapine and pillage for three days.

At this point events in Germany and Italy, which had always been closely connected, combine in a single chain

Richelieu supreme in France.

of cause and effect. The Emperor had called a Diet at Ratisbon, in June, 1630. He had hoped to get his son elected King of the Romans, but he found the Diet in no mood of passive obedience. The bitterest dislike was expressed for the vast power, the unlimited pretensions and the arbitrary conduct of Wallenstein. The Diet demanded his dismissal as the first condition of all concessions on their part. Léon de Brulart was there as French ambassador, with the Capucin monk, Father Joseph, as his unofficial colleague, and they of course supported a demand, the granting of which would so immensely weaken the Imperial power. They gained, by whatever means, an extraordinary ascendancy over the Diet. Richelieu says in his memoirs that the Electors were said to be in the allegiance of the French King, and certainly they adopted the line of policy which was most in harmony with the interests of France. There is no occasion on which the mysterious personality of Father Joseph proved more serviceable to Richelieu. The Emperor found himself forced to submit. Wallenstein retired into Bohemia for a time, and seemed to carry the Imperial sceptre with him. The Emperor found himself deprived of his greatest general at the very time when Gustavus was about to begin his amazing career. And even at this price he did not procure the election of his son as King of the Romans.

It was soon apparent how much the decision told in favour of France. If the Emperor were deprived of the services of Wallenstein he could hardly hope to conquer his united enemies. It would be necessary to conciliate some. Should the Edict of Restitution be withdrawn to conciliate the Protestants of Germany, or should French hostility be bought off by the abandonment of the position that the Imperial troops had won in Italy? Victory in Italy lay by no means so near to the heart of the Emperor as victory in Germany. On the 13th October a treaty was signed at Ratisbon. By this the Duke of Nevers was to be installed in Mantua and Montferrat, despite Colalto's recent victory, and the Dukes of Savoy and

Guastalla were to receive some compensation for the abandonment of their claims. The Imperial troops were to withdraw from the Valtelline. France on her side promised to give no further help, direct or indirect, to the enemies of the Emperor. The negotiations that issued in this treaty and the treaty itself have given rise to endless discussion: for Richelieu no sooner became acquainted with the terms than he protested against them, maintained that in agreeing to them Brulart and Father Joseph had exceeded their powers, and refused to ratify what had been agreed upon. For this refusal he has been charged by an eminent historian with deliberate fraud. But the latest treatment of the subject seems to make it clear that the envoys had really gone beyond their instructions, by which they were confined to Italian affairs[1]; that the pressing anxieties of domestic policy had prevented Richelieu from communicating with them as often as they had expected him to do; and that his indignation with the terms of the treaty was genuine, and expressed in private as well as public. Father Joseph was recalled to Paris; Brulart was sent back to Vienna to negotiate an alteration in the terms. In the end, what had been agreed on for Italy was in the main followed, but we shall see how far Richelieu was from ceasing to support the enemies of the Emperor in Germany. Despite the repudiation of the treaty, hostilities were soon arrested in Italy. After the battle of Vegliana and the fall of Mantua, a truce had been arranged that was to last until October 15th. Hostilities recommenced on that date. The French army, therefore, on the expiration of the term, set out for the relief of Casale, where a French garrison was holding out in the castle against a Spanish force. Marshal Schomberg had received news of the treaty of Ratisbon, but he was sufficiently in Richelieu's secrets to refuse

[1] Fagniez (*Le Père Joseph et Richelieu*, Vol. I. p. 502) thus sums up his judgment on the question: "The Plenipotentiaries had not acted on their own responsibility as much as Richelieu alleged; but they had done so sufficiently to give ground for his disavowal."

to abide by it. He gave orders for the attack. The battle was about to begin, when Mazarin, a Papal agent, dashed between the lines and waved a paper containing the terms of another agreement. Casale was to be surrendered by Spain and France into the hands of the Duke of Mantua, on condition that he maintained there an exclusively native garrison.

But at this point interest in the foreign negotiations and in military affairs was suspended for a time by an extraordinary Court intrigue, which seemed likely at one time to overthrow Richelieu just when the importance of his influence in Europe was beginning to appear. *Richelieu and the Queen-mother. The Day of Dupes.*

We have already noted the paradoxical character of Richelieu's career. Quite apart from the interests that he irritated or trampled on there was something in the undefined character of his position that provoked opposition. His power was not a constitutional one; he had no tradition behind him to appeal to. He was partly the King's favourite and partly his master. It was sincerely believed by some that the King would welcome his overthrow. The number of his enemies at Court was very large. Nobles who had been slighted by him, rivals who had been outstripped by him, Catholics who thought that he tampered with heresy, disappointed place-hunters—all were ready to conspire against him. The centre of the whole conspiracy was the Queen-mother herself, and Gaston, the King's brother, was now as always ready for intrigue against the Cardinal Minister.

The plot began at Lyons, where in September the King lay seriously ill, almost abandoned by the doctors. The last sacraments were administered to him, and everyone was thinking of the new *régime* and of those who would fall and of those who would rise. But the King suddenly recovered enough to go to Paris. The Queen-mother, the Queen, and Richelieu accompanied him, and the plot still went feverishly on, Marie de Médicis especially throwing prudence to the winds in her anxiety to destroy the hated Cardinal. The King's part all through is somewhat difficult to understand. He was a man of lethargic temperament, deficient in energy, whether for speech, thought or action, and yet capable of much stubbornness. Often it seemed that he was persuaded, and yet in the end he clung to his original purpose. He allowed his mother and his wife to rail at Richelieu, and either remained silent or even seemed to agree; but at heart he was convinced that the greatness of his reign was due to Richelieu, and each attack in the end only strengthened the minister's hold on the King's convictions if not on his affections.

At Paris the matter came to a head in an interview between the Queen-mother and the Marquise de Combalet, Richelieu's niece, for whom he entertained a very warm personal affection. Richelieu himself entered during the course of the interview, and her anger flared out against him. He only opposed to it a few deprecating words and withdrew. She then turned passionately on her son, and accused Richelieu of the most improbable crimes, of a design to depose the King and place the Count of Soissons on the throne. The King said nothing, and retired. The next day there was another interview between mother and son, and Richelieu was present. Marie de Médicis declared that the King must make up his mind whether he preferred a valet or his mother; he must part either with Richelieu or with her. Louis XIII was overwhelmed rather than persuaded. He made a show of negotiating through his confessor, and on 11th Nov. 1630 actually signed a decree confiding the command of the Italian army to Louis de Marillac, the Queen's partisan. He then left for Versailles, then a small hunting establishment in the midst of a forest. The Chancellor Michel de Marillac had orders to follow him thither.

It seemed that Richelieu had really fallen. He is said to have thought of flight, and to have been dissuaded by La Valette. But soon there came better news. The King sent a message and wished to see him at once at Versailles.

The King had gone thither rather to escape from his mother than to get rid of Richelieu. The Cardinal on rejoining the King soon regained all his old power over him. A sort of compact was drawn up between them, and the King solemnly promised never to believe anything that was said to the Cardinal's prejudice by those who had on this occasion shown themselves his enemies; never to receive information without communicating it to him; never to employ those who might have both the power and will to injure the State. Hard on the heels of the order that gave Louis de Marillac the command over the Italian army went another, ordering Marshal Schomberg to arrest him; and at the same time the Chancellor Marillac was thrown into prison. The Duke of Orléans was approached, and he consented to abandon the Queen-mother as easily as he had consented to plot with her. He was almost entirely governed by his servants, Puy Laurens and Le Coigneau, who were drawn by promises of places and pensions to the side of the King. Marie de Médicis found herself deserted, but seemed to accept the situation, and went through the form of a reconciliation with Richelieu.

But plotting still continued and would continue so long as the Queen-mother was at Court, and soon Gaston was in the thick of it again. His favourites declared that Richelieu had not kept his promises to them, and Gaston openly declared that all friendship between himself and the Cardinal was at an end. He retired to Orléans, and began to gather a party of malcontents round him. Richelieu suspected—and we now know that he was right—that Gaston had treasonable relations with the Court of Spain. The Queen-mother's early patronage of Richelieu had turned into furious hatred: she would sell herself to the devil, she said, rather than miss her revenge upon him. She entered into and supported all Gaston's plans. Richelieu determined in the first place to proceed against Marie de Médicis. It was a matter of some delicacy, for public opinion would not bear to see the King using force against his mother. A stratagem had to be resorted to. The King and the Court went to Compiègne and the Queen-mother with them. Then next morning, before the Queen-mother was up, the King returned to Paris, leaving guards to prevent her from following him. He wrote to her, saying that "the good of the State" made their separation necessary, and invited her to retire to Moulins, with the government of a province and a pension. But she refused all overtures, and, as she was not allowed to come to Paris, she remained obstinately at Compiègne. Richelieu next turned to Gaston, and, recognizing all the importance that he possessed as the next heir to the throne (for the King remained childless), tried to induce him to return to Court. But his supporters despaired of escaping the vengeance of Richelieu, and accordingly advised him, as his designs were discovered and anticipated, to leave the country. On March 11, 1631, with a few followers, he fled to Lorraine, and was well received by the Duke. His mother soon followed him. Richelieu felt that she would be less dangerous abroad than in France, and it is probable that means of flight were put within her reach. She availed herself of them, and left Compiègne. She had intended to take refuge in La Capelle, but found herself anticipated, and, refusing to return into France, went on to Brussels. She was warmly received by the Spaniards, and thus began an exile that ended only with her life.

Richelieu's triumph was complete. The Parlement of Paris was forced to register edicts against the evil counsellors of the King's mother and brother. A special chamber of justice was established for the trial of their partisans. Many nobles were banished; some fled the country in order to avoid trial. In Sept. 1631 Richelieu was created Duke and Peer and for the future assumed the strange title of Cardinal-Duke; he also received the government of Brittany. Before he could turn his attention again to Europe he had another serious conflict to pass through at home.

Italian affairs had not been seriously disturbed by the palace
intrigues and the Day of Dupes, as the fiasco of
March, 1631, was called. The terms of the truce
by which hostilities had been stopped in October
1630 were confirmed by the Treaty of Cherasco,
signed in April 1631, by which it was stipulated
that the French should abandon all places that they occupied at
the same time that the Imperialists and the Spaniards withdrew.
Thus Pinerolo would cease to belong to France, and the Valtelline and the Grisons would pass into neutral hands, while the
Duke of Nevers would be placed in possession of Mantua.
But diplomacy gained for France what arms had not availed to
win. Charles Emmanuel, the Duke of Savoy, had died in
June 1630, and had been succeeded by Victor Amadeus,
whose feelings towards France were of a much more friendly
character. Richelieu had negotiated with him, and had won
him over to his views. A secret arrangement was made
between France and Savoy, whereby it was agreed that a
large part of Montferrat was to be added to the territories
of Savoy, and in return the French were to be left in
the possession of Pinerolo. But Richelieu's success did not
stop here. No sooner had the Imperialists abandoned the
Valtelline passes than the Grisons chose the French Duke of
Rohan to be their general, and French troops were put in
possession of that all-important gate. The Emperor found
himself outwitted; but his difficulties in Germany were already
so great that he feared to add to his enemies by attacking
France. In this very year, 1631, though Gustavus had already
landed in Germany, the proposal to withdraw or modify the
Edict of Restitution was rejected, and thus there was no possibility of avoiding another and a more terrible phase of the
war. With Gustavus a force of a new kind had come into
German politics. He had indeed personal and dynastic objects
in his fighting, but his zeal for the Protestant cause was real
and passionate. Compromise and personal motives no longer

Gaston of Orléans; the rising of Languedoc and the Duke of Lorraine.

played so important a part as before. The Swedish troops were hardy and well trained, and were kept in a strictness of discipline which contrasted strongly with the terrible laxity prevalent in the German armies, while Gustavus had all the great general's power of inspiring his men with devotion to himself and his cause. He brought, too, fresh tactics into the struggle; his troops were more mobile, and he made far more use of artillery than had been customary with the other commanders in the war. But it is beside the purpose of this book to describe the campaigns and methods of the great Swede, whose career gives him title to rank with the greatest generals and noblest characters in the history of modern Europe. His great victory came on Sept. 7, 1631, when he faced the troops of Tilly at Breitenfeld, near Leipzic, and gained an astonishing and complete success. In the opinion of some, Vienna was at his mercy, and he ought to have marched against it at once. French diplomacy tried to turn him in that direction; but instead of that he turned westward, against the ecclesiastical States of the upper Rhine, and threatened the Duchy of Lorraine. The upper course of the river fell into his power. On Dec. 23 he entered Mayence.

While Richelieu watched the vast convulsion and did something to stimulate or direct it, he found himself again face to face with a serious internal danger. The new opposition linked itself on to the old, which had seemed crushed by the flight of Orléans and the Queen-mother; but it now broadened its basis and took the form of provincial revolt instead of personal intrigue. The causes that made Richelieu hated have been already glanced at, and these had intensified since his victory over the mother and brother of the King. The Marillacs had suffered for the part played by them in that intrigue. The Chancellor, Michel de Marillac, was deprived of his office and imprisoned at Chateaudun, but a harder fate was in store for his brother Louis, the Marshal. He was tried for peculation by a special commission, for Richelieu could not trust the ordinary course of justice. After a long trial he was found guilty—"in a matter of hay and straw," he exclaimed, "for which you would hardly whip a lacquey—" and was executed in May, 1632. But beyond such personal enemies, Richelieu had to reckon with the enmity which his policy had created even in many men of upright and patriotic feelings. He distrusted the powers of self-government which were still left to the provinces, and had substituted direct nominees of the Crown (*élus*) for the representative estates of Dauphiné, of Provence, and of Languedoc. He everywhere overrode the provincial governors of noble birth, and was already developing that system of *intendants* which did more than anything else to destroy the political power of the nobles. Already the Duke of Guise had come into collision with his plans, and had withdrawn from France into perpetual exile. But Henry, Duke of Montmorency, was the most dangerous representative of this provincial hostility to Richelieu. He was a good type of the aristocracy of France, brave to rashness, vain and fond of display, but generous to his opponents, and with much of the spirit of chivalry still visible in his actions. He had been a friend of Richelieu, and had fought well for him both at Rochelle and at Vegliana. But now, as Governor of Languedoc, he put himself at the head of the prevailing discontent, and gathered a party of sympathisers around him. Nowhere was provincial feeling stronger than in Languedoc. The Estates had assembled regularly every three years, and had consisted of twenty-three of the clergy, twenty-two nobles, and sixty-eight representatives of the commons. Beneath these main provincial Estates there had been other similar assemblies for smaller divisions of the province, which together made up a very complete system of local government. Nowhere therefore had Richelieu's autocratic innovations given more offence than in Languedoc[1].

[1] Richelieu writes: "The king's authority was hardly recognized in this country. Troops were raised in the name of the States. The name of the governor of the Province had more weight than that of his Majesty."

By himself Montmorency would not perhaps have been a very serious danger to the Crown. But the storm was blowing up against Richelieu from all sides. Its centre was Lorraine. That duchy was in an anomalous and an unstable condition. It was nominally a part of the Empire, but really dependent on France, which controlled it through Henry II's conquests, Metz, Toul and Verdun. The Duke Charles V, now that the Empire was declining and France increasing in strength, leaned again towards the Empire: but any chance of succour from that side had been ruined by the march of Gustavus. On Jan. 6, 1632, the Duke had signed with France the treaty of Moyenvic, whereby he promised to abandon all alliances with the Empire or with Spain, to grant a free passage to the troops of France, and to give no support to Gaston of Orléans or Marie de Médicis. The last stipulation was of the most immediate importance, for, as we have seen, Gaston had taken refuge at the Duke's Court. He had been betrothed to the Duke's daughter Margaret, and a few days before the treaty of Moyenvic was signed had married her.

The treaty did not restrain the Duke of Lorraine from following his designs. The Duke of Orléans retired to Brussels, from which place he kept up a correspondence with the Duke. He also entered into an agreement with Spain; for Spain thought that she saw in Gaston and the Duke of Lorraine an excellent means of overthrowing Richelieu, or at least of weakening his power so that he should no longer be able to meet and checkmate Spanish plans at every turn. Gaston had an exile's confidence that the country would welcome him back and would rise at his approach. Montmorency promised his co-operation, and hoped to carry the whole of Languedoc with him. The governor of Calais was also believed to be friendly to the plot. But what made the danger greater was the part that Spain was prepared to play in the matter. A successful rising against Richelieu would be worth more to the King of Spain than the winning of a battle, and Gaston received support in men and money from Brussels.

The Duke of Lorraine had no time to play any great part in this scheme. In June, 1632, upon some rumour of what was preparing, an army was despatched against Lorraine, with the King at its head. Upon the 21st Nancy was invested, and the Duke of Lorraine was quickly induced to offer terms. He promised to abandon his projects and to cede Stenai and Jametz to the King for four years, and he sold him the strategically important territory of Clermont en Argonne. But meanwhile the Duke of Orléans, though without any immediate hope of assistance from Spain or Lorraine, had passed through Lorraine and entered Burgundy. He declared that he had come to free the State from "the tyrant who had usurped the authority of the King." But France did not rise as he had anticipated. Dijon shut its gates against him; the Parlement of Paris declared him and the Duke of Montmorency rebels; the other great nobles did not move. When he joined Montmorency he found everything unready; he had come earlier than was expected. The Estates of Languedoc had declared for him, but the province as a whole was by no means unanimous on his side. Schomberg had been despatched against him from Lorraine, and it would probably have been best to avoid a pitched battle. But patience was no virtue in the eyes of Montmorency. He dragged Gaston with him against his will —for at this time they were quarrelling—and met the force of Schomberg near Castelnaudary. On the side of the rebels there was little attempt at an orderly battle. No sooner did Montmorency see the enemy than like a mediæval knight he dashed at them, conspicuous among all by the gay plume in his helmet. He passed through the first lines, but quickly fell, pierced by musket-balls. His fall decided the battle. The Duke of Orléans had taken no part in the fighting, and after it, finding himself without adherents, he adopted his usual method of regaining the King's favour. He betrayed the plans of the allies, sacrificed those who had fought for him, and submitted once more to the humiliating farce of a reconciliation with

Richelieu. Montmorency recovered from his wounds: Gaston pleaded for his life, but in vain. His revolt had been a very dangerous one, and the interest of the State demanded that he should be made a striking and deterrent example to the other nobles; and Richelieu never allowed any private emotion to enter into rivalry with the interests of the State. Montmorency was tried by the Parlement of Toulouse, found guilty, and executed, despite all his intercessions with the King and his favour with the people—perhaps partly in consequence of these (30th Oct., 1632). But while Richelieu punished the leader, he spared the people of Languedoc and restored to them their representative estates, with limitations and conditions. They were to pay a compensation of four million livres to the royal officers who had been displaced; the sessions of their Estates were never to exceed fifteen days; they were to have no power of borrowing money or of levying taxes other than those sanctioned by the King's Government. It was, in fact, merely the shadow of the old Estates that remained. Yet one more consequence of the rising remains to be noticed. Gaston fled once more to Brussels. He made the King's treatment of Montmorency the excuse, but there is no doubt that the real cause was that he had sworn that he was not married to Margaret of Lorraine, and the King had found that his word was, as usual, valueless. Montmorency had before his death told the King that the marriage had actually taken place. The Duke of Orléans was still the heir to the throne, and it seemed impossible therefore to treat him with the severity that his crimes deserved[1]; but it made Richelieu's task all the more difficult, that he saw that if the King died power would pass into the hands of this frivolous and vicious enemy of himself and the greatness of France.

[1] Yet Richelieu writes in his memoirs, "It is a mistake to imagine that a man may trouble the realm with impunity because he is the brother or the son of the King. The Princes of the Blood are subject to the laws like any one else, especially in cases of high-treason."

Richelieu supreme in France.

The noise and danger of the internal struggle might well have diverted Richelieu's attention from the European situation, but he had followed it with close attention and had interfered with much effect.

France as an indirect agent in the European struggle.

Gustavus Adolphus was too great a man, too original a genius, to become a tool, even in the hands of Richelieu; and towards the end of his career there were wide differences of opinion between them. The death of the great Swede came therefore in many ways as a relief to the Cardinal. But France had already gained great advantages from Gustavus's career of victory. His march on the Rhine had completely broken up the Spanish power there, and contributed not a little to the discomfiture of Gaston and Montmorency. All along the Upper Rhine the power of Spain seemed annihilated, and the alternative for the ecclesiastical princes seemed to be to accept the Roman Catholic power of France or the Protestant power of Sweden. The Elector of Trèves was the first to decide. He had been busy now for many years, strengthening his position without much regard to the Empire, and since 1627 had been in very close relations with France. He now, in May, 1632, allowed the French to garrison the two great fortresses of Ehrenbreitstein and Philipsburg, and in August, when there was a rising on behalf of Spain in Trèves itself, he called in the French there also. It was a very important advance towards the goal that Richelieu always had in view, the extension, namely, of the frontier of France as far as the Rhine. But it was only the beginning of acquisitions there. The part that the Duke of Lorraine had played in the enterprise of Gaston and Montmorency gave a legitimate ground for an attack on him, and the importance of the district persuaded the King and the Cardinal to make the attack. In August, 1633, the King laid siege to the great fortress of Nancy, reckoned then to be as important as Metz itself. The Duke despaired of any help from Spain, and, despite the strength of the place, thought it best to hand it over to the King, to be held by him "until the present troubles were past." Only one failure clouded the Cardinal's triumph: Margaret of Lorraine had managed to escape from Nancy in men's clothes, and joined her husband at Brussels: but the marriage was annulled by a declaration of the Parlement of Paris. Lorraine passed wholly into the power of France. A Parlement was established at Metz; everywhere the lilies of France displaced the eagles of the Empire. It was a wonderful gain for France, and more was to follow. The Duke of Würtemburg surrendered Montbèliard in September, 1633, to the French, in order to save it from enemies whom he detested more. Other places came into the hands of the French in Alsace. Count Salm ceded Haguenau, Reichshofen, and many other places of smaller importance. All these great advances had been won with little noise, and with almost no bloodshed.

But the huge scale of events in Germany turned men's eyes away from these acquisitions. Gustavus Adolphus had turned east from the Rhine, and had plunged invincibly into Southern Germany. In April he defeated Tilly on the Lech, and the aged marshal perished of wounds received in the battle. Gustavus entered Munich on May 17th. No resistance seemed possible, unless Wallenstein were called out from his retirement. Even his former foes demanded his recall now. The magic of his reputation swiftly collected an army. The decisive battle between the two greatest soldiers of the age was fought at Lützen, near Leipzic and the former field of Breitenfeld, on Nov. 16, 1632. Wallenstein was defeated after a terrific struggle, but Gustavus, exposing himself like a common soldier, fell in the battle. The death of the Hero-King changed the whole aspect of affairs. It was at first thought that his whole army would disband, and that the Emperor and Wallenstein would be left without opponents. French diplomacy took up the direction of the struggle that had slipped from the hands of Gustavus. In March, 1633, the French ambassador, Feuquières, was present at a meeting of the Protestant States at Heilbronn. At first Richelieu had feared that the Protestant States would make separate arrangements with the Emperor, and thus remove from his path the chief obstacle. Feuquières' instructions, which were drawn up by Father Joseph, were to use every effort to prevent the dissolution of the Protestant League, and he succeeded in his object. It was very largely through his intervention that the Protestants were induced to accept the leadership of the sagacious Swedish Chancellor, Oxenstierna, in spite of their growing dislike to the dominant position that the Swedes were assuming in Germany. In April the treaty between France and Sweden was renewed, and thus it was certain that the war would continue. Bernard of Saxe-Weimar succeeded to the command of the Protestant armies, and showed himself not unworthy to succeed Gustavus. But Wallenstein soon drew all men's eyes upon himself. His power was so great that there seemed no limit to his advance. His soldiers were devoted to him personally, not to him as the Emperor's representative. He disdained the orders of the Emperor, and it seemed quite possible that he might turn his arms against him. He negotiated with the Swedes and with the French, and his overtures were eagerly welcomed by both. The agents of Richelieu offered him a subsidy in money and diplomatic support if he would break openly with the Emperor. A vast change in the European situation seemed more than possible, for there was no army in Germany capable of defeating Wallenstein. But devotion to the Empire still counted for something even among his troops, and in Feb. 1634 he fell by the hand of an assassin. The result was to strengthen enormously the power of the Emperor; for the troops, deprived of their leader, passed over to the Emperor and were placed under the command of his son, Ferdinand, King of Hungary. In Sept. 1634, Bernard of Saxe-Weimar and the Protestant army were defeated at Nordlingen. All the work of Gustavus seemed for the time undone, and the influence of Sweden in Germany was almost annihilated. Diplomacy, too, increased the gain that the battle of Nordlingen had brought to the Emperor, for at last, in the treaty of Prague, he consented to modify and practically withdraw the Edict of Restitution. The measure produced its effect at once. Saxony came in to the Emperor, and the resistance of the Protestants was much weakened. Yet still there were some that would not yield. The Calvinists were excluded from the terms of the treaty, and there were many States that were for different reasons left outside its provisions. The Emperor prepared to deal a blow at these with freer hands and greater force. If any further resistance were to be made to him it could hardly come from any other source than France.

Already Oxenstierna had made overtures to Richelieu in order to induce him to garrison German towns with French troops, and accept the direct responsibility for the war. Hitherto he and Father Joseph had refused to take such a step, and had preferred the *rôle* of seconds to that of principals; but now they would have to take the lead, or it would be taken by no one.

While Germany was agitated by these convulsions, Richelieu was gaining a stronger hold upon the Duchy of Lorraine, and the open rupture with Spain was inevitably approaching. The year 1634 had seen the consolidation of the power of France upon her eastern frontier. In January, Charles of Lorraine had found his position of subserviency to France intolerable. He abdicated in favour of his brother, the Cardinal Nicholas Francis, and proceeded to put his military talents at the service of the Emperor. But Nicholas Francis did not long keep his power. It was questionable whether Lorraine was subject to the Salic law or not, and whether in consequence the rightful heir was not the princess, his cousin. In order to make his position secure, Nicholas Francis, who though a Cardinal, had not yet taken higher orders, married his cousin Claude, assuming that the Pope would grant him the necessary dispensation. France protested against the many irregularities of the marriage, and declared it void. A French army was sent to Lorraine, but the Cardinal and his bride fled from Nancy and took refuge in Italy. The whole of Lorraine at once passed under the direct control of the French Crown. While France thus won full power over Lorraine, recent events, as we have seen, had given her a very strong hold in Alsace through some of its most important fortresses. This was not only a great gain to France; it was also a great loss to Spain and the Empire, for it threatened the communication between Spain and the Netherlands. The strength of the Dutch navy made the sea route dangerous, and, if France were firmly established in Alsace and Lorraine, the land route would be blocked as well.

Spain, or rather the Count Olivarez, who directed the affairs of Spain almost as absolutely as Richelieu those of France, recognised that the indirect and diplomatic struggle must pass into open war. He hoped, despite recent experiences, that an attack on France would be rendered easy by rebellions within. Gaston of Orléans would in any case be a most useful ally, and Gaston, in May, 1634, had promised, in case of an open rupture between France and Spain, to make no reconciliation with his brother until a general peace. But we have seen how little promises bound him. His position in Brussels was becoming intolerable to him. His followers quarrelled with those of the Queen-mother, and fought among themselves, and he complained also of his treatment by the Spaniards. Richelieu saw an opportunity of luring him back to France, and opened negotiations with that end in view. Gaston gave a promise to allow the validity of his marriage with Margaret of Lorraine to be examined, and then in October, 1634, he and Puy Laurens galloped away from Brussels, and never halted until they had crossed the French frontier. Neither Gaston nor Puy Laurens kept his promises. Puy Laurens was soon thrown into prison, and died there. Gaston however abstained from treason for an unusually long time.

It was a great thing to have secured the King's brother within the boundaries of France. Richelieu further strengthened his position by alliances. In November, 1634, a treaty was concluded with the Swedes and the German Protestants, whereby France promised to break openly with the common enemy, to supply a numerous army for action on both sides of the Rhine, and to subsidise the Swedish army; while France for her services was to have the right of appointing a general to the army in Germany, to occupy at once certain places in Alsace, and to receive Breisach, if it could be taken from the Spaniards. In Feb. 1635 a treaty was signed with Holland for a common invasion of the Spanish Netherlands.

Open hostilities began with the year 1635. In January an Imperialist force attacked Philipsburg, which was held by France, and took it. In March, Trèves was surprised by a Spanish force, and the Electoral Archbishop was taken prisoner. Richelieu thought this a favourable opportunity for the declaration of war. On May 19 a French herald presented himself at Brussels, and with antiquarian ceremonies declared war against the King of Spain. It was generally believed in France that the war would be short and triumphant. Few were prepared for the long and evenly-balanced struggle which was to follow.

France, under the direction of Richelieu, thus confronted the Spanish and Austrian power, and began a struggle that was to have far-reaching consequences for both victors and vanquished. The result of his interference was eventually to procure for the Protestants, and especially for the Calvinists, better terms than were offered by the Treaty of Prague, and to free Germany from the retrograde and coercive power of the Austrian House; but such was not certainly his immediate intention; it may even be doubted whether such a possibility weighed with him at all. He was a French, not a cosmopolitan statesman, and fought the Austro-Spanish power not because it crushed German Protestantism, but because it threatened the

The European War to the Death of Richelieu.

free development of France. Europe was amazed at the vast preparations that he had made. Henry IV's army of 60,000 men had been reckoned a very great force in the last reign, but Richelieu was prepared to take the field with 132,000. And his projects corresponded in grandeur with the force that he proposed to employ. In Italy, France in alliance with Parma, Mantua and Savoy, was to attack Milan. Lorraine was to be guarded by the army under Duke Bernard, which entered into the pay and service of France. But the chief effort was to be made in the North. France and Holland were to join hands for the invasion of the Spanish Netherlands, and it was believed that they would find the inhabitants ready to assist them by rebelling against Spain. But these grandiose projects resulted during the first year in complete failure. The attack on Milan failed entirely. Charles of Lorraine attacked the French on the eastern frontier, and, though their troops were under the command of Bernard of Weimar and Cardinal Lavalette, he gained some victories, and took from them Spires and Worms and other places. Still more disastrous was the campaign in the North. It had opened well. The French and their allies had taken Tirlemont in June; but as they proceeded to use against the inhabitants, whom they had nominally come to defend, all the atrocities that the Thirty Years' War had made familiar, any enthusiasm that was at first felt for the invaders soon turned into hatred. An attack on Louvain failed. The enemy meanwhile captured the important fortress of Schenk, and the whole scheme of invasion broke down.

Thus the campaign of 1636 opened darkly for Richelieu. His enemies, among whom the Duke of Orléans was still to be counted, were working against him, and their policy had a better chance of succeeding with the King now that Richelieu's policy abroad had received a decisive check. But the Cardinal had not lost heart. In March the treaty with Sweden was renewed, and the Swedish army was launched against Bohemia and Silesia, and again Richelieu prepared to

face the enemy upon the different theatres of the war. But the
French armies were ill-disciplined and badly-officered, and no
match at present for the veterans of the Thirty Years' War.
France had as yet no really capable generals; it was not
until the end of the war that Harcourt, Turenne and Condé
began to make their influence felt. In Italy the Spaniards
were defeated, but the French did not profit by their victory.
Franche Comté was invaded, and Dôle was besieged, but, before
the place could be reduced, news came of a great disaster upon
French soil. Piccolomini and John of Werth had laid siege to
Liège, but suddenly broke up from before the place to undertake
a more important enterprise. The road to Picardy was open,
and the Spanish army poured down it. No effective resistance
could be made. La Capelle and le Catelet were taken. The
invaders pushed on to the Somme, and laid siege to Corbie.
The place capitulated on August 15, and meanwhile the wild
troops of John of Werth were exhibiting in the fertile lands
between the Somme and the Oise all those habits of cruelty
and rapacity that had desolated Germany. The alarm in Paris
was naturally great, and was increased by exaggerated rumours
that the provinces were in revolt and the capital itself indefensible. At first it seemed as though the popular alarm would
cause an explosion of animosity against Richelieu. His display
of wealth gave offence: he was said to have pulled down some
part of the fortifications of Paris to find room for his gardens:
he was charged with giving important posts to his relations, and
with winking at frauds on the public treasury. For a time he
feared to show himself in public, and, finding the King more
morose and suspicious than usual and inclined to attribute the
disasters of France to his Minister's policy, he talked even of
resigning. It was Father Joseph who drew him from this
depression by appealing to Richelieu's religious feelings, and,
assuring him of Heaven's favour in his holy enterprise, induced
him to face the danger with his usual intrepidity. He went
unattended to the Hotel de Ville, and appealed to the patriotism

of the people. There was a moment's hesitation, and then the patriotic enthusiasm of Paris showed itself equal to the occasion. Troops were enrolled and sent up to the front. Piccolomini and John of Werth were not prepared to crush a national movement. They fell back from the Oise, back from the Somme, and regained the frontier. The French army undertook the siege of Corbie, and it fell in November. Richelieu's position was safe again. Gaston and the Count of Soissons, both of whom were engaged in the campaign against Spain, had thought to use the opportunity to overthrow Richelieu, but Gaston had not the nerve to succeed in his favourite *rôle* as conspirator. The plot failed; Gaston fled at first, but was subsequently reconciled to the King (Jan. 1637). The Count of Soissons retired beyond the frontier.

In Feb., 1637, the Emperor Ferdinand II died, and was succeeded by his son Ferdinand III, though France and Sweden refused to recognise him. The change made little difference in the war. Richelieu strained every nerve to improve the numbers and the discipline of the French armies, and this year the fortune of war, though still uncertain, began to show itself less hostile to France. In the North, Cardinal Lavalette retook la Capelle, and the Prince of Orange captured Breda. Neither was of the first importance to France, but after the experiences of the last year it was something to gain victories at all. Franche Comté was overrun by Bernard of Weimar. Most welcome success of all, the French fleet, upon which Richelieu had bestowed so much care, showed that it had to be reckoned with. The Lérins islands, off Fréjus, had been occupied by Spain in the previous year—an insult and a danger to the coasts of France. The French fleet, under Count Harcourt, attacked the Spanish garrison, and forced the enemy to surrender and to evacuate the islands. The Spaniards attempted to invade France from the South, and laid siege to Leucate; but the place held out stubbornly, and gave time for the troops of Languedoc to collect and relieve it, defeating the

Spaniards sharply. But there were serious losses to be placed against these victories; for both in Germany and in Italy France had suffered disasters. Upon the Italian frontier the French commander, Rohan, had negotiated between the Grisons and the Valtelline a treaty which would have excluded the Spaniards, but gave great privileges to the Protestants of the Grisons. Richelieu and Father Joseph refused to ratify this treaty, and ordered Rohan to amend it. But, before he had time to do so, the Grisons, suspicious of his intentions, turned against him. His own army mutinied and arrested him, and in the end he had to capitulate for the best terms he could obtain. Thus this much-debated territory passed under the dominion of Spain, and at the same time Mantua, upon the death of the Duke, made its peace with the Empire. A disaster equally great occurred on the German frontier. John of Werth blockaded and reduced the great fortress of Ehrenbreitstein, and mastered the whole Electorate of Trèves. The same year also saw disturbances at home. The taxes were heavy, and the mode of collecting them made them heavier still. The peasantry rose in Perigord, and had to be crushed. But if the fortune of war had been doubtful in 1637, its tide began to flow steadily in favour of France in 1638. It will make the situation plainer if we follow the course of the war continuously in each theatre of the war down to the year 1641. But there is one domestic incident that must not be forgotten amidst all the fighting, for it had a profound influence upon the future of France. For twenty-three years Louis XIII's marriage had remained childless, and Richelieu saw all his plans threatened by the possible accession of Gaston of Orléans to power. But in 1638 the child was born who was afterwards to fill so vast a place in European history as Louis XIV. Hardly any victory, not even the capture of Breisach, so delighted Richelieu as the receipt of the news that a child was born who might give permanence to his policy.

To reach the Rhine and to establish it as the frontier

of France was one of the fixed ambitions of Richelieu's life. But since the declaration of war *Germany.* he had achieved no successes in that quarter. The year 1638 opened inauspiciously, for Bernard of Weimar, whilst he was besieging Rheinfeld, was sharply defeated by John of Werth, at the end of February. He held his troops together, however, and on the 3rd of March he was able to assume the offensive, and completely defeated John of Werth, almost on the same spot where he had been previously defeated. The commander himself, whose name had been such a terror to Paris in 1636, appeared there now as a prisoner. Rheinfeld, Freiburg and the Breisgau were the rewards of the victory, and Bernard could press on to the blockade and conquest of the great fortress of Breisach, which was then held to be the most important fortress in Europe, commanding as it did upper Alsace, and, when in Austrian hands, helping to secure the connection between Spain and her possessions in the Netherlands. All attempts to relieve it were repulsed, though they were made again and again. At last, on December 18, 1638, the garrison capitulated[1]. It was by far the most important acquisition that Richelieu had made for France during his career; it was, he himself says, "the end that crowned the work." Yet it seemed as though its capture would lead to grave difficulties between Bernard and the French, for Bernard refused altogether the proposal that he should place Breisach in French hands. Though he was fighting against the Emperor, he was still loyal to the idea of the Empire, and he would not be the first to dismember it. But in July, 1639, while the grave question was still unsettled, Bernard was attacked by disease, and he

---

[1] Father Joseph died just before the capture of Breisach. His death was a very great loss to Richelieu, but not so great as it would have been if it had come five years earlier; for now the time of diplomacy was passing and the time of action had come. Had he lived a little longer he would almost certainly have been made a Cardinal, and would probably have been recognised as Richelieu's successor.

succumbed on the 15th. His death deprived France of her greatest commander, but it made the situation much less difficult. Duke Bernard's army was induced by the promise of good pay to take service with France; Longueville and Guébriant took the place of the Duke as commanders; and Breisach passed of necessity into French occupation. France assumed a more commanding position in Germany than ever before. In May, 1640, an alliance was made with Hesse and Lüneburg. There was little chance now that the Emperor would be able to enforce the Treaty of Prague throughout Germany. In Jan. 1641, the Diet, which was held at Ratisbon, was threatened by the French and their allies. More and more it became evident that neither party in Germany would gain a complete victory.

Equally striking was the ascendant that the French gained in Italy. And yet the position was at first a very difficult one. We have seen already how France had lost the Valtelline and failed to make any impression on Milanese territory. Victor Amadeus, the Duke of Savoy, had died in September, 1637, and had been succeeded by his widow, Christine, sister of the King of France. The two brothers of the late King, Prince Thomas and Cardinal Maurice, refused to recognise her right to the regency, and allied themselves to the Spanish power. Piedmont was invaded. Turin and Nice were taken. The Regent and her infant son took refuge among the mountains of Savoy; but even there she refused to subordinate her country wholly to France. In 1640 the French at last sent her relief. Casale was being besieged by the Spaniard Lleganez, and must be saved at all risks. Count Harcourt crossed the Alps at the head of a strong army. He is the first of the long line of French generals whose exploits fill the remainder of the century, and gain so marked an ascendancy for French arms, and he had with him Turenne, who was destined to follow in his steps and far outstrip him. Lleganez believed himself to be so strongly posted at Casale that he despised the French attack; but the French broke the lines of circumvallation in several places, and Casale was relieved. Harcourt next marched on to Turin, where a French garrison was still holding out in the castle, while the Spaniards were in possession of the city. He drew up his lines round it, and, if he could maintain his position, the fall of Turin was certain. But so great a prize could not be allowed to fall into the hands of the French without an effort to prevent it. Lleganez tried to relieve the siege by cutting off all provisions from the French army, and, upon the news of the arrival of French reinforcements, made a desperate attack on their lines. But he was beaten off, and Turin yielded on September 22. It was the greatest feat of arms that had been accomplished by a French general during the course of the war. France was now unquestionably the strongest power in the peninsula.

While France was thus establishing her ascendancy in Western Germany and in Italy she struck also right at the heart of Spain, and tore from her her command over the sea, over Portugal and over Catalonia.

Spain.

Spain's existence as a world-empire rested on her command of the sea. England and Holland had already outstripped her there, and in consequence her grasp on her possessions in the New World was loosening. But France had hitherto not entered into rivalry on the seas. When therefore Richelieu turned his attention to the creation of a French navy it was an event of immense importance to Spain. We have already seen how the French fleet had managed to regain possession of the Lérins islands, but that was only the beginning of its successes. In September the French fleet attacked a Spanish force of equal strength in front of the harbour of Genoa. A desperate struggle ensued, but the Spaniards were defeated and their admiral slain. In August of the same year the French army laid siege to Fontarabia, and the French fleet, under Sourdis, Archbishop of Bordeaux—one of the many ecclesiastics whom Richelieu employed in his wars—attacked a number of Spanish galleys that were coming to the relief of the place, at Guetaria, in the Bay of Biscay, and succeeded in burning and destroying nearly the whole of them. No part of the victories of France was so welcome to Richelieu as these naval successes; he devotes a greater space to them in his memoirs than to the better known battles on land. But the French army, under Cardinal Lavalette and Condé, which was besieging Fontarabia, was a few days afterwards entirely defeated. The French invasion of Spain was thus for the moment repulsed, and Lavalette, threatened with a prosecution for his failure or his treason, thought it prudent to retire to England, and was condemned to death during his absence. But a greater disaster awaited the Spaniards. In 1639, a very large Spanish fleet put out from Corunna to carry relief to the Spanish Netherlands. The Dutch fleet met it in the Channel, drove it on to the English coast, and, in spite of the English King, attacked it there and wrought a huge havoc upon it. The loss was said to be as great as that which the Armada had suffered from the English and the elements in 1588. The Spanish navy did not recover from the blow.

But worse was yet to come. The unity of Spain had been established by Castile, in opposition to the privileges and separatist tendencies of the various provinces. And now the declining power of Spain offered an opportunity of throwing off the galling yoke. Nowhere was the yoke felt to be more galling than in Catalonia. In language and character Catalonia differed widely from Castile. Her privileges had been neglected, her rights of self-government trampled on. The last insult came when Spain insisted on quartering troops on the inhabitants—a burden from which Catalonia was specially exempted. She threw off her allegiance in June, 1640, and entered into negotiations with France. Richelieu welcomed so splendid an opportunity of striking a decisive blow at the strength of Spain. By a treaty, signed in December, 1640, Louis promised to give the Catalonians support in men and money, and officers to command their troops. In January, 1641, the Cortes of Catalonia went further still, and consented to be incorporated with the Crown of France. Louis XIII was declared Count of Barcelona, and French troops were sent to the assistance of the insurgents. An attempt to regain Barcelona was easily beaten off, and Harcourt, at the head of the Catalonian army, laid siege to Tarragona, which was held by troops faithful to the King of Spain. Olivarez, the Spanish Minister, who for a long time had been nearly as powerful in Spain as Richelieu in France, made desperate efforts to relieve the place, and, after several failures, a Spanish fleet managed to force its way into the harbour. While the throne of Spain was thus shaken in the north-east, it received an even more serious blow in the west. Portugal had been annexed to the territories of Spain by Philip II, in 1581, but had by no means forgotten her former greatness and independence, for she had been cruelly oppressed and her commerce almost destroyed, and now there was a proposal to destroy her separate legislature. John, Duke of Braganza, a descendant of her former Kings, was resident in the country. Stimulated by French diplomacy, the people rose in rebellion against the Spanish Government. In Dec. 1640 the Duke of Braganza was declared King as John IV, and received an oath of loyalty from the whole population, and nearly the whole of the old Portuguese colonies. Spanish detachments which attempted to crush the rising were easily defeated. If Spain, while still undisturbed at home, had found the war with France too great an undertaking, what was likely to be the result now when she was between two dangerous fires in her own peninsula?

Compared with these great events, the war in the Netherlands was unimportant. But even there the Spaniards were losing ground. The French had failed to reduce St Omer in 1638, but in 1640 Arras surrendered to them, after a long siege, and in 1641 Aire also fell.

The year 1641 thus saw Richelieu successful everywhere.

The last year of Richelieu's life: domestic intrigues and foreign war.

But these remarkable triumphs did not cause any diminution in the difficulties that he had to face in France itself. Rather the approaching triumph of all his plans caused his enemies to rally for his overthrow. Spain had found to her cost how the foreign enemy could make use of her internal discontents, and she again prepared to fight Richelieu with his own weapons. There seemed a possibility of success in this direction; for the war had brought with it heavy taxation, and the peasantry groaned under their burdens. There had been a serious revolt in Normandy. The malcontent nobles were as far from reconciliation with Richelieu as ever. Gaston was still ready for intrigue. The Duke of Soissons had retired from Court, and nourished his old grudge in Sedan. His royal blood gave him an importance that his character did not support. He planned the overthrow of the Cardinal and managed to draw in the Duke of Bouillon and the Duke of Guise, while Spain readily entered into his schemes and put troops at his service. Overtures were made to the Duke of Orléans, and were not at first rejected, but subsequently he betrayed them to the King. Nevertheless the plot went on: Soissons seemed near enough to the King in blood to raise a rebellion against him. The conspirators effected a junction with Lamboi and an Imperialist army, and marched from Sedan into France. Richelieu, meanwhile, had acted with his usual promptitude, and had been supported by more than his usual good fortune. Châtillon met the invaders at the wood of Marfée, near Sedan. A strange, confused battle followed. There was disaffection in the French army, both among officers and men, and Soissons and Lamboi gained a complete victory; but before the battle was decided Soissons was shot in an obscure scuffle. His death deprived the victory of all its importance. Bouillon and Guise were not prepared to go on without some leader of the blood royal, and at once retreated to the frontier. Bouillon negotiated and obtained terms. Guise refused to ask for pardon, and retired to Brussels. The Cardinal had triumphed, but at once found himself threatened by another plot—the most dangerous that he had to face throughout his whole career.

The King's character was so prone to *ennui* and melancholy that he was very dependent on others for amusement. Thus while the Cardinal maintained an immense hold over him in all questions of politics and war, there was usually some favourite, whether man or woman, who exercised in personal and private matters an influence that was important and often hostile to the minister. The efforts made by Mademoiselle d'Hautefort in 1635, and by Mademoiselle la Fayette in 1636 to undermine his influence form a very curious and interesting chapter in the life of the Court, but may be neglected here. But the next favourite of the King had a very tragic career. Henri d'Effiat, Marquis of Cinq Mars, had been recommended to the King by Richelieu himself. His handsome face and great personal charm soon gained the affection of the King. He was promoted to a prominent place at the Court, but he was not content with this, and dreamed of playing an important political *rôle*. He insisted on being present at the interviews of the King with the Cardinal, and demanded admission into the Council. Richelieu steadily refused to give his own relations public appointments, and was not likely to yield to the ambition of Cinq Mars. So there had sprung up hostility between them. Cinq Mars' head was turned by the great affection that the King manifested for him, and he began to dream of stepping into the Cardinal's place. The result was a very dangerous conspiracy. He had been in communication with Soissons, and had feared that he might be implicated in his fall, but his secret was not revealed, and he resumed his plots. Gaston of Orléans was cognisant of them, and approved. It seemed at last as though the King himself had been won over to the idea of getting rid of his minister who had overshadowed his whole reign: he showed, it was said, no sign of disapproval when Cinq Mars recalled to his memory the methods by which Luynes had got rid of Marshal d'Ancre. Louis had a way of seeming to be more in agreement with those who spoke to him than he really was; he appears certainly to have allowed Cinq Mars to rail against the Cardinal and to have shown pleasure at his sarcasms. But Cinq Mars was not satisfied with his chances of success on these lines. He played the diplomatist, opened negotiations with Bouillon through his friend de Thou, and even entered into relations with the Court of Spain. The two parts of the plot contradicted one another, and their contradiction gives us the measure of Cinq Mars' ability.

And yet the success of the plot appeared very probable. The King's fondness for Cinq Mars seemed to increase. Richelieu still directed public affairs, but at Court the shadow of coming disgrace seemed to be passing over him. Perhaps the danger was not really so great as it seemed, but certainly Richelieu was in no little anxiety. Then came a sudden discovery that saved him. His secret police, who served him so faithfully, obtained a copy of the treaty that Cinq Mars had made with Spain. Richelieu sent it to the King, who thus found to his chagrin that his favourite who was so loud in protesting his devotion to himself was at the same time seeking the alliance of his bitterest enemy. There was little hesitation now. King and Cardinal met at Tarrascon, and were completely reconciled; "We have lived together too long to be ever separated," said Louis. Cinq Mars and de Thou were arrested. Gaston trod the now familiar path of humiliation; he bought forgiveness for his treason to the King by treason to his confederates, and gave the required evidence against the prisoners. They had been arrested at Narbonne, for the King and his Court had moved to the South of France to superintend the war against Spain. Richelieu took them with him by river to Lyons. The picture of that journey has fixed itself deep in the mind of posterity; the Cardinal, who had just received the title of Lieutenant-General of the Kingdom, was so weak that he could hardly sit upright, and lay in his barge, behind which was towed another barge containing the two handsome and vigorous nobles whom his dying hand had overthrown. They were tried before a commission at Lyons, were found guilty, and were executed on September 12th, 1642. The youth and bold carriage of the sufferers evoked and have continued to evoke much pity. But no sentence of death was ever more fully justified than that upon Cinq Mars, who for his personal ambition would have wrecked his country and caused vast confusion and much bloodshed. De Thou was not so guilty, but he had known of the plots, and had approved of them, and could claim no exemption from the sentence.

Richelieu had triumphed at home, and saw from his death-bed the final victory of his schemes approaching on every side. Europe would probably have been spared a struggle of many years and the shedding of much blood if his life had been prolonged. The difficulties of Spain were increasing. Hardly an attempt was made to regain Portugal, and the rebellion in Catalonia spread. The French invaded Roussillon and laid siege to Perpignan, and, after defeating the Spanish efforts to relieve it, captured it in September, 1642. Roussillon passed thus a second time into the hands of France, and was destined to remain there. The Spanish attempt to regain Catalonia failed for the present entirely.

The news from Germany was equally favourable to France. In January, 1642, Guebriant, at the head of the army which had once followed Duke Bernard of Weimar, had defeated Lamboi at Kempten, captured him and sent to Paris 162 flags that had been taken from the enemy. They were exhibited in Nôtre Dame, and were the first of many similar trophies that France was destined to win during the next century. And soon the Germans suffered an even severer blow. The Swedes under Torstenson overran Silesia and Moravia, and alarmed Vienna, and when the gathering forces of the Empire forced them to retire, Torstenson laid siege to Leipsic and inflicted a crushing defeat upon the Imperialist army that attempted to relieve it (the second battle of Leipsic, Nov. 2, 1642). Things had gone well, too, in Italy. The Duke of Savoy had come over to the side of France, and she now reigned in the North of Italy without a rival. Disaster, too, had fallen on Richelieu's personal enemies. Not only was Gaston drinking the very dregs of the cup of humiliation, but Marie de Médicis, the Queen-mother, lived to see all her schemes of ambition defeated and her plans of revenge foiled. She died at Cologne, in comparative poverty, in July, 1642.

Amidst this blaze of glory Richelieu himself was dying. The decision and energy of his character remained with him even on his death-bed. He peremptorily insisted that the physicians should tell him the real state of his case, and when they said that the end would come within twenty-four hours, he gave his last orders with the utmost coolness. When his confessor asked him whether he pardoned his enemies he answered, "I have had no enemies except those of the State." And when the consecrated host was brought he exclaimed, "Here is my judge, who will soon pronounce my sentence. I pray him to condemn me if in my ministry I have had any other object than the good of religion and the State." Strange utterances for one whom some Catholics called an atheist, and whose career was thought by many to have been marked by personal vindictiveness! But a close study of his career hardly allows us to doubt his sincerity in either point. He died on December 3, 1642, and he was followed to his grave by Louis XIII, on May 14, 1643. With the death of these two men a very important and distinct epoch in French history closes.

It is not necessary to add much to what has been said about the diplomatic and foreign work of Richelieu. Under him France became the first power in Europe. In arms she was already the successful rival of Spain, and in diplomacy she was without a rival. But Richelieu's work was almost equally important for the domestic development and administration of France, though in this respect his achievements were of a more questionable kind.

The sum of his domestic policy may be briefly stated. He carried much further the system of centralisation, and almost completed the organisation of the monarchical government as it existed down to the time of the Revolution. It was his object to put the power of the King above all—above representative assemblies, above the nobility, above religious organisations; and we cannot question that he believed that the King's authority thus placed above all would be "for the good of all."

Domestic policy of Richelieu.

We have already seen how the Crown had triumphed over many of its rivals. The States General had never been called together since 1614, and an edict of 1641 had forbidden the Parlement of Paris to busy itself with affairs of State, and had insisted on immediate registration of all edicts when once the King's will had been clearly pronounced. The Notables had been summoned on two occasions (1626 and 1627). Their debates had been free, and they certainly had not been the subservient instruments of the Crown. But the very fact that they were one and all the mere nominees of the Crown took from their meetings all constitutional importance. The right of the King to make what laws he wished was hardly disputed while Richelieu held the reins of power. But it was not only with regard to the central institutions of France that an absolute autocracy was substituted for representative forms. The same thing was going on in the provinces. These had hitherto been, as we have seen, of two kinds, the *pays d'élection*, where the taxes were levied directly by the Government through their agents, called *élus*, and the *pays d'états*, where there were assemblies roughly representative of the inhabitants, who granted taxes to the Monarchy after free deliberation, and collected the taxes that they granted by their own agents. Once all the provinces had been *pays d'états*, but by the seventeenth century all the central provinces of France had lost their representative institutions. It was only in the provinces that lay on the circumference of France that they were maintained; Languedoc, Dauphiné, Burgundy, Brittany, Normandy, were the chief, though there were others. We have already seen (p. 236) how the estates of Languedoc were first crushed and then restored with crippled powers. What happened in Languedoc was typical of what happened or was attempted elsewhere. The action of the Estates in Normandy was regulated by the Crown. Those of Burgundy were heavily fined for playing with rebellion, and placed under the surveillance of a body of troops. In Provence little was left of the Estates but the name. Dauphiné and Normandy still retained the title of *pays d'états*, but in Dauphiné the States never met from the time of Richelieu to the Revolution, and the Estates of Normandy, after a period of obscurity, were entirely suppressed in 1666.

It is still more important to notice how the authority of the nobles was wrecked under Richelieu's administration. The Monarchy in its rise had found in them its most dangerous competitors, and each advance that it made was a curtailment of their privileges. Their power was diminished by Richelieu in many ways. We have seen how their fortresses had been overthrown: an edict against duelling, issued in the year 1626, had in theory curtailed what they regarded as a privilege, though in fact little difference was made in their turbulent habits for some time to come. We read that in the Regency of Anne of Austria nine hundred and thirty gentlemen met their death in duels, and doubtless a much greater number than was reported had died in that way. Far more important than the destruction of castles and the edict against duels was the practical exclusion of the nobles from the work of the administration. The chief hopes of the nobles, their best chance of establishing something like the independence of feudal times, lay in their occupancy of the position of governor in the various provinces. These posts, as we have seen, owed their origin to Francis I, who

Richelieu supreme in France.

established them in a moment of extreme danger as a temporary expedient; but during the troubles of the civil religious wars the governors had made their authority in the provinces strong and permanent. Despite the blows that Henry IV had struck against their power, it was still very great when Richelieu's term of authority began, and in his "Succinct Narration" he regards them as one of the chief causes of the weakness of the Monarchy; "they acted," he says, "as though they were possessed of sovereign authority." Not content with the power that they had, they were ambitious of making their offices hereditary, and one of them had actually suggested this to Henry IV. France seemed threatened with a new feudal tyranny. The nobles stood, therefore, as the chief obstacles right in the path of Richelieu. Acting upon his advice, the King refused to appoint them to important posts, and gave his confidence to men drawn from the ranks. The high nobles had no place in his councils, and in the provinces officers directly appointed by the Crown more and more displaced the governor of noble birth. These royal officers are the important *Intendants*. Their origin is very obscure. They are closely associated with Richelieu's name by history, and they were so associated by contemporaries. But such officials had been known as early as the reign of Henry II, and there is no edict that definitely establishes them. The system in fact developed gradually and at first secretly; but soon the effect was plain. The nobles, whose estates, traditions, and high birth seemed to give them a claim to exercise power in certain provinces, found themselves for that very reason thrust on one side by these *Intendants* (*intendants de justice, police, et finances* is their full title), who had no sympathy with the nobility, and to whom the King's will was the only law. It is not necessary to analyse their functions with any minuteness. They represented the King, and their power was practically almost unlimited. They encroached on the powers of the governors by superintending the raising and sometimes the drilling of troops, and by taking wholly into their hands the assessing and raising of taxes. By their judicial action they encroached on the local Parlements, for they constantly judged both civil and criminal cases, and especially represented the King in cases of appeal. It was not until the age of Louis XIV that they became the universal and open agents of Government: in Richelieu's time they were chiefly agents for the more economic and energetic carrying out of the measures that the war made necessary. But from the first they were hated by the classes whom they displaced in power. The nobles, finding themselves overmastered, left their estates rather than remain to be governed by low-born *Intendants*, and they thus quickened the tendency to absenteeism that was already visible. Their action varied with the Government of which they were the passive instruments, and was often highly beneficial; but down to the Revolution they were always regarded by the nobles with the bitterest detestation, "as an instrument of despotism more suitable for Turks or Persians than for Frenchmen."

The authority of the nobles was further diminished by the organisation of the King's Council. What was done in France by Richelieu has some analogy to what was done in England by the Tudors. The Royal Council, which during the late disorders had become fluctuating and formless, begins to have clearly-defined duties and a careful organisation. It met on different days for different subjects, always under the real or nominal presidency of the King. The Chancellor and the Superintendent of the Finances are still nominally the chief officers, but by their side and in almost equal power begin to appear the four great Secretaries of State. Richelieu in fact forged the weapon with which Louis XIV subsequently ruled. We may postpone an examination of its working until we come to his reign.

This by no means brings us to the end of Richelieu's changes in domestic organisation. He vastly improved both army and navy, and thus prepared the way for Louvois and

Colbert. He made vigorous but unsuccessful attempts to increase the commerce of France by the foundation of commercial companies. It was directly due to Richelieu that the first newspaper, the *Gazette*, appeared, and it was he who gave official sanction to the Academy that was destined to exert so great an influence over the language and the thought of France. There was unfortunately one branch of the national life where his reforming and organising zeal left no traces. The finances, far from improving during his administration, grew worse as the strain of the great war necessarily increased the expenditure of France. Yet it is quite certain that the expenditure was not so much to blame for the widespread misery and degradation of agricultural France as the way in which the revenue was collected. If we look carefully we see there the disease which eventually produced the financial collapse that led to the Revolution. The rich and noble escaped their fair burden on the ground of privilege; there was no certainty as to what each man would have to pay. The system of farming the taxes made the burden far greater than the gain to the treasury. The maximum of irritation was combined with a minimum of advantage to the State. The whole system of taxation—*tailles, corvées, aides, gabelles*—acted as a permanent check upon the expansion of the energies of France.

Richelieu could not be unaware of the sufferings of the people. He speaks of them in his Memoirs, and if an interval of peace had made such a course possible he would probably have turned to the questions of finance with the same energy and insight which he applied to other departments of the national life. But no such interval of peace came before his death. The financial system of France, despite the vigorous efforts of Colbert, sunk ever deeper into corruption, until the Revolution came to cleanse the Augean stables.

The judgments passed upon Richelieu's work by both French and foreign observers have been widely different. Some have seen in him the organiser of tyranny, and the ultimate cause of the decay of France in the eighteenth century. To others he is the embodiment of all that is greatest in the public policy of France, the supporter of religious toleration and of the balance of power, the statesman who, by centralising the Monarchy, began the work which the Revolution and Napoleon completed. No one, however, has questioned the far-reaching influence of the work he did. He more than any other man is the founder of the "Age of Louis XIV," which bears the stamp of his spirit in its national pride, in its intellectual interests, in its efforts to spread a uniform culture throughout France. Our judgment of Richelieu's work therefore will depend largely on our feelings about the "Age of Louis XIV." English observers have often been more impressed with its decline than with its greatness, and have been careful to point out its more questionable features, such as its exaggerated worship of uniformity and absence of spontaneity; and their judgment upon Richelieu has been correspondingly severe. But if, as will be maintained in a subsequent chapter, the "Age of Louis XIV" is, with all its shortcomings, a great and glorious epoch in the history of European culture, comparable with Augustan Rome or Elizabethan England, Richelieu's name will shine with the glory reflected from such an achievement. The structure of society and government in France has never lost the traces of his work.

CHAPTER IX.

MAZARIN AND THE FRONDE.

IN the short interval between the death of Richelieu and his own death, Louis XIII had made arrangements for a regency that should prevent reaction and ensure the dominance of the ideas of Richelieu during the minority of Louis XIV. The Queen-Mother was to be the president of the Council of Regency, but was to have no power of independent action apart from it. The Duke of Orléans and the Prince of Condé were to hold places next in importance to her own. The other four members of the Council were to be Cardinal Mazarin, trusted and recommended by Richelieu; Seguier, the Chancellor; Bouthillier, the Superintendant of Finances; and Chavigny, the Secretary of Foreign Affairs. The three last had all been docile agents of the policy of Richelieu.

Mazarin's rise to power.

But Anne of Austria succeeded in breaking these limitations without any difficulty, for on all sides the people were eager for change. Her own character and aims were as yet uncertain; but her hostility to Richelieu was well known. Few were inclined to resist her advent to power, since she was likely to use that power to inaugurate a reaction against the policy of the dead Cardinal. Parlement was appealed to, and was flattered by the appeal, which was in striking contrast to Richelieu's repression and neglect. On May 18, by an unanimous vote, it annulled all previous arrangements for the regency, and gave Anne of Austria a free hand.

Those who had been opposed by Richelieu believed now that their turn had come. The Duchess of Chevreuse, an old friend of the Queen's, who had been exiled during the last reign, appeared again at Court after an absence of six years: she assumed that she would have for the future a great influence on affairs. There appeared too the Duke of Vendôme, with his two sons the Dukes of Beaufort and Mercœur, the Bishop of Beauvais and others, who believed that they would have good fortune under the new reign because the last had been unfavourable to them. They were doomed to disappointment. All turned upon the character and wishes of the Queen. Her portrait has been drawn for us by Madame de Motteville in the brightest and most flattering colours. Her beauty, her good taste, her kindness, her liberality are insisted on. It is, perhaps, more important to notice what defects are recognised by her admirer: Madame de Motteville admits that the Queen was of a lethargic temperament, that she was averse to active exertion, and that her education was deficient. A woman of such a character was not likely to be the real governor of France, but she was quite capable of reposing confidence in anyone who commanded her affection and convinced her of his devotion. The outside world received a hint as to who this favourite was to be, when, shortly after the session of Parlement mentioned above, the Queen appointed Mazarin First Minister. The new Minister was an Italian by birth, and his first experience of diplomacy had been in the service of the Pope. His ability had been recognized by Richelieu, and Mazarin shortly was transferred to the service of France. Richelieu on his death-bed had recommended him to the King; he knew no one, he said, more capable than Mazarin to fill the place that he left vacant. We have many descriptions of him

both by friends and foes. He never succeeded in assimilating
the manners or the pronunciation of France: his Italian accent
is often alluded to in the satires that poured upon him during
his career. In policy he maintained and carried further the
traditions of the policy of Richelieu, but in appearance and
temperament he was wholly unlike him. He had nothing of
Richelieu's inflexible directness, nothing of the swift but most
politic and patriotic severity with which he crushed all
opposition. He preferred to win his way by persuasion, and
even by bribery and deceit, rather than by an an appeal to force.
His contemporaries found something mysterious in this
foreigner, who rooted himself so firmly in France; so pliant,
and yet so strong; so often beaten, and ultimately so victorious. Historians have not had less difficulty in decipher-
ing his character and his aims. Madame de Motteville
knew him well and did not like him. She describes him as
charming, even to those who had reasons for disliking him;
always ready with promises and often with real service to those
who sought his favour; the least vindictive of men to his
declared opponents; singularly tolerant of all personal attacks
upon himself. We must add, to complete the picture, that his
foreign policy shows a vigour and insight that render it not unworthy of being compared with the policy of Richelieu. He
soon gained a complete ascendancy over the Queen's mind.
She supported him as steadily as Louis XIII had supported
Richelieu, and it is plain that the support was due to affection
as well as to policy [1].

---

[1] The picture that Cardinal Retz draws of Mazarin is a very notable
one. "On the steps of that throne from which the fierce and terrible
Richelieu had crushed rather than governed mankind we saw a gentle and
kindly successor, who never wanted anything, who was exceedingly sorry
that his dignity as Cardinal prevented him from humiliating himself before
you as much as he would have liked, who used to drive in the streets with
a brace of lackeys behind his carriage." Retz tells us too that it was the
French *u* which gave Mazarin most difficulty. He illustrates it by the

Whilst the new arrivals at Court were assuming that the future belonged to themselves, and were procuring themselves the nickname of "les Importants" in consequence, Mazarin was preparing for their overthrow. A plot to carry him off, perhaps even to assassinate him, was discovered, and the Duke of Beaufort was at the head of it. The Duke was accordingly arrested and imprisoned (Sept. 1643), and the Queen soon banished from the Court the chief of those who had sympathised with the object, even if they had not joined in the plot. Vendôme, the Bishop of Beauvais, and the Duchess of Chevreuse were all dismissed after a very short dream of power. Clearly Mazarin was to possess authority so far as Anne of Austria could secure it to him. For the next eighteen years all that is important in the history of France is closely connected with his name. His career has a double character. If we look at his dealings with foreign policy we see him, in spite of all difficulties, external and internal, conducting France successfully to the goal that had been indicated by Richelieu. If we look to the domestic history of France we see a spectacle of the greatest possible confusion. There is a rally of all the forces of discontent against the authority of the Monarchy. When one motive fails another succeeds: when the energies of one class, or of one part of France, are exhausted in the struggle, another is found to take it up. But all parties and all provinces seem to join in detestation of Mazarin; and yet in the end he emerges victorious, and even with a certain measure of popularity.

following story. Mazarin was one day pestered by a supplicant for some rich church benefice. He said to his attendant, " Souisse! prends ton arquebouse et va touer un abbé pour que je donne oune benefice à cet homme." I have not alluded to the story that the Queen was actually married to Mazarin, and yet the balance of probability seems to be in its favour. See for a summary of the evidence M. Hanotaux's Essay on "La Minorité de Louis XIV," in his " Études Historiques sur le XVIme et le XVIIme Siècle en France."

It will be well first to follow the history of foreign affairs down to the Peace of Westphalia.

The death of Richelieu came when France was in the full tide of success; but neither he nor his royal master lived to see the greatest triumph of their common policy. In the spring of 1643 the young Duke of Enghien had been placed in command on the Northern frontier. He was only twenty-two years of age, and his great military talents were not yet suspected. He brought to the army the prestige of a princely name, but it was expected that the real conduct of the war would lie with those who were given him as guides—the marshals L'Hôpital and Gassion. But they soon found that it was impossible to restrain his fiery impetuosity. Other plans were suggested, but Enghien determined on attacking the Spanish army, which was at the time laying siege to Rocroy, and with some difficulty induced L'Hôpital to consent to his plan : from Gassion he had throughout the most eager support. The Spaniards, under Don Francisco de Mellos, were superior in number and very strongly posted. The battle was at first mainly a cavalry engagement. On the right Enghien and Gassion carried all before them, and then fell on the Spanish centre and crushed it. But meanwhile L'Hôpital on the left was engaged in a fierce and losing struggle with the Spanish right. It was not until Enghien came up that the battle became favourable to the French in this quarter. When the Spanish cavalry was broken, the veteran Spanish infantry—4500 men, under the Count of Fontaines—still stood their ground. Three desperate charges of Enghien's horse were driven back. It was not until the reserves were brought up and the Spanish leader killed that at last the Spanish ranks were broken and scattered. The news of the victory was received with the utmost enthusiasm in Paris. The age of the victor, the striking incidents of the struggle, and the contrast it afforded to the tedious and indecisive campaigns that had hitherto characterised the war made Enghien the hero of all France: and when, soon afterwards, he succeeded to the title of Condé on his father's death he was saluted by public opinion as 'the Great.' The self-conscious reserve of his manners, his hawk-like features and his penetrating glance are described and praised in the Memoirs of the time. The rest of the year was not so favourable to the French. Enghien did indeed capture Thionville, after Metz the most important town on the Moselle, and the Spanish navy was defeated off Carthagena. But on the German frontier things had not gone so well. The Swedish army, under Marshal de Guébriant, was defeated and their leader killed, at Rothweil, in the Black Forest: a division sent to their relief from Enghien's army was almost annihilated. By the end of the year France seemed already to feel the want of Richelieu's firm hand.

In 1644 there was little fighting in most of the theatres of the war. The French were unfortunate in Spain, where they lost Lerida in July. On the northern frontier the capture of Gravelines was the most important incident. But in Germany a great battle was fought. There the two greatest soldiers of France were in joint command: for Turenne, who was at first sole commander, was subsequently joined by Enghien from the Flemish frontier. These two men, destined to a long rivalry, were a very great contrast to one another in all except general ability and courage. For while Enghien was impetuous to foolhardiness, egotistic, and incapable of loyalty, as prodigal of the lives of his soldiers as he was ready to risk his own; Turenne, on the other hand, had studied every detail of the military art, and, though willing to run great risks where they were necessary, preferred to trust to science and skill rather than to mere courage and dash. His care for his soldiers was proverbial, and gained him their warm devotion. He was seduced from the path of loyalty for a time during the disturbance of the Fronde, but afterwards was the very type of self-respecting loyalty. It may be questioned which of these two was the greater soldier, but unquestionably Turenne was the greater man, and he ended by being the more popular hero in France. The Imperial troops were commanded by Mercy, no mean opponent. Freiburg fell into his hands on July 28, 1644, and it was close to the town that the great battle was fought. Mercy was very strongly posted, but Condé insisted on attacking him. After a fierce and indecisive struggle, Mercy took up another strong position near at hand, among the mountains of the Black Forest. Here he was again attacked on August 5. After a murderous struggle the French were driven off, but Mercy had suffered so severely that he determined to retire into the Black Forest and abandon the course of the Rhine to the enemy. Turenne and Enghien took full advantage of the situation. They embarked their artillery upon rafts and dropped down stream. In a short time they had taken Philippsburg, Worms, Oppenheim, and Mayence. The course of the Rhine was in French hands, to serve either as a barrier or as a sally-port.

Negotiations for peace had been earnestly begun in 1644, but fighting still went on in all directions during the year 1645, though with some slackening of energy. It will be well to follow the course of the war before turning to the diplomatic struggle. The French gained during 1645 some successes of a not very decisive kind in Spain. Turenne and Enghien were engaged as before on the Rhine frontier. In May, Turenne was sharply defeated by Mercy, at Marienthal; but in July, with Enghien, he advanced to attack Nordlingen, and forced Mercy to give battle in order to save the place. The battle was fought exactly a year after the battle of Freiburg, which in many respects it resembles. There was the same impetuous attack on a difficult position, the same murderous fighting, and for some time the same balanced fortune. But Mercy was killed by a musket-ball, and John of Werth drew off the Imperial troops towards Donauwerth. The victors had suffered too severely to follow up their advantage; but in November, Turenne, crossing to the left bank of the Rhine, invested and took Trèves.

The year 1646 was more occupied with negotiations than with fighting. It was felt now to be probable that, so far as Germany was concerned, peace might soon be re-established. But fighting still went on, at least in three theatres of the war. In Spain the French, under the Count of Harcourt, were beaten off from Lerida. But this severe check was compensated for in the north, where Enghien gained very important successes. He attacked Courtrai and forced it to capitulate in June. He followed this up immediately by an attack on the still more important fortress of Dunkirk. It held out three weeks and surrendered on October 11. Turenne, meanwhile, had been engaging in operations peculiarly characteristic of him. He effected a junction with the Swedish general Wrangel, and then, by skilful strategy rather than by fighting, he obliged the Archduke Leopold, whose forces were numerically superior, to evacuate Swabia. Turenne and Wrangel then took up their winter quarters on the confines of Bavaria. The Elector of Bavaria saw his territory once more in danger of being ravaged. In March, 1647, he and his brother the Elector of Cologne accepted a treaty wherein they promised to remain neutral during the rest of the war. The campaign that had produced this result is reckoned one of Turenne's masterpieces. But Spain showed no intention of admitting defeat, and the war against her was continued in 1647 and 1648. In 1647 the incidents that deserve chronicling were not very numerous. The most important was that Condé (for owing to his father's death Enghien succeeded in this year to the title), suffered the first check of his career. He had been sent, somewhat against his will, to succeed Harcourt in Catalonia. He undertook the siege of Lerida and pressed it with his usual impetuosity. But the natural strength of the place was too great to be overcome. In June Condé had to confess victory impossible. In the same year Naples rebelled against Spain. No blow could be more serious, for now that the United Netherlands were gone and the communication with the New World was made unsafe by the collapse of the naval power of Spain, Naples and Sicily were the most valuable dependencies of the Spanish Monarchy. The revolt, so dramatic in its incidents and so interesting in its character, hardly belongs to French history. A French adventurer, the Duke of Guise, whose family possessed hereditary claims to the Neapolitan Crown, was for a time at the head of the insurrection. Mazarin distrusted him and refused to support him; but the revolt weakened the strength and showed the diminishing prestige of Spain. With the year 1648 came the last campaign of the terrible Thirty Years' War. Both Turenne and Condé distinguished themselves during its course. Turenne, with the Swedish general Wrangel, again turned against the Duke of Bavaria, who was accused of having broken his promise of neutrality, and in May fought against the Imperial general, Montecuculi, the battle of Zusmarshausen near Augsburg. Turenne and his ally gained a complete victory. Prague was occupied by the Swedes. Danger thus came very close to the Emperor, and hastened the conclusion of peace. Another great victory had meanwhile fallen to Condé. The Spaniards had taken Courtrai and laid siege to Lens. Condé tried in vain to save it, and finding the Archduke Leopold too strongly posted returned without attacking him. But he was followed by the Archduke and attacked. The battle at first went in favour of the Spaniards. But Condé, with the rapid insight and decision which were his great characteristics as a general, brought up his second line and by a vigorous cavalry charge turned the fortune of the battle. The Spaniards were entirely defeated, with a great loss of men and guns. The greater part of their flags and standards fell into the hands of the enemy. *Battle of Lens, August 20, 1648.*

This was the last serious engagement before the signature

The Peace of Westphalia. of the Peace of Westphalia. The scope of the book does not allow us to follow in detail the negotiations that led up to the Peace. They had been going on for four years and a-half at Osnabrück and Münster. At first Mazarin had hoped to establish a general European peace; but Spain held out too stiffly to make that possible, especially after Philip IV had recognised the independence of the United Netherlands, and thus deprived France of a valuable ally; for when the Dutch received this recognition they had no longer any motive for continuing the war. Mazarin had, therefore, to confine his attention to the pacification of Germany. The difficulties were great; the postponements and disappointments numerous, but at last peace was signed.

The Peace of Westphalia is the greatest international arrangement of modern times. The modern map of Europe depends on it. But it is impossible here to do more than notice some of its more important general results, after which we may examine in rather more detail the alterations introduced into the French frontiers.

1. The period of the Reformation ends with the Peace of Westphalia. During the latter part of the Thirty Years' War religious and theological disputes had been thrust into the background by political and dynastic interests. Henceforward the clash of Protestantism and Catholicism was not again to be a chief disturbing force in Europe. The great religious struggle ended in a drawn battle.

2. The effort of the Empire to concentrate and strengthen the Imperial power in Germany had entirely failed. Austria remained a great power: the Empire was hardly a power at all. The number of practically sovereign states within its limits, lay and ecclesiastical, was fixed at 343. That fact is sufficient to show how entirely the effort to give unity to its organisation had failed. The defeat of the Empire was a defeat also for the allied and related power of Spain.

3. While the Empire and Spain declined, France and Sweden rose. With Sweden we are not concerned here. The supremacy of France, founded by Richelieu and carried forward by Mazarin, had become clearly marked during the last years of the war. She had gained many striking victories; she had suffered no serious defeats. Her superiority in diplomacy was as great as in arms.

4. It remains to be noted what were the special gains which France made by the Peace. No part of the negotiations was more difficult than that which concerned the cessions which were to be made to France. The reluctance of the Empire, the claims of France and the protests of the territories concerned presented a problem which it seemed beyond the power of diplomacy to settle, and at last clauses of vague and elastic meaning were introduced which proved a most fruitful source of disputes and wars in the future. In the end two separate documents appended to the treaty of Westphalia defined the gains of France from the Empire. The Empire renounced its rights over the cities and Bishoprics of Metz, Toul and Verdun "with their districts"; the city and fort of Breisach; Upper and Lower Alsace; the Sundgau; and Pinerolo. Of these Metz, Toul and Verdun had been in the effective possession of France since the reign of Henry II, and Pinerolo had been ceded to France by the Duke of Savoy in 1631; now the Empire renounced all claims to sovereignty of any kind. But in spite of the elaborate phraseology of the documents the exact result of the cessions was very doubtful. What for instance was the meaning of the word 'districts' as applied to the three Bishoprics? It was quite doubtful whether it included all that fell within the ecclesiastical province of the Bishoprics or not. There were similar obscurities with regard to the cessions in Alsace. The document indeed definitely mentioned the Sundgau, Breisach, both Upper and Lower Alsace and the ten Imperial cities (Haguenau, Colmar, Schlettstadt, Weissenburg, Landau, Obernheim, Rosheim, Münster,

Kaiserburg and Türkheim), but again these places were to pass to France "with all the rights that had formerly belonged to the Empire" and further "with all the country and all the rights which depend on the praefecture of these cities (omnesque pagos et alia quaecunque jura quae a dicta praefectura dependent). We shall see that in the reign of Louis XIV the sword had to be invoked to define the meaning of these obscure phrases. In addition to the above clauses the Empire promised to give no further assistance to Spain, to allow France full rights of commerce on both banks of the Rhine, and to build no forts on the right bank from Bâle to Philipsburg.

Mazarin had thus gained a very brilliant diplomatic success— one of the very greatest indeed in the history of European diplomacy. But it produced little effect in France at the time, for the war with Spain had still to run its uncertain course, and a domestic and constitutional struggle had broken out which distracted the attention and lowered the energies of the people. It is to this struggle that we must now turn.

The Fronde is in its most general expression the last rally of all the discontented or injured classes against the establishment of a strong Monarchy. It seemed to many that the work which Richelieu had done was due only to his own energy and genius. The opening of a new reign seemed to offer a chance of overthrowing his system. But after a prolonged struggle it was seen that many forces were working for a centralised and strong government, and that Richelieu had only cooperated with the tendency and needs of the time.

The Fronde.

The period of the Fronde is in its domestic aspects very confused and hard to follow—far more so than the contemporary Revolution in England, for personal motives and ambitions count for much more, and principles for much less. But it is possible to analyse the chief forces and ambitions whose conflict and interaction produced the struggle.

First, there was the people at large, broken with taxation.

The appointment of *Intendants* made them attribute their burdens to the action of the central government, not of the Nobility. The provinces were ripe for rebellion. Omer Talon tells us in his Memoirs that the whole realm was starving. "If the peasant enjoyed the possession of his soul it was simply because he could not put it up for sale." The peasantry however counted for very little, and their voice was not destined to enjoy any political importance for more than 140 years.

Much more important was the irritation of the Nobility. The work of Henry IV and Richelieu was too recent to allow them to forget their old power. They were still great landowners: they claimed large feudal rights over their peasants: but they found men of middle-class origin or, worse still, foreigners preferred to themselves in the councils of the King, and in their own provinces the reality of administrative power passing to the King's *Intendants*. The nobles had not shown any talent for government in the brief period of confusion that had followed the death of Henry IV. They showed none during the Fronde. Their action is usually prompted by personal motives: at most they fight for their class, never for their country: and an examination of their conduct during these years makes us acquiesce fully in their overthrow and the triumph of the Monarchy. But they had courage, energy, and high military qualities, so that they were able to throw the kingdom into confusion if incapable of ruling it.

The Parlement of Paris was more immediately important than the Nobility. After Richelieu had done his work the Parlements remained almost the last **Parlement.** channel of constitutional resistance to the edicts of the Crown. The chief function of the Parlement of Paris was, as we have seen, not indeed political at all but judicial; its only direct political power consisted in its right to register the King's edicts before they could be regarded as binding upon the people of France. Under a strong Government, registration was usually accomplished as a matter of course, but one of the first signs that the prestige of the Crown was shaken was the resistance offered by Parlement, and its claim to debate upon and modify the edicts of the King. Of course it represented the nation in no way at all: for most of the members held their seat by purchase and by hereditary right. But since Sully had imposed the *paulette* they were irremovable, except for misconduct as judges, and there were in their ranks at the time some men of great ability and high courage. The Parlement failed indeed in its resistance to the Crown, but the action and character of men like Omer Talon, Broussel and Molé made its failure an honourable one.

The constant drain of the war was very heavy, and the King's financial necessities were the immediate cause of the outbreak. Richelieu had been no economist, but Mazarin squandered money with very much greater lavishness. It was part of his policy to *buy* support among the malcontents, and the Queen out of good nature or policy squandered money among the nobles. In the spring of 1644 the ordinary resources of the State seemed exhausted. Emery, who had charge of the finances, sought for fresh expedients. In July he proposed to revive a forgotten edict of 1548 which forbade the building of new houses within a certain distance from the centre of Paris. The forbidden ground was now crowded with houses, and Emery proposed to make all owners of such houses pay a fine (*la taxe du toisé*). The Parlement resisted this and other financial edicts, and Mazarin had recourse to a 'bed of justice.' The seven year old King was brought down to the Parlement. He was made to say that he was acting "of his own accord and out of the plenitude of his power," and the edicts were registered. But another edict, brought forward in the same year for the levying of a tax upon the wealthier classes (*la taxe des aisés*) met with so much opposition that it was withdrawn. During the next three years there was friction between the Court and the Parlement, but nothing of much consequence happened. The war was critical, and resistance to the Government might seem unpatriotic. The crisis came in 1648, and many things seem to have helped to produce it. It was clear that the war in Germany was coming to an end, and there was therefore less reason for acquiescing in everything that Mazarin proposed. The Revolution in England and the victory of the English Parliament produced a profound impression in Paris. The contemporary rebellion of the people of Naples against the Spanish Government was not without its effect.

Resistance began with the beginning of the year 1648. The Government sent down to Parlement six financial edicts of no great importance. But the temper of the city was very irritable, and Mazarin had to have recourse to a 'bed of justice' to enforce their registration. Quiet reigned for a time, but the ambition of Parlement had been roused, and the members gradually awoke to the possibility of playing a great political part. As the Government persisted in demanding the acceptance of financial edicts, it was determined on the 13th May, by the Edict of Union, that deputies from all the chambers of the Parlement of Paris should meet representatives of the other 'sovereign courts'[1] of Paris, to deliberate on the situation. The Court protested against so bold and threatening a step, issued *lettres de cachet* against some of the members, and ordered the members to withdraw; but they persisted in their action. The attempt of the Court to conciliate the Parlement by certain concessions was equally futile. The concessions were refused, and the sessions of the United Courts were held in the Chamber of St Louis, at the Palace of Justice. The Conference made certain proposals, which were subsequently accepted by the Parlement. They amounted to a direct attack

[1] The four sovereign courts were, the Parlement of Paris, the Chambre des Comtes, the Cour des Aides, and the Grand Conseil. To unite them was, it has been remarked, to reestablish the ancient *Conseil du Roi*, out of which the Parlement and all the other sovereign Courts believed themselves to have developed. (See Chap. I.)

on the system of the Monarchy. The chief demands were (i) the removal of the Intendants, (ii) the abolition of all financial arrangements made with the 'Partisans'[1] for the collection of taxes, (iii) the *taille* to be reduced by one quarter, and no further tax to be imposed without the registration of the 'sovereign Courts,' (iv) the abolition of arbitrary imprisonment (an attack on *lettres de cachet*), and the introduction of something like a Habeas Corpus Act.

The exclusive legislative authority of the Crown was thus directly challenged: and yet at first Mazarin and the Queen hoped that conciliation might be possible. Emery, the unpopular Controller-General, was withdrawn: a promise was given that the *Intendants* should be removed. But the Parlement showed itself little grateful for the concessions, and soon the Monarchy recovered courage to strike. On the 19th August Condé gained the great victory of Lens, and the Government determined to see whether the prestige of the victory would not allow them to crush the Parlement. On August 26 orders were given for the arrest of three prominent members. One escaped, but Blancmesnil and Broussel were arrested.

There was nothing contrary to the tradition of the Monarchy in these arrests, and neither Mazarin nor the Queen seems to have feared the results. But recent events had had their effect on the minds of the Parisians; the notion that the power of the Monarchy ought to be limited was widespread and popular, and the news of the arrests at once produced a violent commotion. The streets were barricaded. Paris breathed defiance against the Monarchy. New actors began to appear on the scene. Of these, the most important was Gondi, coadjutor to

---

[1] These were capitalists who bought from the Government certain taxes, or the taxes of a certain district, which they then collected themselves. Their exactions are a frequent cause of complaint and distress down to the Revolution.

the Bishop of Paris, and afterwards Cardinal de Retz[1]. He had been destined for a military career, but family convenience had turned him aside into the Church. He has left Memoirs, of very great value as literature, that reveal his character—his restless, intriguing spirit, his cleverness in intrigue and his love of it for its own sake, the absence of any high motive or fixed plan in all he did, his exclusive desire to advance himself and attract the eyes of men. Other figures come to the front with him— the Dukes of Elbeuf and of Bouillon, anxious to gain territorial advantages out of the confusion; the Duke of Beaufort, grandson of Henry IV, and a popular name with the masses; above all the Duchess of Longueville, the sister of Condé, powerful by her birth, and still more by her beauty, whose interest in the Fronde was wholly personal. Protest was quickly made against the action of the Court. The Parlement went to the Royal Palace to petition for the deliverance of their colleagues. They were at first satisfied with vague promises, but the populace barred the streets, and would not let them pass until they brought the actual order for the release of Broussel and Blancmesnil. In the end the prisoners were set at liberty: but the excitement did not subside. The Queen withdrew to Ruel with Louis XIV. The financial administration of the country collapsed. Mazarin was everywhere unpopular, and an edict of 1617 which excluded foreigners from the Ministry was reaffirmed by the Parlement. A conference was held between the Parlement and certain princes, under the presidency of Orléans and Condé, with the result that certain demands were put forward. Most of these were financial. The administration of the finances was to be rendered more public, and many abuses were to be abolished. The last demand was that every person arrested should be confronted with his judges within 24 hours. Somewhat to the surprise of Paris the Queen

[1] He will for the future be called Cardinal de Retz in this chapter, though he did not receive the title until 1652.

consented to sign these articles. Her decision gave her a moment's popularity, and at least a short period of tranquillity seemed assured.

But the calm was illusory. The Queen had regarded the concessions as "an assassination of the royal authority," and now found that instead of bringing the contest to an end they had emboldened Parlement and public opinion. De Retz and the discontented nobles were known to be plotting vigorously. Mazarin determined to strike. In the night of the 5th January, 1649, the Queen, Louis XIV, and Mazarin fled from Paris to St Germain. The next day came an edict ordering the Parlement to transfer its sittings to Montargis. Parlement answered the challenge boldly. It denounced Mazarin as an enemy of the King and the State, and a disturber of the public peace. Money was voted to carry on the resistance. The Parlement was joined by a considerable number of the great nobles, who saw in any revolt a chance of striking a blow for their own privileges. The command of the city forces was given to Conti, the brother of Condé. The Dukes of Elbeuf, Bouillon, and Beaufort gathered round him. Madame de Longueville brought her beauty and her talents to the support of the party. At the same time the rising in Paris caused sympathetic movements in the provinces. All the other Parlements declared in favour of the action of the Parlement of Paris. Many of the great towns, such as Reims, Tours and Poitiers, protested against Mazarin's action, and Normandy and Provence broke out into open revolt.

Outbreak of war.

The Court on its side entrusted the command to the great Condé, the hero of Rocroy, who, after coquetting with the Fronde, had been won over for the time to the royal side, and in the military scuffles which followed the advantage on the whole lay with him. The most important incident was a combat at Charenton (Feb. 1649), in which the Parisian force was easily driven in. But it speedily became clear that the struggle would not last long. Food was soon scarce in Paris. The news of the execution of Charles I cooled the eagerness of many by showing them to what lengths civil struggles might lead them. Most important of all, there grew up a divergence between the aims of the Parlementarians and the nobles. For Parlement, intimately bound by its traditions to the royal power, desired nothing better than the restoration of order, if only certain reforms could be established. The nobles, who filled the Hôtel de Ville with gaiety, wished to use the Parlement as an instrument for the breaking of the monarchical system. They were willing even to enter into an alliance with Spain, and were irritated with Parlement for refusing to contemplate the idea. Under such circumstances it was natural to think of a compromise. It was determined to hold a conference at Ruel at the beginning of March. Molé was the chief representative of Paris, and it was largely due to his courage and firmness that the cause of peace triumphed so quickly. He refused to make any concessions to the claims of the nobles or the passions of the Parisian populace. The Queen promised a general amnesty, the restoration of all confiscated property, and certain financial concessions. At one time it had seemed as if there might be a deadlock with regard to Mazarin, for Paris demanded his removal, and the Queen was determined to retain him. In the end Paris gave way. The Peace of Ruel was signed on March 11th, and was accepted in Paris on April 1 (1649). The First Fronde was at an end, and all but the Nobility were delighted that it should be so.

The treaty of Ruel gave little stability to the Government of France. The action of the Parlement, which had given to the movement of the Fronde its most respectable features, falls into the background. *The intrigues and ambitions of Condé.* Henceforth the Fronde is mainly an aristocratic intrigue, in which Condé plays by far the most important part. His military exploits had filled him with an overweening confidence in himself. He was irritated to think that Mazarin, a foreigner and a Churchman, should have more influence in the State than himself. His importance, great by reason of his military reputation and talents, was increased by his royal blood and by his important relationships. He received assistance of the most valuable kind from women. His mother, the Princess of Condé, showed herself as energetic as her son. His sister, the Duchess of Longueville, assisted him not only by her real talents for diplomatic intrigue, but also by bringing to his side nobles who joined his cause in order to win her favour. For this reason the Duke of Rochefoucauld joined Condé, and the same motive made Turenne, just before the Peace of Ruel, swerve from his loyalty to the King in a way which contrasts strikingly with the general tenour of his career. In the ranks of the Nobility the sense of loyalty to the Crown was hardly developed at all; they had no pricks of conscience in fighting for their own order against the Monarchy.

The Court returned to Paris in August, 1649, and friction arose at once between Mazarin and Condé. For Condé regarded himself as the real cause of the Queen's victory over the Frondeurs, and claimed almost to dispose of the fortunes of the Crown. In particular, he demanded high rewards for himself and his relations. Mazarin refused to grant important posts to the nobles who had been against the Crown in the late disturbances, and Condé and his large following opposed and insulted Mazarin in consequence. In September there was an open rupture between them in the presence of the Queen. In October there was the appearance of reconciliation, but the old opposition continued. France, meanwhile, was restless. The Peace of Westphalia had brought no reduction in the taxes: the war with Spain still demanded all the resources of the State. In Nov. 1649 the detested Emery was restored to the control of the finances. The material seemed ready for another outbreak. The whole machinery of intrigue still subsisted in Paris, and many of the Frondeurs hoped for a return of the disturbances.

Towards the end of 1649 the quarrel between Condé and the Court reached a point at which peace became impossible. He not only asked for places and incomes for his personal supporters, but demanded that the Government should take up his personal quarrels and assist him in striking at enemies or rivals. Even Mazarin, who loved to elude his enemies rather than to overthrow them, saw that the time was come to strike a blow against his powerful rival. Overtures were made to de Retz, and he readily offered his support to the royal cause, and promised to induce Paris to acquiesce in the attack upon Condé and his party. On January 15, 1650, when Condé came to the royal council he was arrested, and his brother, Conti, and his brother-in-law, the Duke of Longueville, along with him. Turenne, Bouillon, and La Rochefoucauld were to have been arrested too, but escaped. Those who were thus struck at were not merely some of the highest nobles in the land, among them were also the most trusted and successful generals of the army.

The arrest of Condé.

The military fame of Condé was so great that the news that the "hero of Rocroy" was in prison roused much sympathy and indignation; but at first little dangerous opposition was made to what had been done. The Duchess of Longueville, after vainly endeavouring to induce Normandy to rise in support of Condé, joined Turenne at Stenay. The Paris Parlement seemed to acquiesce readily in what had been done, for they had hitherto regarded Condé as the chief agent of the Court in resisting their aspirations.

A very confused period follows, in which it is extremely hard to disentangle the causes of the events, and to trace the motives of the chief actors. Their conduct was governed not by policy but by intrigue, and the purpose of the intrigue is often very hard to follow. But the chief elements in the situation remain the same: Mazarin was unpopular with nearly everyone: the nobles were ready for any intrigue or rebellion, partly for their own sake, partly in the hope of weakening the power of the Crown. Parlement vacillated, both in opinion and action, and was itself divided into factions: some of its members were for supporting the Court: some were violently opposed to the illegal arrest of Condé and his companions, and were prepared therefore to offer to the policy of Mazarin a firm resistance: some were imbued with the most violent sentiments of the time, and despite the experiences of the first Fronde were prepared to embark upon another. The result of all these conflicting opinions and efforts was a temporary check for Mazarin, and a victory for Condé. The military situation, too, seemed dangerous: there was revolt in the South, while in the North, Turenne and the Spaniards were threatening Paris. The presence of "the great Condé" at the head of the French army seemed necessary.

While Turenne cooperated with the Spaniards in the North, the Princess of Condé had gone to the South, in the hope of raising the country on behalf of her son. She succeeded in inducing the great city of Bordeaux to champion her cause, and from Bordeaux, when once she had been admitted within its walls, she began to negotiate with Spain. Mazarin and the Court turned first against this danger; but, as the Queen went in full state, their advance was remarkably slow and the action of Mazarin at the juncture was extremely lethargic. Here, as always with his domestic enemies, he preferred negotiation to force, and after some delay he was successful in inducing Bordeaux to return to its allegiance. But by that time the danger in the North had assumed alarming dimensions. In June (1650), Turenne and the Archduke Leopold had occupied La Capelle, Vervins, and Rethel, and Mouzon fell into their hands in October. In December, Turenne's Spanish army was sharply defeated by Duplessis Praslin, but even after that the Spanish army was decidedly superior on the northern frontier, and Paris felt itself threatened. Greater irritation than ever was felt against Mazarin: he was accused of causing these disasters by the slowness of his movements, and more than ever men's thoughts turned to Condé's almost unbroken career of victory. On January 20, 1651, Parlement petitioned the Queen for the liberation of the Princes, and was not satisfied when she answered that she would set them free as soon as Turenne and Madame de Longueville had disarmed. The Duke of Orléans, the constant and singularly incapable conspirator against Richelieu's power, again dreamed of playing a political *rôle*. He joined himself to the Parlement, refused to listen to Mazarin's overtures, and became the spokesman of the discontents of Paris. De Retz, too, had not received from the Court the rewards that he had expected, and again threw his influence on the side of resistance.

The Court had no adequate force and no capable general to rely on; Mazarin determined to bow before the storm, and perhaps to gain some popularity by doing with an appearance of willingness what would probably have soon been forced from him. On Feb. 16, 1651, he left Paris in disguise, and making his way to Havre, where Condé and his associates were imprisoned, himself ordered their release. If he expected to earn their gratitude he was disappointed, for Condé opposed him more bitterly than ever. Paris had been greatly excited by Mazarin's retreat, and suspected, doubtless with good reason, that the Queen intended to follow him. A crowd assembled round the Royal Palace and refused to disperse until some of them were admitted into the Palace and shown Louis XIV asleep in his bed. When the news of Condé's liberation arrived, Parlement declared him and his associates innocent of the charges brought against them and restored them to their honours and their offices. The expulsion of Mazarin from the kingdom was still demanded. He thought it best to yield still further, and at the beginning of April he quitted the soil of France and took up his residence at Brühl, in the Electorate of Cologne.

Was it then a victory of Condé and the aristocratic party in France? That issue was by no means settled yet. Mazarin and the Queen had only drawn back in order to spring the further. From Brühl Mazarin exercised as complete a control over the councils of the Queen as when he saw her daily. The middle months of 1651 were filled with intrigue. Parlement suspected the designs of the nobles; the nobles despised the pretensions of the lawyers. The Duke of Orléans tried to drive out the present Ministers of the Queen, Servien, Lionne, and Le Tellier, whom he denounced as agents of the detested Mazarin; but his efforts were in vain. The Court negotiated with de Retz, who represented himself as master of Paris. The Queen promised to support him in his application for the Cardinal's hat if he would induce Paris to declare against Condé. He promised, and his task was rendered easier by the behaviour of Condé, who seemed to regard himself as the ruler of France. There was a rumour that he dreamed of deposing the little King and himself seizing the throne: it is certain that he claimed powers which would have made him too powerful for a subject. He demanded the governments of Guienne and Languedoc for himself, that of Provence for his brother, and fortresses, dignities, and pensions for his friends. The excitement in Paris was at a very high pitch. It is impossible to be sure of the strength of the various currents in the mobile Parisian society, but it seems clear that the feeling in favour of Condé was not nearly unanimous, either in Parlement or among the people; and that de Retz in the hope of succeeding to Mazarin's influence, worked hard to make the Queen popular. On August 17 the Queen summoned the Parlement and other Courts to the Royal Palace, and submitted to them a declaration in which she accused Condé of negotiations with Spain and other acts of high treason. A scene of great uproar ensued, and clearly opinion was much divided. It was very uncertain what would happen in Paris, but early in September Condé, fiercely irritated against the Court, of whose continued dependence on Mazarin he was convinced, distrusting the temper of Paris and hoping for a more rapid success in the military sphere that was more congenial to him than the cabals and intrigues of Paris, left the city and went to Guienne. Bordeaux declared for him. War was clearly imminent and Paris was in danger of being caught between two armies—Turenne and the Spaniards on the north and the army of Condé in the South.

The confusion of interests was extreme. The war was clearly a struggle between the Monarchy and its most conspicuous soldier, but what part would Paris take? What was the feeling of the nation at large? What would be the action of the Parlements? At this juncture an important ally came to the aid of the Crown. Turenne was weary of faction and soon felt that his championship of the cause of Condé was a mistake. He offered his services to the Queen Mother and Mazarin, and they were of course eagerly accepted. Parlement maintained a neutral position. At first, on December 4, they had declared Condé guilty of high treason. But then there came the news that Mazarin, their special foe, had left Brühl and was advancing into the heart of France with an army which he had raised out of his own vast fortune. On the 29th Parlement, in a violent passion, declared him a disturber of the public peace and a traitor to the State, and at the same time offered a reward of 150,000 livres to anyone who would bring him to Paris dead or alive. The Duke of Orléans meanwhile vacillated helplessly between the opposing parties, anxious to play a great part for which he had neither character nor intelligence. All his life long he was directed by some favourite or relation: now he fell under the influence of his daughter, "*la grande mademoiselle*," who played a very adventurous and romantic part during the incidents that follow. He was induced to make alliance with Condé and to declare against the Crown.

In spite of the edict of Parlement Mazarin joined the Court at Poitiers (Feb. 1652); and with him to negotiate and Turenne to direct the campaign the outlook of the Court was hopeful. The only considerable gain of Condé was when the city of Orléans, through the agency of *la grande mademoiselle*, declared for him. But two armies prepared to act against him. Harcourt opposed him in Guienne, while another army under Turenne escorted the Court in a campaign on the Loire. Meanwhile Condé, weary of the indecisive struggle in Guienne, traversed the south of France alone, and in the disguise of a valet joined his army upon the Loire. His presence was at once manifested by an energetic attack on the royal forces at Bléneau, a little south of the Loire, which they had crossed at Gien. At first Condé was successful: if the royal party had fallen into his hands the result would have been overwhelming, but Turenne came up with another division of the army, and by skilful strategy restored the fortune of the day, and held Condé at bay while the Court fell back on Paris. Condé at once embarked on another adventure. If Paris could be induced to join him that would compensate for the loss of half-a-dozen engagements. He left his army upon the Loire and went to Paris, where he presented himself to the Parlement on April 12. But his reception was a cold one. Mazarin was still hated, but Condé's name had lost its ancient glamour, and Parlement was not prepared to support a man who was in alliance with Spain.

The general position then at the end of April, 1652, was this. Condé lay outside of the walls of Paris with an army that he had recruited with difficulty. The King and Turenne pressed on him from the south and defeated his forces in small engagements. Everything seemed turning against Condé: a Spanish force marched to his relief, but was induced by Mazarin's bribes to retire: in Guienne his supporters were defeated. His last hope therefore lay with Paris, and if he gained the support of the city he could treat with the King on something like terms of equality. Paris was decided for neither party, but was a prey to the most violent excitement. There was a constant war of pamphlets, satires, and *Mazarinades*.

The Parlement drifted further away from Condé and

Mazarin and the Fronde. 289

chiefly desired the restoration of peace. The Duke of Orléans, as usual, seemed likely to betray the party to which he had joined himself, and de Retz, having now procured the Cardinal's hat, which had been the great object of his ambition, had no longer any very strong motive for maintaining his intrigues. Decisive incidents occurred in July. Condé determined to move from St Cloud, where his army had hitherto been posted, to the confluence of the Marne and the Seine. To reach the place he had to march round Paris, for the authorities would not admit him into the city. Turenne, who had hitherto been posted at St Denis, moved to intercept him. Condé fell back upon strong entrenchments outside of the Porte St Antoine. Turenne wished to postpone the attack until the arrival of his artillery, but the young King, who in 1651 had attained his majority at the age of 13, ignorant of war but eager for an immediate victory, insisted that the assault should be begun at once. A most desperate conflict ensued. Condé never displayed greater energy nor skill, not even on the field of Rocroy, but at last after a frightful carnage the entrenchments were stormed by Turenne, and Condé's forces were driven under the walls of Paris. In spite of desperate fighting from street to street, and house to house, it seemed that Condé must soon surrender with his whole army. He was saved by a movement of his partisans within the city. Mademoiselle, the daughter of the Duke of Orléans, urged first her father and then the Municipality to save the Prince of Condé. The sight of the wounded and the dead gave emphasis to her words, and in the end she carried her point. Just when Condé seemed ruined and Turenne was pressing hard upon him, the gates were thrown open, and from the Bastille the cannon opened upon the Royal forces (July 2, 1652).

Though the Royal army had gained a complete victory, Condé was safe and Paris seemed to have declared for him. But the gates had been opened in a moment of great excitement and under the influence of the moving appeal of *la grande mademoiselle*: the action of the city still remained uncertain. An assembly of representatives of Paris was held at the Hôtel de Ville on July 4, but the general tone of the meeting was far from favourable to Condé. During their deliberations the hall was stormed by the mob, and some fifty of the representatives were killed. The mob was certainly under the guidance and probably in the pay of Condé and the Duke of Orléans, and all resistance to them was for the moment suppressed. On the 13th a meeting of the Parlement was held, but was very thinly attended: those who presented themselves were forced by threats to appoint the Duke of Orléans Lieutenant-General, and Condé Commander of the Forces.

Again Condé seemed victorious, but his entire collapse was now very near. The decisions recently taken did not represent the feeling of Paris; still less did they represent the feeling of the Parlement, and the Court knew it. Mazarin saw the opportunity for negotiating and seized it. Parlement was summoned by the King to meet at Pontoise, and though very few presented themselves at first, the numbers soon increased. A reaction, as after such violent scenes was inevitable, set in at Paris. The wretched condition of the country was a strong argument for peace. The victories of the Spaniards tended to make Condé unpopular. Mazarin saw that he himself was the chief obstacle to a compromise. On the 19th of August he again withdrew from France and took up his residence in Sedan. After his withdrawal the Royalist sympathies of Paris soon gained decidedly the upper hand. Condé was entreated to make peace, but he refused, or insisted on such conditions as were equivalent to a refusal. But the desire for peace increased rapidly, and Condé, seeing that the game was up, left Paris and went to join the Spanish army. Soon there was no doubt as to the real feeling of the people. On the 18th of October a conference was held with the King, and Paris determined to accept him on his own terms. He entered Paris on the 21st, summoned Parlement to the Louvre on the 22nd, and forced them to register an edict forbidding them henceforth to concern themselves with the finances of the State or with affairs of public policy. On the 15th November another bed of justice was held and an edict registered declaring Condé, Conti, the Duchess of Longueville, and the Duke of Rochefoucauld guilty of high treason. Cardinal de Retz regarded himself as one of the chief agents of the King's victory, and expected honour and power as a reward. But his intrigues with the enemy and his open opposition to the Crown were not forgotten, and his assumption of power and his hope to replace Mazarin made the all-powerful Minister decidedly his enemy. In December he was arrested and imprisoned at Vincennes. In Feb. 1653 Mazarin returned from his self-imposed exile. There were no signs of his former unpopularity. He was cheered on his entry into Paris.

The details of this curious movement are described for us in a series of very brilliant memoirs, which present the complicated intrigues and adventures with much personal and romantic interest. But the struggle itself was an ignoble one. After the first effort of the Parlement of Paris to secure guarantees for personal liberty and restrictions on the Crown, there was no principle represented by the rebellion. Condé's action was personal and egotistic throughout, regardless of honour and of patriotism. The events of the struggle sank deep into the heart and memory of Louis XIV. He never forgot how the opposition of the nobles and the Parlement had made him a fugitive from his capital and had endangered his crown. Despite an act of amnesty he pursued the leaders of the Fronde with great vindictiveness. He resisted the claims of Parlement with decisive vigour, and even showed resentment against the city of Paris, fixing, as we shall see, his residence at Versailles instead of at the Louvre. But the movement of the Fronde had not really been a dangerous one. The resistance to the Monarchy was not deeply rooted in the life of the nation, and had owed most of its success to the personal force of Condé. The failure of the movement made the way of the absolute Monarchy smoother. The nobles were crushed and discredited: Parlement by its constitution was cut off from the life of the nation: the time of the people was not yet. Their cause was indeed better represented by the centralised Monarchy than it would have been by the States General: for States General would have meant at this moment the rule of the aristocracy, and events had thrown into clear relief how little the nobles, even the best of them, cared for the well-being of the people, or even for the military security of the State.

The Fronde was at an end, but the war with Spain still continued, and presented a very difficult problem.

The war with France to the Peace of the Pyrenees.

It is strange that the Spanish Government did not take greater advantage of the internal disorders of France, and their slackness in the matter can only be explained by their financial embarrassments, the lethargic character of Spanish policy, and the suspicion that was always present to the minds of Spaniards that the demands for their assistance were not sincere. Turenne had first fought with them, and then had been won back to his allegiance to the French Crown. Why should not Condé do the same? But still they had gained important advantages during the civil wars of France. We have already noted the victories gained in 1650, when Turenne was with them. In 1652, while Condé was in arms in the south, their victories were still more important. Since the beginning of the war, indeed, though it had lasted seventeen years, France had suffered no such series of misfortunes as those of 1652. In May the Archduke Leopold took Gravelines. In September he captured the very important fortress and port of Dunkirk. In October Marshal de la Mothe surrendered Barcelona to a general bearing the once famous name of Don John of Austria. In the same month Casale capitulated to the Governor of Milan. And now Condé had thrown himself into the arms of the enemy, and was wearing the colours of those whom he had defeated at Rocroy and Lens. It could hardly be doubted, after the experience of recent years, that the military strength of France was greater than that of Spain. But the finances of France were in extreme confusion. It is impossible to give any clear statement of the financial position, for its chief characteristic was disorder, and system was non-existent. The efforts of the finance Ministers since Emery had been directed merely to meeting the wants of the day: they were satisfied if by some temporary expedient they could squeeze out money for a year or a campaign. No one knew the exact state of affairs: not certainly Mazarin nor Emery, for there was no yearly balancing of accounts: nor the *Chambre des Comptes*, before whom all accounts were supposed to go, for the secret expenditure of the Crown and Ministry (the *acquits au comptant*) had grown at such a rate that, whereas in 1648 they had been limited to three million livres a year, they had risen subsequently to as much as eighty millions. In February, 1653, the notorious Fouquet was appointed finance Minister, and succeeded in relieving the pressure, though at an enormous cost. The future was sacrificed to the present: money was borrowed at fabulous interest, and, worst of all, the Government shut its eyes to the way in which the capitalists who advanced the money repaid themselves at the expense of the peasants. Now, if ever, the criticism and protest of the Parlement would have been useful; but the Fronde had opened the King's eyes to the danger of Parlementary opposition, and after the collapse of Condé's movement he found himself strong enough to enforce his wishes. When in March 1654 the Parlement ventured to resist the proposals of Fouquet, the King, who was about to hunt, hurried down in his hunting dress (but apparently without the legendary whip in his hand), and at once enforced registration. The failure of the Fronde could not have been more openly proclaimed.

The war meanwhile dragged slowly on. On both sides there was lack of money, and on the side of Spain there was constant disagreement between Condé and the Spanish generals, Fuensaldagna and the Archduke Leopold. The events of the year 1653, such as they were, left a balance in favour of France. Condé had hoped to take the French between two fires, for while his adherents in Guienne were to march from the south, he hoped with a Spanish army to attack from the north-east. But the plan failed. Guienne and Bordeaux surrendered to the King in July. In Bordeaux the movement had taken a violent and democratic character: the rebels had adopted *Vox populi, vox dei* as their device, and had then collapsed through their own violence. The royal forces were thus at liberty to watch the northern frontier. Turenne advised that for the present no great enterprise should be undertaken, but that Condé's force should be watched and any siege he undertook broken up. The plan succeeded entirely, for Condé was unable to force Turenne from his defensive positions, or to induce him to give battle in the open. Rocroy was the only place that fell into Condé's hands. Turenne captured Rethel and Mouzon, and for Condé it was a defeat to have done so little.

The next year (1654) witnessed the same dragging campaign, marked however by one military event of importance. At the beginning of the year, in March, Condé was formally condemned to death. Many of his friends had made their peace with the Crown. Madame de Longueville, weary of intrigue and disillusioned by her experience of a political career, retired in the fulness of her beauty and popularity into the Jansenist convent of Port Royal, and was soon followed by her brother Conti. The Duke of Orléans retired to Blois, and there finished his fretful and dishonourable career. Cardinal de Retz, after his arrest, had been imprisoned at Nantes. In August, 1654, he escaped; but he passed the rest of his days in exile. The last hopes that Condé entertained of help from within the boundaries of France thus vanished. In the middle of the summer Turenne laid siege to Stenay, and Condé to Arras. Turenne counted on bringing the siege of Stenay to a successful end in time to interrupt the siege of Arras. His plan worked out well. Stenay capitulated, and on August 25 he attacked Condé in his lines at Arras and completely defeated him. Henceforth the military prestige of Condé pales before that of Turenne.

In 1655 hardly any military event of importance occurred. Turenne took Landrecies in July, but it was retaken by Condé in August. But the chief interest shifted from war to diplomacy, when both France and Spain sued for the alliance of Cromwell. In both countries there must have been a sense of humiliation in appealing for the support of the great regicide; in France especially, where the royal family was so closely connected with Charles I. But both countries were weary of the long war and intensely anxious to conclude it at an advantage, and it was clear that the money and the troops of the great English leader would in all probability turn the scale. Cromwell hesitated between the two applicants for his favour, but in the end he decided for France, and in November 1655 a treaty of commerce was concluded. Mazarin pressed for a political and military alliance, but for the present could gain nothing further. The year 1656 was chiefly notable for a considerable French disaster. Turenne laid siege to Valenciennes and expected to capture the place, but on July 16 he was attacked in his entrenchments by Condé and Don John of Austria. The situation was closely analogous to that at Arras in August, 1654. A part of Turenne's force had to capitulate; with the rest he managed to effect his retreat. In 1657 new and very important elements were introduced into the long and weary war. For in March Mazarin managed to convert the commercial treaty with England into an offensive alliance against Spain, and a considerable force of Cromwell's now world-famous veterans passed over to Flanders. The current at once began to run decisively in favour of France. Mardyck with St Venant and Bourbourg fell into the hands of Turenne. In this year, too, the Emperor Ferdinand III died. Mazarin seems at one time to have hoped to rob the House of Austria of the elective crown, though when he put forward Louis XIV as a candidate he can hardly have thought success possible. The best chance was that the Elector of Bavaria might be chosen. But this hope also failed, and the Austrian Archduke Leopold, the ally and general of the Spanish forces, was duly elected on the 18th July, 1658. There was a danger then that the work of the Peace of Westphalia might be undone and France threatened again upon her eastern frontier. But the danger was cleverly averted by Mazarin. The German princes asked only for peace, and Mazarin succeeded in combining the Electors, Bishops, and Dukes of western Germany in 'The League of the Rhine,' whereby they bound themselves together under the presidency of France for the maintenance of the Peace of Westphalia, and promised mutual assistance in case of attack. It was a great diplomatic success for France, which now assumed for western Germany the position of pre-eminence that had formerly belonged to the House of Austria.

In 1658 there came at last a decisive success for France. Dunkirk had been promised to the English as the price of their alliance, and in May Turenne and the English army under Lockhart proceded to lay siege to it. Condé and Don John of Austria marched to its relief. A great battle was fought—the battle of the Dunes; Condé and the Spanish were entirely defeated; and Dunkirk capitulated on the 25th of June. The whole district was soon swept by Turenne and his English allies. Dixmuyde, Gravelines, Oudenarde, and Ypres all fell into the hands of France. The only drawback to these triumphs was that, in accordance with the treaty, Dunkirk which would have been so valuable to France had to be handed over to the English.

Spain could struggle no longer. Jamaica had been captured by the English. Spain could procure neither money, nor troops, nor allies; and peace became a necessity. Nor was France on her side unwilling to entertain the idea. In addition to the exhaustion

The Treaty of the Pyrenees.

of the war the nobles were still discontented, the provincial Parlements acquiesced in the power of Mazarin less readily than the Paris Parlement, the peasantry were reported as being driven by starvation to the verge of revolt. In September, 1652, Cromwell died, and the whole conduct of the negotiations was therefore left to Mazarin, for England contained no one that could succeed Cromwell. There were some difficult questions to settle besides the changes in frontier. Would Spain recognise the independence of Portugal? Would France receive back Condé and grant him his old position in the State? Both points were at first answered in the negative. Mazarin had had for some time another object in view as well. He desired not only peace and territorial concessions from Spain, but further a matrimonial alliance. Down to the end of 1658 overtures with this view had produced little result. But then Mazarin forced on a decision by suggesting the marriage of the King with a princess of the House of Savoy. At once Spain sent Pimentel as ambassador, with a proposal that Louis XIV should marry the Infanta of Spain. Louis XIV's heart or his fancy was already engaged elsewhere: he was devoted to one of Mazarin's nieces. But neither Mazarin nor the King, though Louis struggled against the decision for some time, could in the end allow a private affection to outweigh reasons of State, and the offer of Spain was eagerly, if not joyfully accepted.

Negotiations began in the Island of Pheasants on the river Bidassoa, the south-western frontier line of France. By November all the terms had been settled, and the treaty was signed on Nov. 7. This 'Treaty of the Pyrenees' was the complement of the Peace of Westphalia, and put the seal upon Mazarin's diplomatic successes. On all sides France gained both territory and prestige, and her claim to be the most powerful State in Europe became indisputable. The chief stipulations of the treaty were the following: (1) on the side of the Netherlands all Artois except Aire and St Omer became French, and many places in Flanders, Hainault and Luxemburg were surrendered by Spain. Chief among the towns that thus came into her hands were Arras, Gravelines, Béthune, Landrecies, Montmédy, and Thionville. (2) Catalonia was abandoned to Spain, but Roussillon and Conflans remained French. (3) In Italy France retained Pinerolo. (4) All the stipulations of the Peace of Westphalia were confirmed, which meant especially that Alsace was recognised as French territory. (5) The Duke of Lorraine was to recover his territory, but under such conditions that it would be quite incapable of resistance or attack. Already France possessed Metz, Toul, and Verdun, the real keys of Lorraine. Now she was to retain Clermont, Stenay and Jamets, with the Duchy of Bar; and the Duke was compelled to raze the fortifications of Nancy, and to grant to the troops of the King of France a free passage to the Rhine. If France retained her present power, Lorraine was clearly destined to become hers before long. (6) The concessions that France made on her side were in comparison trifling. She withdrew from Franche Comté, Catalonia, and Italy. She consented to abandon the alliance with Portugal, and finally consented to take back Condé and to grant him the governorship of Burgundy.

There remained only the marriage of Louis XIV with the Infanta Maria Theresa. Before that could take place there was some haggling about the dowry, and more as to whether the Infanta should renounce all possible claims that she might ever possess upon Spanish territory. The renunciation was insisted on, on the side of Spain, and in the end Mazarin gave way. In view of the immense importance that this renunciation subsequently assumed, certain circumstances about it deserve notice[1]. In the first place though it was made with

[1] It may be well to quote the chief sentences of the marriage contract which bear on the renunciation:—"Moyennant le payement effectif desdits cinq cens mille éscus d'or...ladite Serenissime Infante se tiendra pour contente du susdit dot, sans que par cy-après elle puisse alléguer aucun sien autre droit, pretendant qu'il luy appartienne ou puisse appartenir autres

every solemnity, it was from the first dependent on the payment of the dowry; and the dowry was never paid. And in the second place many recognised, and Mazarin certainly among them, that, if ever the opportunity came for pressing such claims, the solemnity of the renunciation would not prevent France from pressing them. If we may trust Madame de Motteville, even the King of Spain spoke of the renunciation as a foolish trifle.

So the marriage took place. The King entered Paris in August, 1660, amidst general enthusiasm. France had hardly a rival in Europe, and the Monarchy had certainly no rival in France. The last grumblings of the provinces had been crushed by the suppression of the revolt in Marseilles. Mazarin had done his work. The plans of Henry IV and Richelieu were completed. Much inferior as Mazarin was to them in nobility of character, and in his handling of the domestic problems of France, the lucidity of his diplomatic plans, and the skill with which he carried them out, assure him a high place among the great statesmen of France. He was fortunate, too, perhaps in the occasion of his death. Louis XIV would not probably have been his docile pupil much longer. But eight months after the King's entrance into Paris Mazarin died (March, 1661). Avarice had always been his besetting sin, and he died possessed of an enormous fortune.

In addition to diplomacy, war, and civil strife, the period of the Fronde was also marked by a religious move- The
ment of great interest and importance, for it was Jansenists.
during these years that Jansenism became an active force in France.

---

plus grands biens, droits, raisons et actions par cause des heritages, et plus grandes successions de leurs M^{tez} Catholiques ses pere et mere...ou pour quelque cause et titre que ce soit, soit qu'elle le sçust ou qu'elle l'ignorast ...et avant l'effectuation de ses epousailles elle en fera la renonciation en bonne et due forme." The next clause of the contract stipulates that the Kings of France and Spain shall make an equally solemn and binding renunciation. (Vast, *Les grands traités du règne de Louis XIV*. vol. I.)

Cornelius Jansen, who gave his name to the movement, died without knowing that he was the founder of an important religious society or of any society. He had studied theology in France, but he was of Dutch origin, and when he died in 1638 he was Bishop of Ypres, in the Spanish Netherlands. During a great part of his life he had been devoted to the study of the works of St Augustine, and at his death he left in manuscript a long work on the subject, which was posthumously published under the title of *Augustinus*. It was a bulky work, in three large volumes, not at all likely to become generally popular, or in ordinary circumstances to arouse the interest of a very large circle. But Jansen had long been in conflict with the Jesuit order, and upon the publication of the book vigilant members of the society did not fail to find heretical doctrines in it. Jansen's work, on the other hand, did not lack champions, and as the controversy more and more engrossed the attention of Church circles, a Jansenist party, and soon a Jansenist movement, developed.

The ground was well prepared for Jansenism. The chief strength of the movement is to be found in the expression that it gave to the latent hostility to the Jesuit order, which was in certain districts and circles of society deep and widespread, for the Jesuits had now almost acquired the control of the Church. They were the confessors of Princes and nobles, the most able and most popular of schoolmasters, and they encroached upon the instruction given in the Universities. They had not gained this power solely by persuading the nation of the justice of their principles. They had allied themselves to the Monarchy, and had forgotten their old, almost democratic opinions; and the Crown had rewarded them for the valuable support that it had received from them. Opposition therefore had been crushed, though it was often strong both among the clergy and laity. But though opposition to the Jesuit order was the most important root of Jansenism, it was not the only root. Just as Protestantism in the sixteenth century was often a cover for political opposition to the Crown, so Jansenism profited by and in turn stimulated the political discontent that found an expression in the various movements of the Fronde. It is very noticeable that Conti, Madame de Longueville, and other leaders of the Fronde drew close to the Jansenist movement, when the Monarchy finally triumphed over all opposition. But while it is possible to analyse in this way the origins of Jansenism, we cannot for a moment deny to the movement and to its leaders a deep sincerity and an earnest piety. A movement that includes Angélique Arnauld, St Cyran, and Pascal cannot be regarded as a mere piece of opportunism.

The Jansenists resented no accusation so bitterly as the charge of sympathy with Protestantism. Jansen, in the preface to his *Augustinus*, submitted himself wholly to the Pope. His followers were very active in controversy against Protestantism. They were thrust out from the Church wholly against their wills, and to the last regarded themselves as faithful and orthodox members of the Church. Their sincerity is unquestionable, and yet it is equally plain that in many respects they approximated to Protestantism and even to Calvinism. For though they did not regard the Bible as the sole religious authority, they appealed always to earlier against later traditions, and were active in translating into French the Bible and the early Fathers. They resembled the Calvinists, too, in the austerity of their moral code and in their dislike for dancing and the drama. The very fact of their hostility to everything that belonged to the Jesuits brought them into line with Protestant reformers on certain points. They opposed the doctrine of 'grace' to the Jesuits' insistence upon the freedom of the will, and they supported a simpler form of ritual against the elaborate innovations of the Jesuits.

The centre of the Jansenist movement was the Community of Port Royal. This was a foundation which dated back to the time of the Crusaders, but which had in the interval fallen into much decay. Abuses had crept in, the discipline had become lax, and the right of appointing the head had become the property of a noble family. But all this was changed under the rule of Angélique Arnauld—La Mère Angélique, as she is called. She received the appointment at the age of seven, and at first took the duties of her post as lightly as her predecessors. But later on there came a change. Penetrated by a new religious ardour, she introduced a rigorous discipline, and soon Port Royal became known for the austere and simple life of its occupants. St Cyran, the friend of Jansen and the champion of his views, became the confessor of the Monastery, and thus the place was soon identified with Jansenist opinions. There came, too, to Port Royal men who were attracted by the form of religious thought prevailing there. Schools were established: new methods of teaching were employed. Men of note, such as Tillemont, the historian, Pascal and Racine, joined the band of solitaries. They submitted themselves to a severe discipline, and gained the regard of the religious in consequence. Some years later we have a description of the place from Madame de Sevigné: "Port Royal is a Thebaïd: it is a paradise: it is a desert where all the devotion of Christianity is to be found: a sanctity is spread from the place for a league round....Everything connected with the place—their ploughmen, their shepherds, their workmen—everything has an air of simplicity. I assure you that I was charmed with the sight of this divine solitude of which I had heard so much."

The Jansenists however were not allowed to go on with their work in quiet. The Jesuits appealed to the Holy See against their opponents, and in 1652 there was issued a Papal Formulary condemning five theses of the *Augustinus*. The acceptance of this formulary was made obligatory on all Catholics. The Jansenists, we have said, were not Protestants, and their dilemma was a painful one. They did not wish to resist the authority of the Pope, nor could they declare heretical the views expressed in a book that was to them so valuable. The attitude they adopted in the end was this. They declared themselves ready to admit that the doctrines condemned were heretical, but they professed themselves unable to find them in the *Augustinus*. There ensued a controversy, not quite sincere on either side, as to whether the Papal authority extended to matters of fact or was limited to questions of faith. The formulary was presented to the nuns of Port Royal. They offered to accept it with the proviso that they could not say whether the theses, denounced as heretical, were really in the *Augustinus* or not. But the acceptance, pure and simple, was demanded, and already a certain amount of persecution was being used against Port Royal when Mazarin died.

The controversy produced, naturally, numerous works on either side, but only one of any permanent importance. Pascal's *Provincial Letters* were published in 1656, and were by far the most effective indictment of the Jesuit order that had appeared or was destined to appear. The gist of his charge is that, in their anxiety to secure the authority of their order, the Jesuits had watered down the principles of morality and had almost effaced the difference between right and wrong. Drawing from the acknowledged works of Jesuit teachers, he revealed certain devices whereby, he alleged, they allowed their penitents to sin with a free conscience. The reader must go to the pages of *The Provincial Letters* to understand the casuistic methods of avoiding sin by the doctrine of 'probabilism'; by directing the intention to those parts of the act that were not sinful; by defining the sin in such a way that the act did not fall under the category. If the accuracy of the quotations is sometimes questionable, the argument is always powerful, and is supported by every sort of literary artifice handled by one of the most consummate masters of style. Pascal allows us to understand, in the end, that he would have preferred a stronger stand on principle to the elusive answer that the Jansenists had offered to the formulary.

The Jesuits found and still find their defenders against Pascal's attacks. It is alleged that he misquoted, and that he took exceptional opinions, or such as had actually been condemned, as typical of the views of the whole Jesuit order. We need not enter into the controversy. It is hardly disputable that the Jesuits felt the effects of Pascal's attack for more than a hundred years, and that it prepared the way for their overthrow in France in the year 1764.

Conclusion.

The year 1659 brings one clearly defined period to an end and inaugurates another. The domestic struggles of the Monarchy were over; it had beaten down one enemy or rival after another. The organisation of the Church, the ambitions and traditions of the nobility, the local aspirations of the provinces had been mastered in turn. The system of representation had not availed to secure victory to the States General nor fixity of tenure and legal prestige to the Parlement of Paris. The Protestant Movement, joining hands as it did with many of the enemies of the Crown, had seemed at one time likely to prove the most dangerous enemy of all; but that danger was over and Protestantism in 1659 was dependent for its existence upon the toleration of the Crown with little of its former social and intellectual prestige remaining. The next century was to see other and more dangerous enemies rise up, but for the present there was no cloud upon the horizon. The strength and the pride of France were concentrated in her King, and the device of the sun which Louis XIV subsequently adopted was well chosen to signify the dependence of all classes upon the Monarchy. And if France thus presented no dangerous rival to the Crown, Europe hardly seemed to offer a rival to France. Germany would for many a long year feel the wounds that she had received in the Thirty Years' War: Spain seemed still a splendid power but her foundations were undermined; Holland was piling up wealth and neglecting her defences; England was soon to pass through anarchy to the Restoration and under

Charles II would seem content to forget the high dreams of the Cromwellian period and follow ingloriously the lead of France. Rarely has any country possessed such an ascendancy in Europe as France had at this time; and as France seemed personified in her monarch the next half century of European History bears justly the title of "The Age of Louis XIV."

APPENDIX I.

The French Kings of the House of Valois, from Charles V to the extinction of the line.

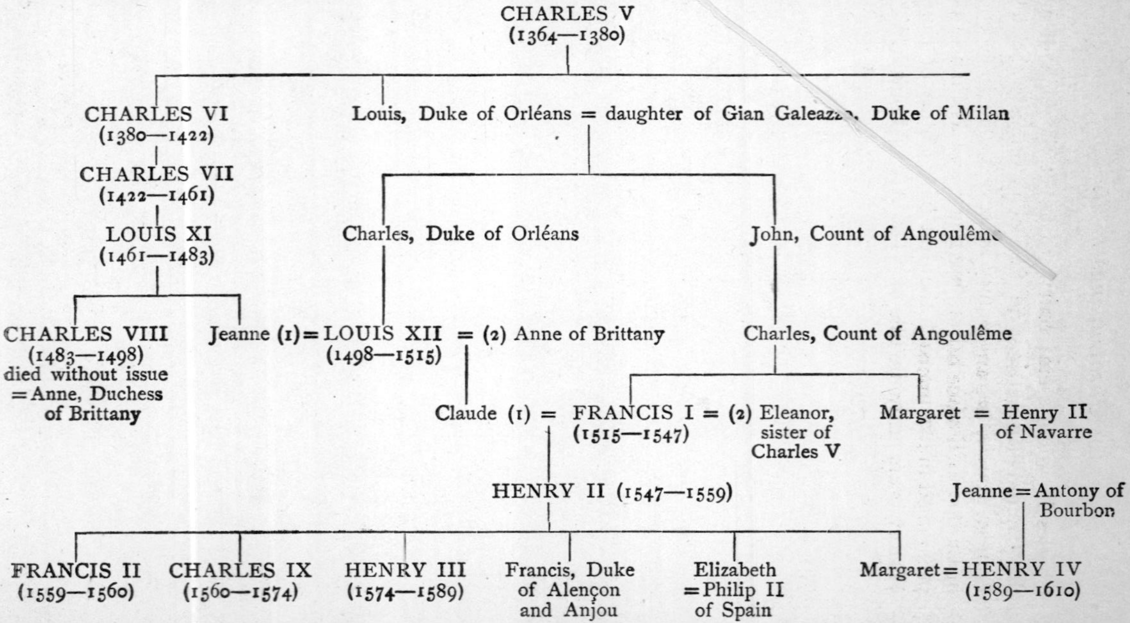

CHARLES V (1364—1380)
│
├── CHARLES VI (1380—1422)
│   │
│   └── CHARLES VII (1422—1461)
│   │
│   └── LOUIS XI (1461—1483)
│   │
│   ├── CHARLES VIII (1483—1498) died without issue = Anne, Duchess of Brittany
│   │
│   └── Jeanne (1) = LOUIS XII (1498—1515) = (2) Anne of Brittany
│   │
│   └── Claude (1) = FRANCIS I (1515—1547) = (2) Eleanor, sister of Charles V
│   │
│   └── HENRY II (1547—1559)
│   │
│   ├── FRANCIS II (1559—1560)
│   ├── CHARLES IX (1560—1574)
│   ├── HENRY III (1574—1589)
│   ├── Francis, Duke of Alençon and Anjou
│   ├── Elizabeth = Philip II of Spain
│   └── Margaret = HENRY IV (1589—1610)
│
└── Louis, Duke of Orléans = daughter of Gian Galeazzo, Duke of Milan
    │
    └── Charles, Duke of Orléans
        │
        └── John, Count of Angoulême
            │
            └── Charles, Count of Angoulême
                │
                ├── FRANCIS I (see above)
                └── Margaret = Henry II of Navarre
                    │
                    └── Jeanne = Antony of Bourbon
                        │
                        └── HENRY IV (1589—1610)

APPENDIX II.

The Bourbon Kings.

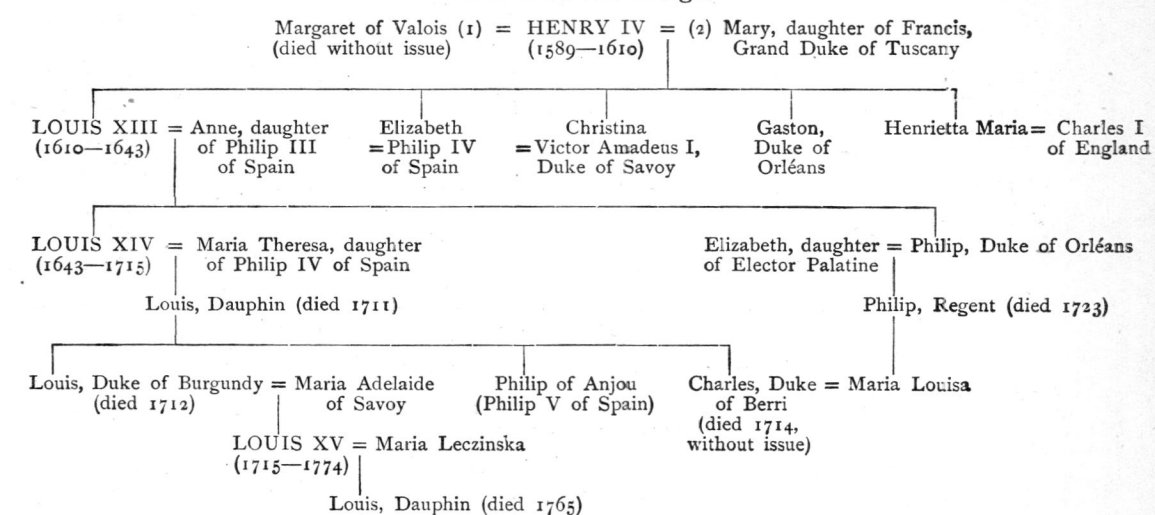

Margaret of Valois (1) = HENRY IV = (2) Mary, daughter of Francis,
(died without issue)   (1589—1610)   Grand Duke of Tuscany

- LOUIS XIII = Anne, daughter of Philip III of Spain
  (1610—1643)
- Elizabeth = Philip IV of Spain
- Christina = Victor Amadeus I, Duke of Savoy
- Gaston, Duke of Orléans
- Henrietta Maria = Charles I of England

LOUIS XIV = Maria Theresa, daughter of Philip IV of Spain
(1643—1715)

Louis, Dauphin (died 1711)

Elizabeth, daughter of Elector Palatine = Philip, Duke of Orléans

Philip, Regent (died 1723)

- Louis, Duke of Burgundy = Maria Adelaide of Savoy
  (died 1712)
- Philip of Anjou (Philip V of Spain)
- Charles, Duke of Berri (died 1714, without issue)

Philip, Duke = Maria Louisa

LOUIS XV = Maria Leczinska
(1715—1774)

Louis, Dauphin (died 1765)

LOUIS XVI = Marie Antoinette
(1774—1792)

APPENDIX III.

The Family of the Guises: to illustrate the Wars of Religion.

Claude, Duke of Guise = Antoinette, daughter of Francis, Count of Vendôme
(died 1550)

- Francis (died 1563)
  - Henry (murdered 1588)
- Charles, Cardinal of Lorraine
  - Charles, Duke of Mayenne
  - Louis, Cardinal of Guise (murdered 1588)
- Claude, Duke of Aumâle
- Louis, Cardinal of Guise
- Mary = James V of Scotland
  - Mary, Queen of Scots

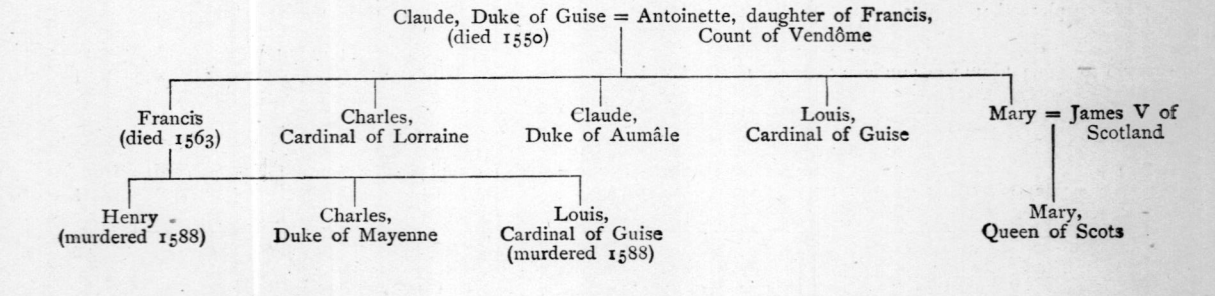

APPENDIX IV.

The House of Condé, and its relation to the House of Bourbon, to illustrate the Wars of the Fronde.

Charles, Duke of Vendôme
```
   ├── Antony of Bourbon = Jeanne D'Albret, Queen of Navarre (died 1562)
   │      ├── HENRY IV, king of France
   │      │      ├── Louis XIII
   │      │      └── Gaston, Duke of Orléans = Mary of Montpensier
   │      │             └── Anne Maria Louise "La Grande Mademoiselle" (died 1693, without issue)
   ├── Charles, Cardinal of Bourbon (died 1590)
   ├── Louis I, Prince of Condé (killed at Jarnac 1569)
   │      └── Henry I (died 1588)
   │             └── Henry II (died 1646)
   │                    ├── Louis II, "The Great Condé" (died 1686)
   │                    ├── Armand, Prince of Conti
   │                    └── Anne, Duchess of Longueville (died 1679)
   └── Margaret = Francis, Duke of Nevers
```

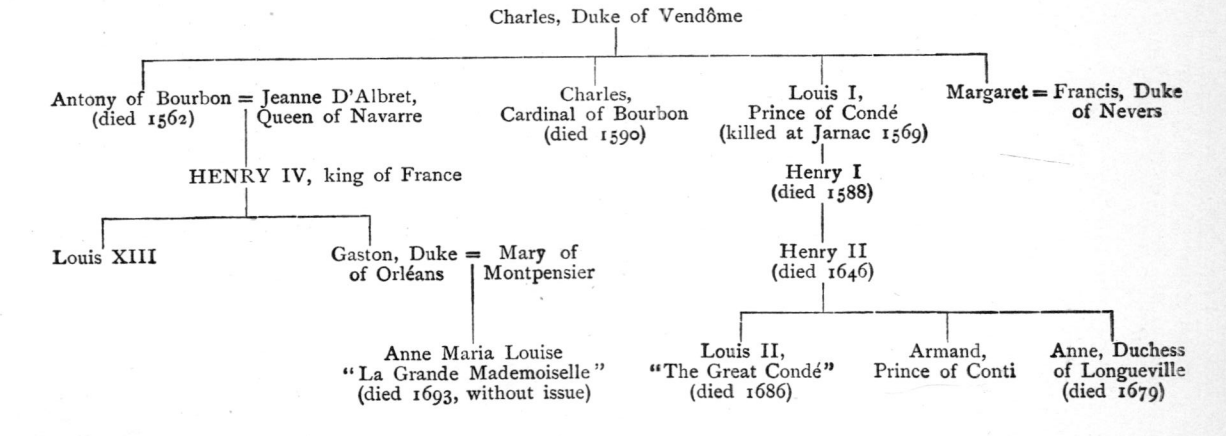

APPENDIX V.

THE PEACES AND TREATIES OF THE WARS OF RELIGION.

1. March 1563. *Peace of Amboise.* This Peace was in the form of a royal edict, and professed to establish an interim settlement of the religious difficulty "until the general council and the majority of the King." (i) All nobles of the highest class were allowed the practice of the "so-called reformed religion in their own houses," for themselves, their families and dependents; other nobles had the same privilege for themselves and their families only. (ii) Liberty of Conscience was allowed for all; and those towns were to be allowed the reformed religious service, in which it had actually been exercised up to the 7th March, 1563. (iii) Elsewhere it was to be allowed in one town in each *bailliage* or *sénéchaussée*: but Paris was specially excepted from this provision. (iv) An amnesty was granted for all offences connected with religion.

2. March 1568. *Peace of Longjumeau.* The terms of the Peace of Amboise were renewed: and all modifications that had been introduced were annulled. The Peace was to be maintained "until it should please God to unite all the subjects of the King in one and the same religion."

3. August 1570. *Peace of St Germain.* (i) The regulations as to the reformed religious services were repeated, with few changes, from the Peace of Amboise: the slight changes were favourable to the Huguenots. (ii) Protestants were declared equally eligible with Catholics for all civil and military posts: all

Appendix V.

Universities and schools were thrown open to them. (iii) In all litigation in which Protestants were concerned, they were to have the right of rejecting a certain number of "presidents or councillors" in the Parlement of Paris and the Provincial Parlements. The Parlement of Toulouse was declared incapable of dealing with cases in which Protestants were involved. (iv) As security for the carrying out of the Peace, the Princes of Navarre and Condé and other Protestant noblemen were to be allowed to garrison La Rochelle, Cognac, Montauban and La Charité. (v) All members of Parlements and all municipal and royal authorities were to swear to observe the Peace.

4. June 1573. (Published as an Edict in July.) *The Treaty of La Rochelle.* The three great Protestant cities—La Rochelle, Nîmes and Montauban—were permitted free exercise of the reformed religion; the great nobles were permitted to celebrate baptisms and marriages in their houses, but not more than ten people were to be assembled on such occasions in addition to those immediately concerned in the ceremony; liberty of conscience and an amnesty were promised to all.

5. May 1576. *Peace of Monsieur.* The unrestricted practice of the reformed service was to be permitted everywhere in France, except in Paris and the neighbourhood. (ii) Chambers consisting of Catholics and Protestants (*chambres mi-parties*) were to be established in all the Parlements for the trial of cases in which Protestants and Catholics were concerned. (iii) Complete amnesty for all, both high and low, who had resisted the King. (iv) Eight places to be garrisoned by Protestants. (v) The States-General to be assembled in six months.

6. Sept. 1577. *Peace of Bergerac.* (i) The reformed service was allowed in one town in each *bailliage* or *sénéchaussée*; and in the houses of the nobility, much as in the Treaty of La Rochelle. (ii) No reformed service was to be held in Paris. (iii) New mixed chambers were to be established in all the Parlements, with special guarantees for justice to Protestants in Bordeaux, Grenoble, Aix and Toulouse. (iv) The Protestants were to keep six of the eight strong places assigned to them by the Peace of Monsieur.

7. November 1580. *The Peace of Fleix.* The Peace of Bergerac was exactly re-affirmed.

CAMBRIDGE: PRINTED BY
W. LEWIS
AT THE UNIVERSITY PRESS

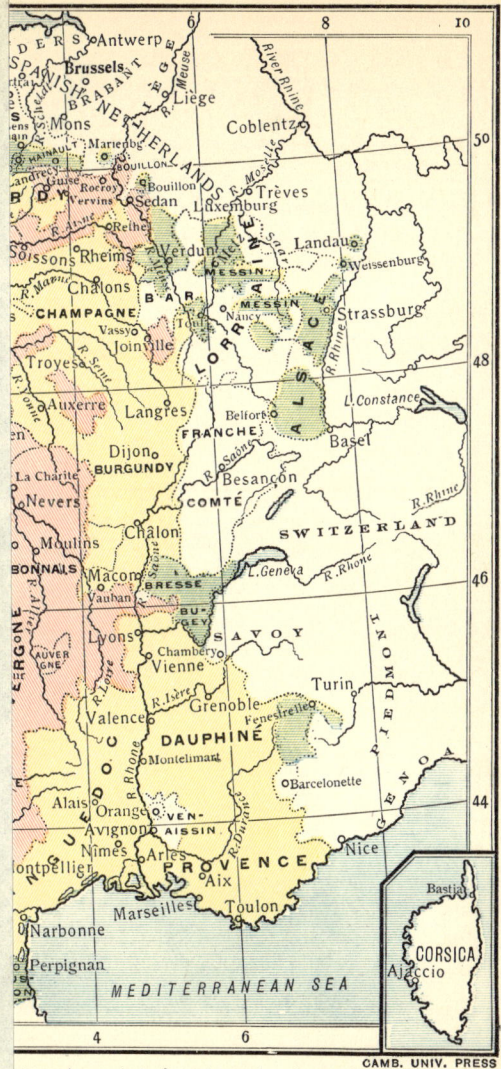

...cts under control of great vassals subsequently brought
France between 1483 and 1659.

1659.

at end of Vol. I. (1)

FRANCE, 1483.

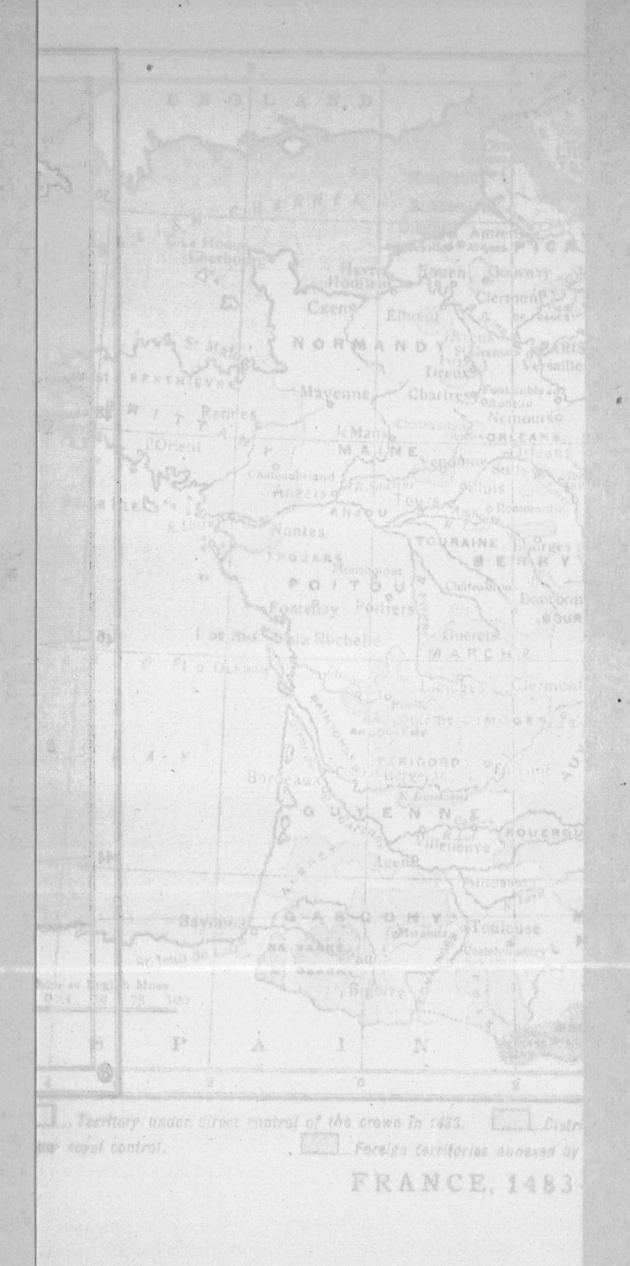